W0028015

For my family

Contents

Foreword

Accounts of new religious movements often focus on their charismatic leaders or distinctive teachings. What impact do these have on the lives of those attracted to them? Wade Fransson offers an uncompromising account of his first exposure and subsequent career in the Worldwide Church of God. Fransson demonstrates a remarkable ability to honestly explore his own feelings and analyze his experience while at the same time show understanding and compassion for those whose paths he crossed. A soundtrack of the music of his life offers a powerful counterpoint that underscores his account, an insightful tale that will interest all students of end-time groups.

—*Henry Sturcke*

Preface

Dear Reader,

Writing a deeply personal story is difficult and painful. It's just plain hard to approach life objectively or to understand your own motives. Is it narcissistic to imagine that an autobiographical review of your personal experiences is of interest? And if a far better writer than I, Rousseau, put his life to the test of truth in *Confessions*, and his reviewer skewered him for failing that test,[1] those familiar with my life might make the same call.

On the other hand, Socrates is famously quoted as having said "An unexamined life is not worth living."[2] He was on trial for heresy and for encouraging his students to challenge the accepted beliefs of the time—to think for themselves. As you read this account you'll understand why I agree with Socrates.

But the real motivation behind this book is Jesus' statement: "Greater love has no man than this, that a man lay down his life for his friends."[3] As I metaphorically lay my life bare for you in the pages of this book, I pray that it will be a blessing to you in some way. And since we always hurt the ones we love the most, I apologize in advance to those featured in this account in ways they might not prefer. It causes me pain to know that in writing this account I will offend some. I ask forgiveness as I seek, imperfectly, to fulfill a higher calling.

This book contains obscure biblical and theological references, essential to the story, which may be puzzling to those unfamiliar with Herbert Armstrong and the Worldwide Church of God (WCG). This may detract from the text the way obscure nineteenth century whaling and zoology information detracts from

---

1.   Time Magazine book review, "The Invincible Loner," Friday, Oct. 21, 1966
2.   Plato—Apology, 38a
3.   John 15:13-17

Moby Dick. Some reviewers praise the recap of key doctrines and my struggle with their accuracy. If you don't, I guess you had to be there.

Finally, your life is unique. You are a treasure to God who, I believe, owns the secret place deep within your heart that is His abode. I realize that I'm on one extreme of the WCG experience spectrum, viewing my time in the WCG as overwhelmingly positive, knowing God guided my steps and used even painful experiences to bring me closer to Him. You, dear reader, may be on the other end of this spectrum, viewing your experience, or that of others in the WCG, as destructive and debilitating. I can only hope and pray that laying down my life may, in some way, be helpful to you, as you continue along your own path, independently investigating Truth.

I'll end this open preface with two quotes. The first is an anonymous quote that recently caught my attention. "The only thing I can change is myself, but sometimes that makes all the difference." My editor provided the second. "The function of music is to release us from the tyranny of conscious thought."[4]

Sincerely,
Wade Fransson

---

4.   Sir Thomas Beecham, English conductor (1879—1961)

1

Yesterday

The birds they sang at the break of day. Start again I heard them say
Don't dwell on what has passed away; or what is yet to be.
Ah the wars they will be fought again.
The holy dove She will be caught again
bought and sold and bought again; the dove is never free.

Ring the bells that still can ring. Forget your perfect offering
There is a crack in everything. That's how the light gets in.

—LEONARD COHEN: ANTHEM—

All religious epics begin with a creation story. Here is mine.

My dad, Lennart, was an adventurous boy in Sweden, was on the shorter side of stature, but destined for bigger things than working his father's farm. Jealous of city kids who swam while he weeded and hoed, he set off at age twenty to find fortune in the big country out West. He landed in eastern Canada on May 7, 1953, and worked on a farm.

Dad is industrious, creative, and ambitious, with a pleasant personality and a natural sense of humor. His playful use of sound bites leads to instant acceptance by those with similar views. In English his first sound bite was "Moo," and Dad enjoys telling people he learned English talking to cows. This bovine-intensive process worked well, and soon Dad to landed a job in machine shop in the big city of Toronto at eighty cents an hour with overtime and eighty-hour weeks. When Glen Carswell joined the team Dad had his first friend in the new country.

Can You Take Me Back

Dad wanted to go west, and convinced Glen to join him. In the summer of 1955 Glen bought a Chevy, Dad bought a Ford, and they hit the road in hot pursuit of the Canadian dream. A brief detour to the south introduced Dad to the U.S. and to Chicago's finest, one of whom taught Dad a lesson about red lights that cost him his last eight dollars. The young adventurers limped back into Canada on fumes, but a week's wages harvesting wheat got them back on the road.

They followed a lead about work at the remote Rocky Mountain House, halfway between Calgary and Edmonton, but arrived too late. Temperatures dropped overnight, cracking the engine block on Glen's Chevy so they headed west in Dad's Ford, pursuing work and a view of the Pacific Ocean. A logging company on the Portland Canal hired the flat broke and starving young men, who enjoyed a free meal on the eight-hour ferry ride to the camp. By winter's end the finance company had repossessed their cars but they had a comfortable stash, and flew to Vancouver looking for work in the big city.

Glen was a good mechanic and found work easily. Without the foggiest idea was an ironworker was, Dad interviewed as one at something called a Union Hall. Asked where he had been working he answered "a logging camp." Asked about welding skills he said "I've done a little." Asked which local he belonged to he answered with a blank stare. Frustrated, the man said the union couldn't help him, just as the union boss, of Swedish descent, came over to find out who was on the other end of the thick Swedish accent. The union boss had also worked in a logging camp and made a phone call to the Dominion Bridge Co., where

Dad learned the ropes, as it were, of his lifelong profession. The rest is history. Examine a bridge or high-rise anywhere in Canada or the Pacific Northwest, and you'll find my dad's boot prints all over the iron.

With English skills and prospects improving, the handsome young ironworker with a dwindling Swedish accent looked around at the ladies. In Surrey, a little town outside Vancouver, Dad and Glen hooked up with local schoolgirls. The one named Edna was destined to become my mom. She was the middle child and, according to Dad, was the smallest and prettiest of three girls who had moved in from Edmonton, Alberta. Edna was a frail and sad (but very sweet-looking) wisp of a ninth-grade girl who wanted to escape from a dreary life.

Gramps was quite a bit older than Grannie, and was a retired hospital orderly with two children from a prior marriage, who were all but a mystery to his new family. Grannie worked in downtown Vancouver at Eaton's department store, riding the bus back and forth to work, as they didn't have a car. Grannie towered over Gramps, and not only in stature. Her boisterous and aggressive personality dominated those around her in a somewhat controlling and not exactly pleasant fashion. She tended to clench a lengthy cigarette holder in her mouth, focused intently on the task in front of her. Her legs were unusually long, the opposite of the Penguin's in the *Batman* comics, but their gait and physical demeanor were reminiscent. In describing Grannie the Penguin always comes to mind.

Dad says Grannie arrived home at 5 p.m., with the proverbial cigarette in her mouth, through the back door. This opened into the kitchen where Gramps sat with a glass of beer listening to a baseball game. Still in her coat, Grannie put the kettle on, and tea in hand, left Gramps in the kitchen to occupy the living room, knitting and watching T.V. By 11 p.m. Gramps headed for bed, through the living room where his wife and the upright piano were sitting. Gramps would sit at the piano and play a little tune, rise and bow to Grannie, and with a "goodnight dear," head upstairs to bed.

When Dad recounted this scenario flashes of memory told me this snapshot conveys the essence of truth. Dad says he never saw them sit down to a meal together, but that Gramps had a nice yard and garden which he liked tending to. Sadly, I never got to know Gramps. My only memories are of me at seven-years-old visiting a sad, ineffectual man, dying of complications from a stroke that left him partially paralyzed and unable to speak. I'm curious about him, his connection to music, and his mysterious prior life. As I understand it, he was born in England, a descendent of the respected Reverend Wright, author of a commentary on *The Pilgrim's Progress*. Grannie showed me a copy once. I once heard that the Right Reverend Wright had a black sheep son who immigrated to Canada. That must have been Gramps.

What I do know is that Edna was unhappy, especially after gum disease claimed her teeth in ninth grade. Dad and Glen were more appealing than finding out if a new set of false teeth would make tenth grade any better. The couples "Glen and Edna" and "Len and Barb" were formed. How they met, when the partners switched, and how they all remained friends, is unclear, but once the couples became "Glen and Barb" and "Len and Edna" the relationships progressed rapidly.

Dad says he was really attracted to Mom, a beautiful girl who liked to have a good time. A good time at that time meant drive-in movies, cruising town, and eating hamburgers at the White Spot drive-in restaurant. White Spot hamburgers are legendary where I came from, and their flavor permeates memories of childhood visits to British Columbia. Dad doesn't highlight this part, but pictures show smoking and alcohol as part of the fun scene, which wasn't destined to last. Dad says he thought about what beautiful children he and Mom might have, and apparently he couldn't wait to find out. At age sixteen Mom was already expecting my older sister.

Dad also recalls getting along fine with Mom's parents, which doesn't quite match the story he told me about Gramps finding out Mom was pregnant. He told Dad to choose between marrying Edna and going to jail. Dad says the threat wasn't necessary, as he was totally smitten, but they had to wait until Mom's older sister Alice was married, on December 21. After what may have been a merry Christmas, my parents were joined in holy matrimony on Boxing Day, December 26, 1957. In the three pictures I have of the wedding, no one looks particularly happy. But it was a match made in [fill in the location after finishing Chapter 1].

You Know My Name

Five months and change later, on June 1, 1958, my sister Cobina Laome (aka Coby) was born. Family legend is that Dad chose her name because he liked the sound of it. That fall the local economy turned bad and the new daddy was out of work for seven months. In the spring of 1959, with Mom again six months pregnant, he got work in far away Fort St. John. I made my appearance just after my big sister's birthday, but before the job ended, on June 2. Dad and I met each other five days later.

In the absence of information about why my name was chosen, my theory is that Dad chose a name his family in Sweden couldn't pronounce. As evidence for this hypothesis, consider that Dad added an "h" to the end of his name, changing it to Lennarth. "Th" is one of two sounds that are virtually impossible for Swedes to pronounce. The other one is "W"—a letter that doesn't exist in the Swedish alphabet. The Swedish word for Sweden is *Sverige*, and in Swedish a "W" is automatically pronounced as a "V." This leads people in Sweden to make a connection with the origin of my name. They're reminded of the calf of the leg, called *vaden* in Swedish, pronounced "vahden." The etymology explains the dual meanings of my name: "wanderer" and "warrior." Shortly you'll understand why all this matters.

With a son to carry on the family name, in a way that his family couldn't pronounce or understand, Dad got serious about his longstanding dream of moving to the United States of America. Within two years Dad had his coveted green card and moved us to San Francisco, where my younger sister was born. Her name is also interesting for a couple of reasons. She is the only one in our family who has a name that works on both sides of the Atlantic, evidence that Dad is capable of learning from his mistakes. Her angry demand not to reveal it in this book foreshadows the trouble ahead.

For a year or two in the mid-sixties, we lived the American Dream. Dad was a credit to his Northern European nature. He was shaped by evolutionary forces to grab hold of adversity and through hard work and sheer willpower not only survive but thrive. Dad's skills as an ironworker were now exceptional and he had standing in the union. His was a lucrative career for someone with the equivalent of a seventh grade education, and he was pulling in large paychecks working six or seven "tens"—sixty to seventy hours per week, at union rates, with overtime pay and benefits.

Dad loved the excitement of being on bridges and high rises—the higher up the better! He disregarded safety belts and other regulations that slowed him down, and though he soon lost the top half of two fingers, remains a risk-taker to this day. If you've seen that classic picture of ironworkers sitting on a beam, swinging high above the city eating lunch, Dad would have been the one seated the furthest out, in the most precarious position, with the biggest smile on his face.

Dad was moving up in other ways too. He followed the advice of the famous real estate investment guide, *Nothing Down*, and completed a successful set of flips, funding a family trip to Sweden for Christmas six weeks after my little sister was born. I have fond memories of dancing and singing around the Christmas tree, and I learned that the Swedes have a practical way of keeping track of grandparents. My Swedish grandfather was literally called Dad's dad, *Farfar*, and Dad's mom *Farmor*, as opposed to Mom's parents who in Swedish were *Morfar* and *Mormor*. But cultural differences, practical or not, can be a two-edged sword.

Our early life was punctuated by accidents not uncommon for children in that pre-child protective world, devoid of car seat and bicycle helmet mandates. My younger sister had hers early, when she crawled too close to the fireplace and seared the palm of her hand on the hot tile. Mine came playing unsupervised on the sidewalk where an older boy with a loud cap gun threatened to blow my head off. Terrified, I ran into the street and right into the bumper of an oncoming car. The couple of pictures that survive showcase a battered face and head, and how close I came to much more serious injuries.

Rounding off the reverse-rundown-terrible-trilogy of childhood close calls, Dad much later confessed to an accident with Coby and a little plastic bathtub on the counter. When he turned to get the towel, down came baby, tub and all. Coby was apparently unharmed, but it's nice to have a retort to her claim that my crash with the car bumper caused certain deficiencies. Humor aside, if these had been the worst of our childhood troubles, our lives would have been far different. Our accidental physical traumas would pale in comparison to the emotional trauma ahead.

We were doing well in San Francisco until Dad learned that ironworkers made big money at Alaskan work camps. It's hard to say what influence music might have had on him, but he loved Johnny Horton and his two megahits from 1958 and 1960: "When it's Springtime in Alaska (it's 40 Below)" and "North to Alaska," respectively. But some risks don't pay off. He went broke sitting on the bench in Alaska for two months. He didn't have any money to get back home and couldn't send money to Mom, who had two kids tearing up the place while she was trying to take care of the new baby. When Dad finally got work he moved the family to Bellingham in northwestern Washington. This was closer to Alaska and to mom's family in Vancouver, fifty miles up the road across the open border.

Country music continued to provide a fitting soundtrack to Dad's life, with its focus on "cheatin." In Alaska, thousands of miles away from his family for months at a time, Dad engaged in cat's-away shenanigans, poison to an already strained marriage. Amongst these mildly prophetic songs on the radio, Dad tuned in to prophecies of a different nature. He stumbled upon *The World Tomorrow*, a half-hour radio program featuring a fast-talking, charismatic, evangelist named Garner Ted Armstrong. This was a surprising turn of events, since neither of my parents had the slightest interest in religion. I only recall attending church once or twice as a child, with friends or neighbors. These were probably hand-offs that helped our parents sleep off Saturday night, to volunteers who feared for our souls.

I wouldn't personally hear Garner Ted Armstrong for several years, but religion clearly hadn't drawn Dad in. It was the snappy, if shallow, intellectualism of the dynamic, compelling, articulate presenter, who had an amazing command of global news, trends, and biblical and historical facts. Dad loved how Garner Ted sarcastically blasted everyone from evolutionists to economists, from preachers to Ph. Ds. Dad insisted on listening to *The World Tomorrow* before he and his friends hit the town. His work buddies were confused as to why this strong-willed, independent, hard-partying personality from Sweden, a country known to be liberal and anti-religious, suddenly took an interest in a smart-alecky, Bible-thumping radio personality. This was a credit to Garner Ted's ability to make the Bible relevant. He had the knack of bringing the Bible into the discussion only after he had captured the listener's interest with an amazing grasp of facts, events, names, numbers and anecdotes woven together into an intoxicating "all the experts are wrong" mantra. To Dad, for whom common sense was more important than education or expertise, this mixture was irresistible.

Garner Ted was the godfather of all right-wing talk radio in America today, spinning the secular and the sacred into a colorful and utterly compelling story. He was an early and more intelligent version of Rush Limbaugh and Glenn Beck, with a subtle religious agenda instead of an overt political bias. Dad found Garner Ted mesmerizing and was gradually drawn to the source of his dogmatism: the Bible. He was making good money now and sending checks home to his wife. That and a daily dose of radio religion helped him feel right with God while he lived the life of a single man.

Can't Buy Me Love

Those who knew my mother in those days all believed she was a good mother. She certainly wanted to be and at first she was. My early memories are of road trips and singing songs about eating worms, a doggy in a window, Fuzzy Wuzzy, and ants marching. With a mom like that, and an absentee father, it's not surprising that I was a bit of a momma's boy, nor that I clung for many years to the idea that Mom was, in fact, a good mother. But Mom was ill prepared and far too young to be raising three kids. This was true even if she hadn't been alone, in a new town, a border away from her family, and thousands of miles from her increasingly tarnished white knight.

Mom also had to deal with an unhealthy child. I was in and out of doctors' offices being tested and x-rayed for asthma and stomach problems. I remember the chalky sweet taste of penicillin bottles in the fridge, artificially flavored cherry and banana, and recurring painful canker sores in my mouth. No one at the time made a connection between the ever-present, second-hand cigarette smoke, which I remember viscerally hating. Mom wasn't satisfied with being stuck at home on a never-ending treadmill of feedings, diapers, illness, and bickering kids. Her life was made palatable by a pursuit of intoxication of a different kind from Garner Ted. Nights on the town were far more fun and rewarding than her life at home.

Our bickering was not surprising since my parents weren't getting along. My only memory of Dad and Mom together is from when I was about seven years old. It plays like a scene from a movie, set at our table at breakfast: *The mood in the room is tense and growing angry. An argument ignites, which gets louder and then scary. I'm frightened at the emotions and sit transfixed, watching Mom and Dad yelling at each other. Suddenly, it turns ugly, as Mom picks up a glass of tomato juice from the table and flings the contents in Dad's face. Quick as lightning, Dad grabs Mom, pinning her arms to her sides to immobilize her and drag her away from the table. Mom wrestles her left arm free, grabs the metal coffee pot, and hits Dad upside his head with it.*

The scene goes dark after that. Perhaps it got worse and I blacked it out. And though I say it plays like a movie, all these years later, I'm not sure the scene as I remember it is exactly what happened. The few times I've asked Dad for information, facts, or details about our early life, he claims no memory. Not even of basic facts like what time of day I was born, much less reassuring or affirming stories about what we were like as children. Information about our childhood has been painfully dragged out of him. In fairness to Dad, his marriage wasn't just painful for the kids. Regardless, as this is primarily my story, what's important is that my father's idea of providing for a family started and stopped with putting food on the table. He is a man of action, but verbs like *nurture* and *cherish* or even *educate* and *train* were not in his Swedish or English vocabularies.

This introduces a key distinction between Dad and Mom. Just as people defend my mother as a person by saying she was a good mom, others defend my Dad as a person by saying he is a good man. They describe them in this particular way because it's more difficult to apply these compliments the other way around. Mom was certainly a pretty good mother in our early years, despite her very visible problems. But objective or even supportive observers of Mom would be forced to admit that she fell seriously short of a minimum standard of motherhood. And Dad is a good man—so hard-working that he elevates work to the level of worship. He's hard on himself and those around him, and is honest to a fault. He does what he feels is right, even if it hurts him or his family, which it often did. And since he was always doing the right thing, no apologies were ever required.

People can and do repress unpleasant memories, but healing can often result from processing them properly and thoroughly. I've struggled to piece together the necessary history to write this book, not only because it's been difficult to get information from my dad or other family members, but also because of missing memories from my childhood. I'm not a psychologist, but I'm sure this is largely due to self-protective adaptation, since human beings are wired for survival. If I was learning to protect myself psychologically at this early age, that was good, because things were about to get a lot worse. But there would be a heavy price to pay for this instinctive response mechanism and I would be dealing with its baggage for decades to come.

This is a reflection of what Mom was doing with alcohol: numbing the pain of an unhappy situation and blocking out the fear and agony of failing and unhealthy relationships. But she also took action. She divorced Dad when I was eight years old and was awarded custody of my sisters and me.

Strawberry Fields Forever

My only vague memory of the divorce is Mom sitting me down to explain that Dad wouldn't be coming home. I don't recall having a negative reaction to this news. Dad was never there anyway, and when he was, he tried to change behavior he didn't approve of in family members from whom he had been absent and was disassociated. He was the source of fear and negativity associated with harsh, uncaring correction and discipline. Knowing that he wasn't going to be around to trouble Mom or any of us was not, under these circumstances, an emotionally unpleasant realization.

The kids didn't doubt that Mom cared deeply about us, since she treated us with kindness and respect, but she was struggling with drinking and the disintegrating effects it had on her life. As her drinking increased, the times when she was able to be a good mother became fewer and further between. But the good times are what I remember of Bellingham. During the summer I turned nine, Mom hooked Coby and me up with our first job: strawberry picking! I enjoyed the job largely because of how much I loved eating strawberries and how much fun I had throwing them. Soon I spent more time eating strawberries or in strawberry fights than putting strawberries into the crates. Just a few weeks into my tenth year I found myself unemployed.

The $12.78 I had earned burned a hole in my nine-year-old pocket, and Mom let me spend it on whatever I wanted, despite, or perhaps because of, having just been fired. Now what would a young, red-blooded, Canadian-Swedish-American boy want as July approached? Fireworks, of course! I blew it all on the biggest stack of fireworks I had ever seen. And I had an enormous, stupendous, fantastic time seeing my entire life's savings go up in smoke.

Later I would learn about delayed gratification, but like any normal nine-year-old, the biggest, baddest fireworks came first. But Mom sat, patiently, until long after dark, watching me light every last one of thirty or forty little black and multicolored pellets on a block of wood on our lawn. She observed unwearyingly, smoking a cigarette as those pellets slowly wiggled and grew into big fat worms made of ash. I loved Mom, and even what was to follow hasn't erased these positive feelings.

The next morning, July 5, 1968, is also indelibly etched upon my memory. I was sitting in our living room carefully extracting burnt gunpowder from fireworks used in the prior evening's festivities. My mind was working overtime, imagining uses for the dirty, pungent, spent remainders collecting in a little plastic bucket. Like Dennis the Menace, or Calvin of *Calvin and Hobbes*, I had misguided and unrealistic ambitions. Bombs were high on the list of imagined possibilities, but explosives are not, actually, the most common method of blowing apart the lives of children.

While Mom was at work, my sisters and I were at home with a babysitter when Dad walked in and introduced himself to the young lady watching us for the day. We hadn't seen him in months, and ran to him, calling "Daddy!" He told the babysitter he wanted to take us shopping and get me a haircut. He told us we might be gone for a while, allowing us to take along one toy. I slyly snapped on my swimming mask and grabbed my big book of dinosaurs to read through the mask, proudly bending the "one-toy rule." Dad did, in fact, take me to get a haircut, since the length of my hair, even then, was a point of contention. But after the barber we headed to the airport, not the mall. We had been kidnapped.

This was before the proliferation of computers and instant communications, so we were effectively underground, on a plane bound for Anchorage, Alaska, before the authorities had been alerted. The ironically named Stockholm effect, in which those kidnapped have empathy and even defend their kidnappers for not having physically abused them, was in full force for me at the time. It was fun staying in a hotel with Dad. Having learned from Garner Ted that smoking was wrong, Dad had given up cigarettes and I was able to enjoy a smoke-free environment. Then there was the hotel pool table, eating out, and even going to see a movie.

Disney's *Jungle Book* had just been released, and the title in colorful lights on the façade of the theatre seemed magical. Once inside, I was entranced by the story of Mowgli, an orphaned infant, left in the jungle to be raised by animals. The allure of a young girl calls Mowgli down from his tree to follow the mysterious creature to his true home, rescuing him from a childish desire to stay in the jungle with his animal friends. It's the story of not fitting in, and the troubles you face when you find out where you really belong. From this point forward, my story has eerie parallels to the story of a boy raised in the jungle by another species instead of enjoying a real family.

Band on the Run

We spent a week or so in Anchorage, as Dad struggled to fix a flaw in his master plan. He needed to get us to Sweden, where he, as a Swedish citizen, could contest the custody ruling of the American courts. The problem was, he needed valid passports to get us there, and he was missing one. He had the Canadian passports for Coby and me from our earlier trip to Sweden, but our sister's U.S. infant passport had expired. Reality was crashing in on this federal fugitive, trapped in the wrong country. Kudos to Dad for the creativity, diligence, and perseverance to come up with such a fantastic scheme and get this far, but his situation was very serious indeed. If he couldn't solve the passport problem, it was just a matter of time before his plan would backfire, big-time. The clock was ticking as he weighed his options.

He went for broke. Dad had a friend who worked for Scandinavian Air Lines help us board with the expired passport but from there he was on his own. The most likely outcome was detention at the passport control desk at Stockholm's Arlanda airport and a flight back to the U.S. on the next plane, at

Dad's expense, into the waiting arms of the FBI. In an effort to increase his odds, Dad stacked the passports in descending age order, putting the expired passport at the bottom. He distracted the agent with the story of how the passports mirrored his progression from Sweden, through Canada, to the U.S., the Big Country in the West to which Swedes at that time had a romantic attraction. It worked. The agent didn't check the expiration date of the bottom passport, and the "ka-chunk" of his fourth stamp confirmed my father's daring, international kidnapping as a *fait accompli*.

A crowd of uncles, aunts and cousins gathered at Aunt Karin's house in Stockholm to welcome us and support Dad. Dad was ecstatic to be home free on home turf with immunity from the kidnapping charges while the court reviewed his complaint against the U.S. custody ruling. For us kids, what was actually going on had not yet sunk in. I was an energetic little boy on an exciting adventure. The day after we arrived I went to the local supermarket with Aunt Karin, who spoke no English, to pick up some essentials. In the store, I read the Swedish label on what was obviously a milk carton. Returning to the house, I precociously showcased my command of Swedish to the crowd by badly mangling the unpronounceable Swedish word *mjölk*. Howls of stinging laughter were my first indication that Dorothy and Toto were not in Kansas anymore.

Within a few days the Swedish court agreed to hear the case and granted Dad temporary custody. The three of us were abruptly split up and sent to live with three different sets of relatives, as Dad returned to Alaska to work and provide funding for a long, drawn-out, international legal battle. There was no discussion about what was happening or why, nor any concern shown for how we might feel about it. Like the kidnapping, which ripped us away from our mother without warning, this separation was unceremoniously forced upon us, ensuring that inner feelings of loss, angst, helplessness, and frustration would take root and grow stronger.

Dad's version of the story emphasizes driving nervously around Bellingham for an hour before entering our house. He says knowing he was doing what was right gave him the courage to go ahead with his plan. Mom was involved with a guy she met in a bar, and we were his responsibility. He had tried to reconcile with Mom, who refused. Today Dad blames himself for the divorce, which at the time caught him completely by surprise. Divorce was uncommon in the old country, and no one close to Dad had experienced it.

But kids aren't able to understand the logic, circumstances, or stresses of the adult world. To make matters worse, Dad was genuinely unable to display concern for the opinions, feelings, desires, or even the rights and dignity of others, especially his own children. Stories he has told about his own childhood indicate that empathy and concern for others were not high on the list of things he learned. A tiny bit of Swedish history might be important here.

Swedish mythology says its flag, a cross of gold on a field of blue, was inspired by a golden cross in the sky seen by 12th century Swedish king Eric the Holy as he landed in Finland during the First Swedish Crusade in 1157. Centuries later, through glorious conquest, Sweden had become a great European power, a period of history ironically highlighted in elementary school in a country that otherwise prides itself greatly on being peaceful and completely neutral. In the eighteenth century, Sweden's King Charles the XII, believing God would be with him in fighting the lying, heathen Czar of Russia, Peter the Great, resolutely wasted the wealth and resources of his country in a series of disastrous campaigns against the older and wiser ruler. Its mini-empire in ruins, Sweden struggled to regain its footing as famine and poverty hounded this once-great power right up until the time my Swedish grandfather, Farfar, was born.

Farfar was among the "little people" suffering under this legacy. His dad died of a respiratory ailment when Farfar was four, and by age twelve Farfar was a hardworking "young man." He married, fathered nine children, two of whom died young, and struggled to make ends meet, establishing a farm to support his family and provide a secure future. Farmor held up the domestic side of the bargain.

Work was the air and lifeblood of the family. The kids all worked on the farm, and there was no "quality time" available for those at the tail end of the brood. Dad's position in the birth order, baby number seven, didn't even give him the distinction of being the baby of the family. That honor stayed with his little sister, Ingrid, baby number eight, after the infant death, at eighteen days, of premature baby number nine, Astrid. One distinction Dad wanted me to highlight was that he was born on a Saturday. If you wonder why he feels this is important, don't worry, you'll find out shortly.

This history helps explain why Dad approaches things the way he does, and why he seems unable to relate to others with gentleness or kindness. Dad was always a hard-working, dedicated provider of our basic physical needs, but he showed no interest in understanding, much less caring about or trying to fulfill any of our personal, individual, emotional, or inspirational needs. Because of this, rightly or wrongly, Dad's position on the kidnapping—that he did it out of love for us—has always rung hollow. Those kidnapped have not emotionally felt it to be true. Given the power of our emotional reality, it was easy to reach the conclusion that self-serving motives played a larger role. Much of the motivation may have come from a desire to do the right thing but without a focus on or an understanding of the real needs of others. Having a dad who "does the right thing" is not bad, but when it comes to kids, once basic needs are met, feeling nurtured, safe, and protected emotionally are all very important. It always felt as though a desire to not let Mom get the upper hand, or even to exact revenge for the way in which she had hurt him, played a bigger role than Dad cares to admit. This in turn left me with a grudge I carried for much of my life.

Cry Baby Cry

My sisters and I now lived in a different country, in different towns, each in a different family, with people we didn't know who spoke a language we didn't understand. We were thrown in the deep end of a pool without an emotional life jacket. We had no contact with each other. I don't recall any phone calls or other efforts to bring the three of us together. This sounds strange now, upon reflection, and was probably because our aunts and uncles all had inherited or acquired the same basic characteristics as Dad. Circumstances were what they were and how you felt about it didn't matter. Life was to be gotten on with, not reflected upon. Arrangements were practical; separating us ensured we would pick up the language more quickly and limited the impact on the families receiving us.

It also maximized the continued disintegration of our own family unit, our sense of home, and our sense of security about who loved us, who would care for us, or even who gave a crap about us. Coby had been placed with Dad's next older sister Margereta, who was stern, organized, and productive. She had married Olle Karlsson, a smarter-than-average man with a keen wit and a great sense of humor who was well-liked by everyone. They had wanted children, and were grateful to have Coby. They worked hard to make sure she was happy and well-adjusted. Not to diminish in any way the trauma she was experiencing, Coby's situation was in some ways an improvement over being the oldest of three children living with a single mother.

I was placed with Aunt Ingrid, the baby of the family, right behind Dad in birth order, a female version of Dad in personality and temperament. Ingrid also did what was right for her family, which in her case meant stoically supporting a façade. Her family was not a happy one, and the introduction of an energetic, free-spirited American boy ignited sibling rivalry between my cousins and me.

My new siblings were Conny, fifteen, and his ten-year-old sister, Inger. Neither was particularly happy to have a new kid in the household, much less one from America who was the focus of a lot of attention. When Conny wanted to show me who was boss he did so by cramming his dirty socks in my mouth and holding me upside down by the feet to give me swirlies in the toilet. Inger just tended to glare at me. I'm not sure which was worse, swirlies or the silent treatment!

But it wasn't just sibling rivalry that made the situation stressful and far from ideal. My uncle Leo was a functioning alcoholic who managed to hold down a government job with the state railway, while fooling no one close to him. He stashed beer in the garage and liquor in the basement, making constant nervous visits to both places. He stashed other things too, which I would soon discover.

On the positive side, it was exciting to be in a new country, living with a new family, learning a new culture and a new language. Over the summer, I began to pick up the language and the cultural cues, though it would be awhile before rye bread and pickled fish would win me over. As I adapted to the new situation, the subtle changes in feelings, perceptions, beliefs, and identity that had begun with the laughter at my first attempt to speak the language picked up steam.

My younger sister was placed with Ingemar, Dad's next oldest sibling, who with his wife Gun had an older son and daughter in their late teens and a much younger daughter, a few months older than my sister. The idea was that the same-aged girls would be playmates, but the reality was a sibling rivalry so intense that my younger sister soon moved in with us. At that point it just added more stress, since the house was overcrowded, and our cousins now had to share their world with two foreign intruders.

Sweden's public education system featured a nine-year program, after which kids chose between vocational programs or higher education. Swedish kids started school a year later than in the U.S. and were more mature starting out, while the pace of school was faster and more demanding. It was easy to match Coby with her peers in skill level and age by having her repeat fourth grade.

Rather than drop me back to repeat third grade, it was felt I would benefit from being in the same class as Inger, who resented my intrusion into her world and wanted nothing to do with me. My world was now a foreign, fourth-grade classroom with a cousin who pretended she didn't know me as she turned her friends against me. Besides being a year younger than everyone else, I was just learning Swedish, which made it hard to catch up with my older classmates. I was tiny, even for my own age, and am physically very out of place in class photos. Boys in the class resented the attention this puny American kid was getting, so, yes, I was teased and bullied.

We can all reflect back on our childhood and how and why it shaped us the way it did. In hindsight, I was profoundly and deeply impacted by these experiences, and those about to occur. But it was beyond my capacity at the time to assess or analyze what was happening, or to try to mitigate the effect it was having on me. Ripping us away from our mother without explanation and waging an international divorce war had already opened gaping wounds. I was now different and more emotionally fragile than other kids my age. These differences were greatly magnified by the move to a foreign country, with a foreign language, living with people I hadn't known, and attending school in a class with children all a year older than me. Without positive role models the behavior patterns I was adopting ensured that the impact of the situation would deepen and extend forward in time, as negative behavioral feedback loops were established.

This was immediately true at school where I naturally got an "F" in Swedish. But I had problems in all the other subjects as well. With no background in Swedish history or culture, I earned a "D" in Social Studies. Without a solid grasp of the language, on top of playing catch-up, my math grade was also affected. English instruction began in fourth grade, but even here I was humiliated with a "B," because the teacher said I wouldn't pronounce the words properly. My inexcusable act of defiance against the forces that had conspired against me was to refuse to mimic her heavily Swedish-accented version of British English.

Enough other parts of my identity were under attack without succumbing to this indignation.

Only in reflecting back after all these years do I understand what was happening. She didn't like the disruptive influence of an emotionally wounded, loud-mouthed American, and was probably trying to force the school to move me back a grade and get me out of her hair. I was unable to process what was happening, though my deepest fears were being validated daily. I was unloved and unwanted.

At this time music began to play a role in my life. My teenaged cousin Conny was into music, and the Beatles were all over the airwaves. "Hey Jude" was the song of the moment, holding down the number one spot on the global charts for months. With no one to talk to about the feelings trapped inside, music became more and more important to me.

Hey Jude

I vividly recall roaming the little hills behind our schoolyard, not yet ready to go "home," exploring the little ponds, valleys, and trees—which to me seemed an isolated forest in which I could commune with myself. I was a stranger in a strange land, taken away from my parents, adrift, foreign, and alone. This wandering soul was searching for something or someone, and it was crying out to the universe in an expression of longing.

The way I called out to the universe was to sing "Hey Jude," and other songs that appealed to me, in an early childhood cathartic expression of emotion. With the sound of the chill fall winds whipping past my ears, I sang "Hey Jude" at the top of my lungs, hoping someone, somewhere, would hear and understand. Without really knowing what the song was about or the point of view from which it was written, it spoke to me in important ways. They may have been adult words, but they were English words, and their musical form carried much more meaning than the Swedish swirling around me. It was an instinctive, intuitive, and powerful form of language, and the way the Beatles wielded it spoke directly to my heart. By giving it full voice, I tapped into my own hidden emotions, which were buried, ever deeper inside, masking the profound loss and hurt of my short but eventful life.

Decades later I learned why the musical message of "Hey Jude" was so powerful. Paul McCartney wrote it for Julian Lennon, John Lennon's son from his first marriage. John grew up without a father and with no close relationship to his mother, and was repeating the pattern in his own life. His son Julian suffered the abandonment of a globally famous father's captivation with a world of travel, drugs, and ideas that took him away from his son. When John left Julian's mother, Cynthia, for Yoko Ono, a strange, foreign woman, Julian felt even more abandoned, estranged, and unhappy. "Hey Jude" was originally "Hey Jules," which is what Paul called Julian. Paul was speaking to Julian's heart, asking him to open it to the changes around him.

The song was so intensely appealing to me because Paul wrote it for a boy my age, facing problems strangely similar to my own, offering an emotional life raft. With no Uncle Paul to go to, music became my solace, my expression, the language of my young heart, and was destined to play a crucial role in my journey.

While discovering the power of music, I discovered another powerful influence. While wandering through the semi-secluded wooded area I stumbled upon a hiding place in the bushes and trees. Not far from the empty cans, bottles, and remnants of a small fire, was a hidden soft-cover picture book. Sweden in the early '70s was one of the most enlightened societies, ahead of its time, at the crest of the free love generation. The glossy pictures in the little magazine were a pornographic reflection of their sophistication, and were unlike anything I had ever seen or imagined. This was not your daddy's *Playboy*. Page after tantalizing page featured striking close-up pictures of young women, sporting nothing but vinyl, leather, fur, and chain-link accessories. These items were designed to accentuate, not conceal, the women who spread themselves in erotic poses, revealing all.

At nine, I didn't quite know what to make of this, and didn't fully understand it, but I was still hypnotized. I studied them in detail, including the facial expressions of these women who were willing to share an intimacy that was completely unavailable to me. The pictures of these girls didn't cause a physical reaction or the behavior it might have if I had been older. But their enticing parting of their lips in mock ecstasy, and the staged willingness to invite the viewer in for the most intimate experience possible, reached out and grabbed me. Even the façade of love and intimacy was powerfully appealing for someone already feeling the pain of having lost them, and I was enthralled. I soon discovered that my uncle was both a closet alcoholic and a closet consumer of pornography, and I could locate his hidden treasure and put it back without anyone being the wiser. I knew these pictures were "wrong," but I couldn't resist going after them from time to time, even if my fascination with such a taboo added to the vague feelings of responsibility for Mom and Dad's divorce.

In the spring of '70, my second year with Ingrid and Leo, at the tender age of eleven, I had my first opportunity to explore the feelings and emotions being generated. In a little fort down the dirt road in the forest in back of where we lived, two thirteen-year-old neighborhood girls were experimenting with their feminine prowess, and I was a safe, somewhat exotic, and very willing boy. And maybe I was precocious for my age, being in a class with older girls. While the sexual experimentation didn't go very far, it intensified my deep longing and desire for closeness and intimacy.

Those least emotionally able to handle such situations are most susceptible to exploitation, and after two sessions the girls suddenly wanted nothing to do with me. But they had gotten under my skin and left greasy fingerprints on my imagination. My battered and bruised heart had been wounded in a new way.

Every Little Thing

Many years later I would learn about childhood development and how and why certain events impacted my sisters and me. One of the reasons these experiences were traumatic is that a child has an innate sense of and desire for order. A 2011 letter to parents of pre-school children in a Montessori school program explains it this way: "*The young child possesses a love of order that adults sometimes trample all over, because as we become older this sensitivity is less central to our lives and learning. Learning success for the young child, though, depends on this connection and understanding of order.*

It is the child's innate sense for finding and creating order that helps build later logical thinking. As adults, we disrupt a child's sense of order mainly by being unaware of this order, by changing the child's environment, which includes people, nature and ideas, as well as objects..."

My early negative experiences were laying down a cracked foundation that would affect my life and my health profoundly in a variety of ways. Instead of enjoying the fun, fearless relationships that well-adjusted children develop in a safe, secure, and orderly environment, I was forced to invest my emotional energy into instinctive, self-protective defense mechanisms. What doesn't kill you makes you stronger, but survival came at the expense of burying feelings and emotions, which meant failing to understand and honor them. I swallowed tears, fear, and pride, while building a tough exterior to protect my tender young ego. Erecting these defenses was just the beginning stage. These patterns of behavior would deepen and become more entrenched as the pain became more intense.

Suppression and denial of feelings and emotions are not at all the same as learning to manage them. I shut out love and affection, which are essential to grow, thrive, and give life meaning, but which were not essential, in the short term, to survive. What little I do know about how suppression and repression work helps me to understand from today's vantage point that these things imbedded themselves into my subconscious, and ended up controlling my life in subtle but powerful ways.

The behaviors I evolved prevented the thing I was afraid of losing—loving relationships—from developing in the first place. An innocuous and almost silly example of how insidious this is can be seen by deconstructing the mechanics of my lifelong struggle to remember names. For decades I blamed this on constantly moving but that wasn't the underlying reason. The root cause was self-conscious protection against rejection, preventing me from connecting emotionally with people I met. Since I was more concerned about protecting myself than learning about the new person, I didn't develop this simple people skill. I feared, instead of formed, relationships, and chose, at some level, not to make note of people's names.

In meeting someone again, embarrassment at not remembering his or her name reinforced a self-centered, inward focus. If I did remember the name it would be because of some other personal detail that person would have previously shared with me. Self-centered fear and insecurity focused energy inward, crowding out attention needed to grasp and retain relatively important little matters about others. This became a self-fulfilling negative pattern—not getting to know people in the first place, and being awkward at making new friends. As I moved through seven different schools in multiple countries and states, this pattern repeated itself in a self-reinforcing downward spiral, and I became an increasingly bitter, disillusioned, and disconnected young man.

My sisters and I weren't abused or physically neglected as babies or toddlers, but I faced an uphill battle. Alcohol and cigarette use by my parents, poor nutrition, and too many antibiotics added to genetic and systemic weaknesses that opened a door to serious health issues. And emotional and psychological baggage resulting from the dysfunction and disintegration of my family was already causing a wide range of personal demons to creep into my psyche. You might say there was a shadow hanging over me, which brings us back to the story...

2

Ticket To Ride

Oh little darling of mine.
I can't for the life of me remember a sadder day,
I know they say let it be
But it just don't work out that way.
And the course of a lifetime runs over and over again
No I would not give you false hope on this strange and mournful day
But the mother and child reunion is only a motion away.

—Paul Simon: Mother and Child Reunion—

Back in Alaska, Garner Ted Armstrong explained to Dad through *The World Tomorrow* radio program that God was not only real, He was more active in the world than ever before in history. This was self-evident for anyone with eyes to see and ears to hear.[5] This message was not only shared over the airwaves, but

---

5.   Mark 4:9 and many other biblical references

through an impressive array of written materials offered free of charge by the organization behind *The World Tomorrow*. The Worldwide Church of God was a small but rapidly growing church founded and run by Garner Ted's father, Herbert W. Armstrong, built on the strength of *The World Tomorrow* and the free monthly *Plain Truth* magazine. There were now also countless booklets, articles and a Bible Correspondence Course from the Worldwide Church of God's Ambassador College, with campuses in Texas, California, and England.

Through his growing library of free literature, Dad began to understand God's plan for mankind, which per Garner Ted was destined to reach a climax in the next ten to fifteen years. By studying the Bible using the Bible Correspondence Course and booklets such as *Where is the True Church, What is a True Christian, Pagan Holidays vs. God's Holy Days*, and the powerfully frightening *1975 in Prophecy*, Dad came to understand that he was privileged to know things virtually no one else on the planet could see or understand. That nobody else could see the truth that was so plainly visible was further evidence that it was true.

Give Me Some Truth

The Worldwide Church of God's mission was to proclaim that Jesus Christ was about to return, as conquering king, to take over the affairs of the planet. Their fantastic claim was proven to Dad's satisfaction in his study of the Bible, guided by their literature. Dad's eyes and ears were opened to truth divinely revealed through the only organization aware of when and how Christ would return—the Worldwide Church of God (WCG).[6] The WCG was a tight-knit, well-oiled religious organization with intense focus on its media operations. Its clear mission was to trumpet the gospel of the soon-coming Kingdom of God to the world "As a Witness"[7] before the "Great and Terrible Day of the LORD"[8]. The Day of the LORD was the apocalyptic Armageddon, coinciding with Christ's return, which would bring mankind to its knees by wiping out up to ninety percent of earth's population.[9]

---

6.   See Acronyms Glossary page 214
7.   Matthew 24:14
8.   Joel 2:30-32
9.   Based on a mathematical computation of death detailed in the book of Revelation

Many listeners and readers were fascinated by the idea that readily available writings from 2,000, 3,000, and even 4,000 years ago reveal in intricate detail exactly what was about to happen on the current world scene. As the turbulent '60s were drawing to a close, and his kids were living with relatives in Sweden, Dad was discovering biblical keys to unlock prophecy. Fantastic events were due to shake the world to its foundations in the next ten to fifteen years. He wanted to join the members of the WCG who were doing something about it. But Dad was no fool! He traveled from Alaska to the headquarters of the Worldwide Church of God in Pasadena, California, located on the immaculately landscaped Pasadena campus of Ambassador College, to check these people out. The quality and beauty of the facilities, the happy, friendly, clean-cut students, and the overall atmosphere were enough to remove any remaining doubts he may have had.

From a theological perspective, the WCG was essentially fundamentalist which, according to Wikipedia, "depends on the twin doctrines that their god or gods articulated their will clearly to prophets, and that followers also have an accurate and reliable record of that revelation." A willingness to start from scratch and take God at His Word, through diligent Bible study, was behind an eclectic mix of doctrines quite distinct from those of any other organization. A focus on every Word of God being inspired[10] was behind the view that a thorough grounding in the Old Testament was needed to understand the New.

Jesus was a Jew, and He was not the one behind the religion taking His name in vain, Christianity. Core Christian doctrines such as the Trinity, the Immortal Soul, Heaven, Hell, Christmas and Easter, with all their trappings, were not to be found in the Bible. The WCG could convincingly show from scripture and history that these ideas and concepts were constructs, based in mistranslation and misinterpretation of ancient languages, used to introduce pagan philosophy into Christianity. These perspectives were supported by clear biblical, linguistic, and historical evidence. Instead of classic Christian ideas, the WCG followed the pattern of worship outlined in the Old Testament, as codified primarily in the Ten Commandments. Old Testament elements pointed to Christ, and through obedience to the Law of God it was possible to have an enhanced understanding of the message and purpose of Jesus, and the understanding that He was about to return in power and glory.

---

10.   Proverbs 30:5, Matthew 4:4 and Luke 4:4, among others

WCG theology emphasized that God gives His Holy Spirit to those who obey Him.[11] Obedience brought the person being called into alignment with the will of God. Members of this elite group would be protected from what God had revealed would befall all humanity, in a place of safety being prepared by God.[12] God was calling Dad to, as summed up handily by one of Dad's famous sound bites, "Get in line and stay there." God had a test for those He called to see whether or not they would obey Him. Failing the test meant losing the knowledge He had granted, but passing the test granted additional understanding. The test was the fourth of the Ten Commandments God gave Moses on Mount Sinai. Keep it and you had access to truth.

Eight Days a Week

The fourth commandment reads "Remember the Sabbath day, to keep it holy. Six days shalt thou labour, and do all thy work: But the seventh day is the Sabbath of the LORD thy God: in it thou shalt not do any work, thou, nor thy son, nor thy daughter, thy manservant, nor thy maidservant, nor thy cattle, nor thy stranger that is within thy gates: For in six days the LORD made heaven and earth, the sea, and all that in them is, and rested the seventh day: wherefore the LORD blessed the Sabbath day, and hallowed it."[13] It was the cornerstone of a belief system labeled by detractors as Armstrongism.

The Sabbath was a Sign from God.[14] Passing the test proved you knew and obeyed the true God, and that God recognized you as His special treasure, a chosen one, and hand-selected out from everyone else on the planet. Those keeping the Sabbath were the one and only People of God or, in the context of this book, The People of the Sign. This was a continuation of a pattern God had instituted at creation, the way He had worked with humanity ever since. WCG members observed the Sabbath from sundown Friday night to Saturday sundown. Members were willing to lose their jobs, in faith, over the Sabbath day. And some did. It was virtually impossible to be a member in the WCG and not keep this command, as expounded by the church.

---

11. Acts 5:32
12. Revelation 12:14
13. Exodus Chapter 20:8-11
14. Exodus 31:13

In the days of Noah, God had become so frustrated with how evil man had become, that He had wiped them off the face of the earth, with the exception of Noah and his immediate family members. He entered an unconditional covenant with mankind at that time to assure mankind He would never again take such drastic action, and established the rainbow as the sign of His covenant.[15] Later, under Abraham, circumcision was introduced as the sign of a two-way, conditional covenant. Because Abraham held up his end of the bargain, he secured God's covenant promises for his descendants: benefits of nationhood, fabulous physical blessings, and numerous other physical and spiritual components.[16]

The Ten Commandments were the center of a subsequent covenant with Israel and an important extension of the covenant with their ancestor, Abraham. Israel became the special People of God, with promises of pre-eminence and many other blessings and privileges worthy of such a distinction. By keeping the Sabbath we could secure this status for ourselves, and without it we could not claim to be God's chosen ones, no matter what we believed or did. The importance of the Sabbath to WCG theology cannot be overemphasized. It's why being born on Saturday was meaningful to my dad.

But in addition to the weekly Sabbath, there were seven annual Sabbaths. These Holy Days were the days God commanded Israel to keep when they were rescued from slavery in Egypt. According to the booklet *Pagan Holidays or God's Holy Days,*[17] these days revealed specifics of the plan of God, both physically and spiritually, to those who kept them. This set the WCG apart from Seventh Day Adventists, the Church of God Seventh Day, Seventh Day Baptists, and virtually every other Sabbatarian church group on the planet. WCG members were totally unique as a dedicated group of people who could pride themselves, in a humble, converted way, on being the only human beings who understood the plan of God. Only they could see the hand of God, which was actively guiding world events. They understood the specifics and the immediacy of biblical prophecy.

Dad had no choice but to submit his life to the will of God, bringing himself into conformity with this divinely delivered pattern of worship. He was

---

15. Genesis 9:11
16. Genesis 17:11
17. See Acronyms Glossary page 214

about to join his destiny with the destiny of a group of tribes who had escaped slavery to wander through the deserts of the Middle East some 4,000 years ago, on their way to the promised land. While Dad pondered joining The People of the Sign, the Swedish courts ordered him to personally care for us or lose custody. He moved back to Sweden in the late summer of 1970, just in time to gather his children together before school started.

Come Together

It had been two years since I was transplanted into Swedish society and I had made great progress in adapting to my new country and situation. I was fluent in Swedish and had caught up with my older classmates. Now I was uprooted again and forced to cope with another new family situation, another new town, and another new school. There was another set of older classmates, new teachers, all with a different accent. Coby, who towered over me by about four inches, was in sixth grade with me, which was more awkward than helpful. Our family situation was obviously abnormal, and we stuck out like the proverbial sore thumb.

It was not a return to anything familiar. Dad and Coby both seemed like strangers. Dad had been working in Alaska for years prior to the divorce, and aside from the brief kidnapping incident, we hadn't seen him in two years. In terms of my mental and emotional state, my identity, my security, and other internal issues I was struggling with, this was a step backwards.

Dad was no help, as it was not in his nature to care about our inner health. He was also focused on the challenges of repatriating himself into Swedish society, and dealing with the financial and logistical challenges of making this work. Dad hired a live-in housekeeper who could have been Cinderella's stepmother, if her evil daughters had been two large, smelly, and unruly dogs. This disheveled, snaggle-toothed, and ill-tempered woman and her hounds took over the house until Dad could take it no more. He then tried a young, inexperienced, unwed mother with a three-month old baby and a jealous boyfriend who was not pleased she was living with us.

Dad was also beginning to implement his new understanding on child rearing, an update on the classic "spare the rod and spoil the child" method, reinvigorated by someone he mistakenly considered to be an expert on child psychology, Garner Ted Armstrong. He had penned *The Plain Truth about Child Rearing,* a lengthy booklet on a systematic approach to behavior modification, in which obedience to divine and parental law was taught through age-appropriate corporal punishment. This punishment was to be delivered swiftly and uncompromisingly for each infraction. A touchstone scripture was "Foolishness [is] bound in the heart of a child; [but] the rod of correction shall drive it far from him."[18] Parents had to begin applying the method in infancy in order to correct the foolish nature of children.

Dad, in his zeal, passed himself off as an experienced father, applying this method to his own children and teaching our young and inexperienced housekeeper how to train her baby to sleep. While not out of line with Swedish national history, this was counter to the prevailing social wind in Sweden. The families of which the three of us had been a part had all adopted a more modern approach. The transition was hardest on Coby, who had bonded with Margareta and Olle because they had given her the love and attention she so desperately needed. They genuinely wanted her as a daughter. She had entered puberty and was deeply resentful of how Dad had ripped her away, again, from a more loving environment. They were fighting with Dad to adopt her, and she wanted to stay with them. Dad's implementation of a family version of Christ's rod of iron made Coby's life unbearable. I was eleven, had not yet reached adolescence, and was not fundamentally opposed to a binary obey or be punished approach. In fact, I was about to learn to love the underlying logic behind Garner Ted's booklet.

It was firmly based in the WCG's view of how God approaches humanity. The Sabbath and annual Holy Days illustrated God's plan. The spring Holy Days symbolized Jesus' first coming, as in the lamb slain at Passover to produce a sinless life. Pentecost was the only summer Holy Day and it pictured the time since then, under the Holy Spirit—the promised "Comforter." The fall Holy Days highlighted Jesus Christ's return to rule with a rod of iron, and the humbling of humanity leading to reunion with God. The first two of four fall Holy Days, the Day of Trumpets and the Day of Atonement pictured these events. But the spiritual high point of the year was the Feast of Tabernacles, a seven-day festival opening with a Holy Day, and followed immediately by the final annual Holy Day called The Last Great Day. Together these eight days

---

18.   Proverbs 22:15

were affectionately known as "the Feast" and celebrated at many "Feast sites" around the globe.

As we were reunited in Sweden, the fall Holy Day season was looming, and Dad was determined to attend the Feast. In 1970 Sweden was managed from the WCG's office in Germany, so we crowded into our VW bug to drive through Denmark to the church's office in Düsseldorf. Frank Schnee was the colorful and dynamic WCG leader with responsibility for the German-speaking region of the church. His indomitable, effervescent enthusiasm, and can-do, wheeler-dealer style had led him to charter a plane, turning the journey to and from this spiritual gathering into a joyful community experience. We were swept up in the excitement of the European contingent of WCG members headed for a strange-sounding Feast of Tabernacles in a place called Minehead, England.

That fall, as the Age of Aquarius was dawning, I found myself traveling to the ancient harvest festival God commanded Israel to keep, thousands of years ago, "forever, throughout your generations."[19]

You Really Gotta Hold of Me

Deuteronomy 16:13-15 commanded us to rejoice before God "in the place which the LORD shall choose." For us the LORD God had chosen a holiday camp in southwest England. It was the kind of camp featured in the Who's rock opera, "Tommy," and the resulting movie starring Elton John, Roger Daltrey, Tina Turner, and a host of others. There I had my first exposure to epic, ninety-minute sermons explaining how human beings were at the center of the spiritual struggle between right and wrong, good and evil. God was looking for a few good men (and women) to showcase the right way of living through complete and total submission and obedience to Him and His One True Church.

We were at a critical juncture in history, the prophesied "Time of the End" immediately prior to Jesus Christ's return as "King of Kings and Lord of Lords." We were called into an elite training program to assist Christ in bringing the world into alignment with God's way of life. The planet would fight against Him, but His rod of iron would bring humanity into submission to a re-education program similar to the one we ourselves were undergoing at the

---

19.   Leviticus 23:41, among others

Feast. My vivid memories of the Feast include a night sick with fever, dreaming about giants fighting a titanic battle to gain control of the planet. Those sermons were heady stuff for an impressionable eleven-year-old.

But I also began to see what appealed to Dad about all this. The Feast was a foretaste of the future. *The World Tomorrow* was the name of the radio program, and also later the TV broadcast. *Tomorrow's World* was the name of the more explicitly biblically focused sister magazine to the mass-circulation *Plain Truth*. The term "The World Tomorrow" became symbolic to WCG members of the 1,000-year, benevolent (if dictatorial) reign of Christ on earth, during which the lamb would lay down peacefully with the lion. The eight days of the Feast were a grand, glorious, and powerful community celebration of our faith, our hope, our church, our uniqueness, our identity, and the glorious future that awaited all of us. We would reign with Christ as "Kings and Priests"[20] during this future 1,000 years—a period known officially as the Millennium.

Members saved up ten percent of their gross income, known as a tithe, to use at the Holy Days. Almost all of this money was spent at the Feast where members lived together for eight days at an economic level far above the one they experienced the rest of the year. WCG members felt like royalty in more ways than one, and it was a magical world of abundance for children and teenagers. It compared very favorably to Christmas, which, with the exception of our one Christmas as a family in Sweden years earlier, seemed an empty, consumer-society ritual of frantically opened presents and superficial happiness. Christmas, once the last present was opened amidst a lack of familial warmth, always left me cold.

The Feast, on the other hand, was a balance of spiritual nourishment for parents and physical fun and excitement for kids—and it lasted eight glorious days. Being new to the church, Dad had not saved a tithe, so we were on a tight budget. The German office had funded our flight, but here we were on our own. Dad cooked for us in our accommodations while most participants feasted on catered meals in the main dining area. But we quickly formed warm relationships with the people we met, who were all very interested in this unusual new family from Sweden, a region as yet fairly untouched by the WCG media machine. Several of them delivered goodies to help us celebrate a proper Feast. This unfamiliar generosity felt like the warm embrace of a new spiritual family.

---

20. Revelation 5:10

At the Feast in Minehead, WCG members occupied the entire holiday camp, designed for family vacations. It was off season, so the camp was all but shut down, but there were WCG scheduled church services daily, along with many other activities. But on two nights during our stay, the rides and games were opened, and WCG kids had the run of the camp. Then our new family consisted of everyone in the park. The Feast was unlike anything I had ever experienced—an emotional life raft to a child lost at sea. The positive impact this event had on my life is with me to this day.

During the Feast, Dad publicly proclaimed his commitment to his newfound faith through baptism. The WCG practiced baptism according to the biblical model—adults only, full immersion—a watery grave for the remission of sins, and a resurrection to a new life. The gift of the indwelling of the Holy Spirit was then delivered via the laying on of hands and prayer of the ministry. A minister named John Karlson who worked with Frank Schnee in the German region performed these twin ceremonies. We were now in with God. We were People of the Sign.

Run for Your Life

Upon our return to Sweden, we were officially placed on the WCG member list and we received Volume I of the new *Bible Story* in the mail. This was not a typical collection of random stories from the Bible, sanitized for children; it was a children's version of the Bible, written and illustrated by an internationally known and acclaimed cartoonist, Basil Wolverton. Wolverton's ability to visually convey the horror of biblical plagues and calamities is legendary in the WCG universe. *1975 in Prophecy*, a booklet showcasing the end of Man's autonomous rule by illustrating horrifically the events of the book of Revelation, is the classic example.

The *Bible Story* had been published serially in the WCG's *Plain Truth* magazine for years, and was now a set of volumes sent free, one at a time, a few months apart, to WCG members. Dad started reading Volume 1 to us before bed at night. I enjoyed this activity, as being read to in bed was the kind of childhood experience I had longed for. But more than that, I was instantly fascinated with the narrative and the vivid, high-quality drawings that graphically displayed all of the gory glory of the Old Testament. But family story time lasted only a week or two, after which Coby steadfastly refused to participate in this exercise, and somehow won the argument. This may have been because Dad was not the type to read his children a bedtime story and then tuck them in.

But on my own I read the book cover to cover. Chapter after chapter told of God reaching out to a rebellious mankind turning its back on Him. He taught mankind His way of life, giving them the chance to make right choices. Man disobeyed and God withdrew His protection. Man suffered and God gave new teaching and laws, and another chance to obey. Colorful characters were brought to life by Wolverton, whether it was the nameless faces above the Noachian flood waters before going under, or Job sitting on an ash heap in a ragged loincloth, scraping the boils on his skin with a pot shard.

Wolverton's images made powerful music, but the words were the lyrics that drove the message home. This colorful collection of history and spiritual analogies was the Word of God, recorded for the spiritual education and benefit of mankind. I took it to heart. In a very personal way, this was written specifically for me. I loved these books so much that when book two showed up, I read book one again, before diving into book two. When book three showed up, I feasted on book one and book two again, before treating book three like dessert. It was the source of my early understanding of God's approach to mankind, what He expects of us, and that people typically respond with doubt and rebellion.

God provided man with a path to happiness, but stubborn, immature, foolish man insists he knows better. God then applies Pavlov's method across a vast expanse of history. And history shows that man generally refuses to learn. With Basil Wolverton's clear style, and even clearer illustrations, you would have to be a fool not to want to be on God's side. I had been adrift without the internal compass good parents provide to their children, but no longer.

I wanted each hero—Abel, Noah, Abraham, Jacob, Joseph, Moses, Joshua, and Caleb—to be the one to turn things around for humanity, or at least for Israel. It was high mystery and suspense and I was spellbound! This was a powerful world-view for a troubled eleven-year-old pre-adolescent. And it was so simple. I would be different, one of the few, the special, the chosen. All I needed to do to experience happiness, protection, and blessings, was do what God asked. Regardless of what the rest of humanity did, I would trust in God and be faithful to Him. I was completely sold on the value of joining The People of the Sign.

The *Bible Story* also showcased WCG emphasis on the classic patriarchal model. Sarah was honored because she called Abraham "Lord." The biblical admonition for women to submit to their husbands[21] was required reading at every wedding. Male/female relationships and marriages in the WCG were anachronistic, to say the least. Marriage was binding until death. You could divorce, but to remarry while your ex-spouse was alive was considered adultery. Only a rare church ruling of fraud prior to the wedding could justify an annulment. This meant that if a happily married couple became members and one of them had a living ex-spouse, that couple had to divorce, even if children were involved. Many true believers complied. Dad, being divorced, was not free to remarry, which became one of his first major trials in the faith.

The court case between my parents was winding its way through the Swedish court system. Dad had won, Mom had appealed, and it reached the supreme court of Sweden. Mom had recently remarried, which gave her an advantage over my dad, who was trying to rear us as a single parent. Dad suspected that Mom's happy marriage was a show, contrived to gain an advantage. A female judge asked Dad if he had plans to remarry. Dad, infused with newfound belief that God had his back due to his recent baptism, was perhaps a bit overconfident. He shared his intent to stay single (due to the church's teaching) while insinuating that a woman had no business being a judge.

Dad may not yet have known that WCG speculation held Swedes to be the modern day descendants of one of the lost ten tribes of Israel, the tribe of Naphtali. There is a fascinating story in the book of Judges about a man of the tribe of Naphtali so timid and fearful that God chose to work through a prophetess, Deborah, as the judge that led and protected Israel at that time.[22]

In any case, my mother won. Dad's experience was in line with the *Bible Story*. God doesn't back you up when you're out of line.

Don't Let Me Down

We returned to the U.S. over the winter break of 1970-71, stopping in England to celebrate our reunion. My younger sister was only four when she

---

21. Ephesians 5:22 and elsewhere
22. Judges chapter 4

had been kidnapped and had forgotten English during two and a half years of Swedish immersion, so she and my mom couldn't understand each other. Mom struggled to maintain a happy façade with her new husband and troubled kids. Getting back together with her was supposed to be magical, but the reality was an enormous emotional letdown. It wasn't just that everything was different; something was irreparably broken. It wasn't yet clear what it was, but it hung in the English air like the pending break-up of the Beatles, even in the penny arcades, and like the cold drizzle over London, even in the double-decker buses, and even when the sun was out.

I don't recall alcohol in England, but on the flight home Mom started drinking as soon as the plane was in the air. There were arguments with Don, who tried to slow her down, and over the course of the long, transatlantic flight, she became increasingly loud and unruly. Her interactions with Don, us, passengers, and attendants on the plane were painfully embarrassing, but they were nothing compared to the arrival.

What should have been a triumphant, victorious return to friends and family, including Grannie, aunts, uncles, and cousins who were waiting at the airport, had become a horrible, slow-motion train wreck. Mom had to be helped, staggering, down the stairs of the airplane. Don and Coby were furious and resentful, baby sister was crying, and I just stared in wide-eyed horror.

When Mom came into contact with the people who had given signed affidavits to the court, vouching for her capability as a mother, it was like an elementary school science project volcano, where you pour vinegar into baking soda. The welcoming party was beyond disappointed; it was shocked and angry. Mom responded with belligerence. There was yelling and swearing and a physical tussle to bring her under control. It took several people to get her through the airport and to the car. I don't remember details of what happened after that, except a vague memory of Mom sobbing uncontrollably on the ride home. I do remember the sickening feeling in the pit of my stomach, my fear and worry about what was going to happen next, and the horrible realization that I had not, in fact, gotten my Mom back.

I had lost her forever.

Mom's second marriage was a sham. As Dad suspected, they met over alcohol and married only to fool the courts. Don was a problem drinker, but Mom was now a full-fledged alcoholic. Back in Bellingham, I don't recall more than one or two family dinners, memorable only for the drama of the charade and the drunken arguments. I also don't recall whether Don actually ever lived with us or not, but the marriage was clearly over by the time we touched down on North American soil.

This seemed lost on the local lady reporter who interviewed us to showcase the happy reunion in the papers. The inherent misrepresentation of describing our situation as a happy-ending success story was not lost on me, even as an eleven-year-old. I was very uncomfortable with the celebratory spin she put on our family for her front-page scoop. We were hurting, but were expected to be all smiles and hugs. I recall the disheartening realization that people choose to believe what they want to believe, and will spin things to their own advantage, taking from others what they want regardless of the morality or truthfulness of what they are doing.

Such bitter experiences with irresponsibility and lack of concern in those around me confirmed the value of my brief but powerful introduction to God and His view of sinning humanity. This, being bilingual, and having experienced life in ways unusual for an eleven-year-old, gave me a perspective quite different from other kids my age. These filters began to profoundly impact the way I received and processed information and my interactions with other people. Having learned to manage as an outsider among older kids in an accelerated foreign-language system, I was empowered to stand outside of my situation and question it. For example, I have a vivid memory of my first day back in an American school. I re-joined kids my own age mid-year in sixth grade, and the teacher stood me up in the front of the class and introduced me as the "new boy from Sweden." I was furious! I was an American, and I didn't like being singled out as different, yet again, right from the start.

But I was different; I stood out and stood apart, observing the behavior of other children in class on my first day. In Swedish schools, the teacher was in charge of the classroom and was shown respect at all times. Here, the kids were loud, obnoxious, and out of control, and had drawn and written in colored chalk all over the chalkboard; words like Love, Peace, and a symbol I didn't understand—the peace sign. This wasn't a sign I could relate to. My interactions with the other kids were far from positive. When kids at school reached out to the new kid with a friendly "Say something in Swedish" I shot back with "I'm not your monkey."

Having been on an accelerated track with older kids, I was academically closer to a ninth-grade level. In school I was bored, frustrated, and felt very different from my peers. As an adolescent I began withdrawing into a resentful and aloof shell, built around a complex mix of emotional inferiority and intellectual superiority.

Bellingham was not the same place I remembered from my happy first summer month as a nine-year-old. It hadn't changed, but I sure had.

I'll Get You

As sixth grade ended and summer came, I spent time at a local lake just down the road. I had always loved the water and was not a bad swimmer. I signed up for a swimming program and quickly progressed through the levels. Soon I was precociously swimming in deep water to reach the big kids' diving platform, and gained a sense of freedom and independence. Emotionally I was drawn somewhat to songs on the radio, like "Mrs. Robinson" and "Harper Valley PTA," and I remember the longing I felt listening to "Bridge over Troubled Waters." But there were no bridges on the horizon.

With Mom working and drinking, we were unsupervised and out of control. We watched TV and fought constantly and outside the home I was becoming a juvenile delinquent. I remember the joy of breaking glass, using plastic squirt bottles, paint thinner, and matches to create flame throwers, and climbing up into the open space under the overpass of a major rural intersection to throw dirt clods at cars driving by below.

When fall and seventh grade arrived, I entered junior high. I was allowed a couple of electives, and chose Earth Science, because it sounded interesting and I wanted to learn. I did not want a repeat of my painful experience in the second half of sixth grade, spending day after day in an out-of-control classroom learning nothing I didn't already know. Within the first couple of weeks my hopes were mercilessly destroyed, as a voice-over to an educational filmstrip in Earth Science class intoned: "The Sun is very high in the sky. It is higher than the clouds. It is higher than an airplane."

I looked around at the others in the room, who were either listening intently or didn't care that they weren't learning anything a three-year-old couldn't figure out on its own, and I was horrified. What is wrong with these people? And how could the teacher presiding over this mind-numbing nonsense be so oblivious to the damage it was doing? It was suffocating, and I was trapped in it. I was a twelve-year-old version of Jack Nicholson in the movie *One Flew over the Cuckoo's Nest;* sane, but stuck in an insane asylum. I was literally frightened by the experience, a victim of stupidity being inflicted on the young and defenseless.

In the fall of '71 the three of us saw Dad for the first time since Sweden. He had gained court permission for us to fly up to Alaska and spend the Feast with him. It had been a year since the Feast in Minehead, and almost that long since I had seen the *Bible Story* books, which Dad had brought with him. I instantly re-acquainted myself with them, and when I wasn't at services, eating in a restaurant, or attending some other church activity, I was in our room on the floor, re-reading *The Bible Story*, books one through three, and continuing with books four and five. My life was confusing, and I was deeply unhappy in ways I had been unable to developmentally and consciously appreciate until now. *The Bible Story* was an escape from a Maya-like reality that is but an illusion into a well-illustrated story that depicted reality.

Dad brought his minister by to show off my interest in the *Bible Story*, and the minister said he wished more church kids were like me. Instead of responding positively to such praise, I was annoyed, having learned to immediately question anyone being nice to me. What was in it for them, and where were they when I needed them?

But the Feast itself was a blast, and I actually enjoyed the two-hour church services. They started with hymn singing, a short sermon, and then music performances and announcements about activities, and developments as the WCG pursued its Mission. The main attraction was the sermon, an hour-long romp through the Bible and world events tying ancient texts, spiritual principles, our current experiences, and moral lessons into guidance on how to live a better life. All of this was related to what we were doing right then and there, living a foretaste of the World Tomorrow, the time just ahead of us in which, under Christ's rule, a thousand years of peace and prosperity would be forced upon a rebellious planet.

This well-orchestrated, well-organized, and jam-packed event was a refreshing change from my chaotic, unsupervised, and information and knowledge-starved life back home. And the promise of a better world was like nourishment to a starving boy. Maybe there was hope after all! But even an eight-day-long religious celebration was but a short break from reality. Back in the real world the hope and possibilities that were awakened would soon be a distant memory.

My mother's drinking problem was serious and getting worse. It's pointless for me to speculate how much of this was due to what Dad had done, but it certainly had pushed her over the edge, and I blamed Dad for the mess. I learned later that Grannie had loaned Mom the money to fund the custody battle and buy a house, giving our situation a stable external façade while inside life was coming apart at the seams. Mom worked as a bartender and was drinking heavily all the time. We were left home alone—a lot. We had a cat and a dog that left messes around the house that didn't get cleaned up. There were other kinds of messes too. Mom was making wine downstairs, and while I had learned how to get into that, we three kids had not learned how to properly take care of ourselves.

Coby tried valiantly to hold things together, and while our sister followed her lead, I was having none of it. My choices in food and dress were blatantly unhealthy and socially inappropriate. So were my choices in behavior. I was getting more aggressive with my delinquent pranks, like pelting neighborhood houses with eggs and raw Pillsbury dough slices, or setting paper bags of unpleasant substances on fire on people's porches and ringing their doorbell, so they would stomp into the contents. And it wasn't anywhere near Halloween.

She's Leaving Home

Mom spent some evenings at home. One night I'll never forget she came home drunk to our dangerously messy home and fixated on a houseplant that had died for lack of water. She launched into an angry tirade, yelling at me and Coby for letting this happen, and then put on Carole King's melancholy masterpiece, *Tapestry*, and sat down on the floor.

This album had sad emotional songs like "So Far Away" which laments that we don't "stay in one place anymore." Carole sang "Long ago I reached for you and there you stood, holding you again could only do me good. Oh, how I wish I could, but you're so far away" and set off an emotional vibration of longing deep inside of me. I was still hurt and confused by Mom's anger and stood looking at her, sitting on the floor in the middle of the living room, cross-legged and drunk, hunched over and staring at the carpet. She was only three feet away, but farther from me than she had ever been. I was powerless to reach her, and my own pain was submerged and covered by hers. The weight of the world pressed hard against the top of my shoulders as I observed her hunched position and felt responsible for her misery. Remembering to water the plants would not change a thing.

Then the impact of the title track, with its eerie haunting lyrics about a mysterious traveler in a coat of many colors, penetrated into my heart and soul. I listened while the traveler "reached for something golden hanging from a tree, and his hand came down empty." Carole explained, "It seemed that he had fallen into someone's wicked spell and I wept to see him suffer, though I didn't know him well." The story concluded with the frightening specter of death and Carole's own tapestry unraveling, as she sings, "He's come to take me back."

I imagined a swirling black mist surrounding Mom that became cobwebs and then threads of a dark tapestry wrapping itself around her, trapping her and carrying her limp body off into the air. I had a sense of her receding in the distance and disappearing from my life, while my fate was somehow tied to that of this powerful wanderer who somehow had made this thing happen.

A hopeless atmosphere permeated my situation, and there were troubling physical symptoms as well. It may have been our terrible diet, the emotional stress, or a combination of both that caused a recurrence of the frequent stomach cramps and canker sores I'd had before going to Sweden. In addition, I now had recurring gnawing pains in my calves and thighs that often kept me up at night. Mom said they were growing pains and maybe they were harmless, but to me they were an ominous sign that pointed out the obvious—things were just not right.

In the spring, a few months before Coby's fourteenth birthday, Mom picked up a group of five or six hitchhikers from Holland and let them stay at our house. She was out on the town with one of them, and the others decided to have a dance party at our house. Coby had her girlfriend from across the street come over to join in the fun. When one of the Dutch guests became more aggressively forward than Coby was comfortable with, she left with her friend and never came back. From her friend's house, she contacted friends of our family in Canada who were able to arrange for her to come live with them.

Coby had always been closer to our younger sister, and the girls had stuck together in the ongoing sibling triangulation, in which I was the unloved and unwanted third party. With Coby gone, little sister was on her own, as I was anything but a good older brother. As I recall, Mom had been gone for about three days when my eight-year-old baby sister stood crying in her nightgown on the neighbor's porch. She was trying to explain that she didn't know where her mommy was, and that she didn't know what to wear for school.

From there it didn't take long for the local protective services to finally intervene. Toward the end of seventh grade I was pulled out of class and taken to see the guidance counselor. Once in her office I was told, without explanation, that I wouldn't be going home that day. I had become a ward of the state. My younger sister and I were sent to live in an "interim home"—a temporary orphanage.

As I was approaching thirteen, the main lesson I was learning was that although most people will smile and be nice to you, they are doing so for largely selfish reasons. They won't really lift a finger to help someone in need, especially if that person is standing right in front of them. It's too messy, and the commitment to help goes beyond what they are willing to do. I was not yet outwardly or openly rebellious. In any interaction with those older or in authority I would conform, but internally I was becoming more and more angry and resentful. I resented, for example, that Coby had ended up in a good situation, with friends of the family in Canada, and I grew more and more angry toward Dad.

In my last week of school, a friend at the interim home, the son of the couple who managed the place, met me on my way home to tell me he had learned from his mom that my dad was in town to pick me up. I followed Coby's example and ran away. My friend told the agents at the house with Dad that I was hitchhiking to Seattle to throw them off the track as I tried to make my escape.

But where could this runt of a twelve-year-old boy go? I was headed on foot toward my mother's house when I noticed a vehicle pulling up next to me. As I started to cut across a field, a young man and a young woman got out, calling out to me in a friendly way. They said they were social workers who were there to help me. As we talked they drew me out a bit, asking me why I was running away.

Given the kind and respectful treatment, I decided to open up, and shared that I did not want to go live with my dad. They assured me that if I didn't want to live with my dad no one would make me do so. I should get in the car and go back to the facility to talk about it. I quickly assessed the situation. First of all, I didn't have a choice, and what they said seemed reasonable to my young mind, given that I knew Coby had been able to find a new home in Canada.

Once in the car, I was taken straight to the interim home and handed over to Dad. My new kidnappers walked away, without a second thought about the lies and manipulation they had used, as my old kidnapper demanded to know why I had run away. Humiliated, I refused to answer, as my slow-burning internal anger was being fanned into a red-hot flame.

In my own immature and unprotected emotional world, I was completely wrapped around the axle. I was trapped in a surreal version of the old flower petal game. Everyone had been given a daisy and pulled the petals, one by one, to find out if they were loved. Everyone else had gotten a yes answer at some point, and had left with those who loved them. I was standing center stage with all spotlights on me, pulling the last petal off my little wilted stem. The answers had all been no, and there were no more petals to pull.

As Dad again took my younger sister and me to Alaska, this time with the full blessing and approval of the American Justice System, I was on the verge of turning thirteen, the Bar-Mitzvah age at which Jewish children become responsible for their own actions. Despite the WCG affinity with all things Jewish, this was a non-event. Birthdays were considered moderately pagan, at best distracting from God's Holy Days, and fostering selfishness and materialism among children. Such beliefs appealed to Dad's basic nature. His approach did not include any acknowledgement that his son was an independent individual, with independent thoughts and feelings. Just get in line and stay there! There was no need to express any recognition that this might be difficult, or that my little sister or I might be troubled by all we'd been through.

Living with Dad could have been an improvement, but he wouldn't think twice about squashing any discussion he believed to originate in a bad attitude. Dad was not interested in emotions or psychobabble. Concern or empathy were not only unnecessary, they were counterproductive.

My teen years were not going to be a happy time.

3

Happiness is a Warm Gun

"The fear of the LORD is the beginning of wisdom:
and the knowledge of the holy is understanding.
For by me thy days shall be multiplied,
and the years of thy life shall be increased."

PROVERBS 9:1-11

My life had become a tennis match between bitter rivals in which I was the ball. My little sister and I were again living with my dad, but this time in Alaska, not Sweden. It was even colder there, in more ways than one. There was no female influence in our family, which might have called out a need for some degree of love, understanding, and nurturing. Dad was taking care of us without really caring for us. He provided for our physical needs with no emotional support. He took no interest in what interested us, outside of the limited activities of the church. We were also not receiving any help with our schoolwork, since Dad was a manual laborer with a sixth grade Swedish education and little respect for those who did not earn their living through his definition of hard work.

As hard as this was on me, it was much worse for my younger sister, who had not benefited from an accelerated education in Sweden. I was somewhat self-sufficient in school but she was not, and was less able to protect herself from the damage of being in the shadow of an authoritarian and emotionally unavailable father. As she had previously experienced with English, she had now forgotten Swedish, a result of her pawn-like existence, pushed around by forces and situations she did not control and could not identify with.

All I've Gotta Do

As for me, at the ripe age of thirteen I had learned from bitter experience that people couldn't be trusted, but the members of the WCG I met at the weekly Sabbath Services in Anchorage seemed a cut above average. Church services were structured like those at the Feast, though the sermons provided by the local minister, Mr. Gordon, were typically less than inspiring. They were long on specific instructions on what we should do, and while they were spiked with colorful anecdotes and stories, there was little illuminating exploration of the implications or the reasoning behind the mandates that were being issued. But most of the members made us feel very welcome and a few even showed some genuine interest in me as a person. I also made several friends at our local church and in congregations that met for combined services on the annual Holy Days, turning them into mini-versions of the Feast—additional annual highlights for the spiritual communities of the WCG.

The WCG view of the Holy Days was twofold: a pattern of worship representing a better way of life, and a prophetic roadmap outlining the plan of God. This plan was illustrated by God's rescue of Israel from slavery in Egypt and their obedience and submission to a relatively large number of rules and regulations. Christ's life and sacrifice "magnified the law and made it honorable"[23] which made it even more binding on us. We had to go above and beyond the physical requirements.

For example, the tithe members saved for use at the Holy Days was only part of a law on tithing. It was known as second tithe, because the first ten percent of a member's gross income belonged to God, and was sent to the WCG

---

23.   Isaiah 42:21

to fund the aggressive media campaigns driving its growth. We also kept the laws of clean and unclean meats, from Leviticus 11, as a practical law with spiritual implications. The food laws promoted health while teaching us to be different from other people, setting a distinction between the Holy and the profane. The Sabbath cemented this uniqueness since God used it as a test and a sign between Him and His people. The WCG obeyed, claiming the sign and a special relationship with God, along with many related promises.

Then there were special keys to unlock prophetic understanding, like the modern identity of the lost ten tribes of Israel. Ancient Israel was composed of twelve tribes, ten of which settled in the Northern Kingdom, called Israel. They were unfaithful to God, were taken captive, and since they stopped keeping the Sabbath and Holy Days altogether, they lost their identity. Modern-day Jews are the descendants of the Southern Kingdom, called Judah, where the tribes of Judah, Levi, and some from Benjamin settled. These three tribes were also disobedient; they were sent into captivity as well, but they held tightly to their religious practices throughout history, especially the Sign—observance of the seventh-day Sabbath. They could identify God, who brought them back to Judea prior to Christ, only to see them reject His Son. Still, they held to the Sabbath, so in the twentieth century God again gave them back the Holy Land, as He had promised in prophecies written thousands of years earlier.

But the WCG both accepted Christ and had the Sign. We were Spiritual Israel, the inheritors of the spiritual promises. This was all the more compelling to me after the loss and betrayal by those who should have been caring for me, but failed. God was not like the people in my life. He would care for, protect, and bless anyone who would turn to Him. Even submission to the so-called wrathful and vengeful God of the Old Testament was preferable to what I had experienced at the hands of less dependable mortals. It seemed reasonable to believe that the years just ahead would bring unbelievable calamity and suffering to a rebellious and sinning humankind even as their designated time for autonomy came to an abrupt halt.

Lucy in the Sky with Diamonds

What doesn't kill you can make you stronger. The time in Sweden and in different family situations had heightened my survival instincts. Even at age thirteen I could generally outthink and outmaneuver most peers and some people much older than me, intellectually. This gave me an inner stability, a sense of integrity, and a place deep inside my ego to take a stand. This took place mostly on an intellectual level, fueled by anger, disappointment, and a fighting spirit, and it allowed me to square off with Dad without having to fight or submit to him.

Entering my teen years I began to express myself through open mistrust, sarcasm, and attacks on anyone who tried to get close to me in any way. The odds of me developing close, intimate, loving relationships as an adult were low, and sinking lower. My experiences with love and my emerging consciousness of what love should be was impacted by a deep and pervasive sense of loss. My approach to relationships with others was impaired by the fear of further loss. I was a victim—struggling with a victim complex. I appeared secure, even threatening, on the outside, but inside I was battered and bruised. My defenses were walls built up to protect a seriously wounded, emotionally raw center. I was an abnormally short kid, with a tough, cocky outward stance that masked enormous insecurity. As I grew up I could protect myself from others, but not from myself.

When I turned fourteen in the summer of '73, I traveled to Orr, Minnesota, to the church's Summer Educational Program (SEP). SEP was an insanely well-funded, deluxe summer-camp program, with a well-organized, jam-packed schedule of interesting and challenging activities. I made new friends, learned to water ski, and generally had a great time, but it wasn't enough to help me change the path I was on. I related to one of the big hits of the summer, Elton John's "Bennie and the Jets" anthem about fighting our parents "in the street to find who's right and who's wrong." Teen rebellion had arrived, I was looking for trouble, and SEP brought me an opportunity to try illegal drugs, sort of.

An older boy from another dorm had bought purple haze, a form of LSD (aka acid) on a dorm trip into Canada, and offered it for sale. Phil, my new dorm buddy, agreed to take it with me, so I bought two hits with my care package money. Phil shared vivid stories about what he was experiencing, while

I didn't notice anything. Later Phil admitted he had lied; he hadn't taken it at all, confirming my belief that you couldn't even trust your friends to tell you the truth.

And had the buyer been snookered in Canada, or was I ripped off by another church kid? Regardless, I wanted to get my hands on the real thing. Secret drug use was to significantly color the next five years of my life. Things were destined to get a whole lot worse before they would begin to get better.

After SEP my relationship with Dad mirrored the U.S. and Soviet Union at that time; a cold war based on a policy of Mutually Assured Destruction (MAD). I had deep inner resentment, holding Dad responsible for my emotional pain and for my life being so different compared to others my age. Dad's perspective, however, was that I had nothing to complain about. And if I did, it was all my fault, and certainly not his. Any effort to seek a reasonable dialogue was quickly shut down by telling me to straighten out my "bad attitude." Countless arguments with Dad resulted in me retreating to my room in tears. This was humiliating, so I quit trying to talk to Dad. The tears dried up and I stopped expressing emotion altogether. I began a habit of quoting song lyrics to express myself, which my three or four close friends either enjoyed or tolerated, but which most people found puzzling, impenetrable, and probably annoying.

Entering high school, I was still a short little runt. West Anchorage High School had over 2,000 students, and I was the second shortest kid in the school. The person shorter than me was a tenth grade girl with dwarfism. West High had soda machines that the interconnected junior high did not have. School security stopped me several times when I was trying to buy a Coke, and ordered me back to the junior high. Being forced to show my school ID was humiliating, and was one more reason to act tough, while inside I was painfully aware that I didn't measure up, in more ways than one.

My attitude had, in fact, become very bad. I seethed with anger and resentment, stemming from having been ignored, unloved, abandoned, and then manipulated and lied to by authority figures. I retreated into music, science fiction, and darker pursuits. I was spending a lot of time at a downtown bookstore called the Book Cache, which is where I discovered the fascinating exploits of Xaviera Hollender, also known as the Happy Hooker. My fascination with sexual intimacy was growing more intense, even as I was becoming increasingly emotionally introverted. On top of the growing insecurity about my height, this developing trait dramatically decreased my chances of being able to form meaningful and healthy boy-girl relationships. I developed another escapist fantasy as well. A global audience was about to discover, along with Star Wars story of hero, Luke Skywalker, was about to discover, along with his terrifying archenemy, Darth Vader—the personification of evil—is really his father. I had already arrived at that conclusion about my dad, and began to imagine a grim solution. I specifically remember one afternoon at the Book Cache, sitting in the reading area plotting out how to go about killing my dad, mulling over the possibilities of not only accomplishing it, but also how to get away with it. These thoughts were inspired by what a fellow student had done when his drunken father had physically abused his mother and then fallen asleep on the couch. This fifteen-year-old boy knew where his dad kept a gun, and had walked up to the couch, pointed the barrel at his dad's head, and pulled the trigger.

My emotional perspective at the time was at war with what I had accepted intellectually. The fifth commandment demanded "Honor thy father and thy mother: that thy days may be long upon the land which the LORD thy God giveth thee."[24] WCG sermons emphasized that this was the first commandment with a promise.[25] It was a mini-covenant, and it was conditional. If I didn't obey it, God would neither bless nor protect me. I was internally conflicted—my rebellious rage was at war with my belief in God and the knowledge that the path to a better life was submission to him.

It was painfully obvious to me that my life was not going in a positive direction. My early optimism about being different, about obeying God even if no one else would, was vaporized by adolescent hormones reacting to childhood experience. Aside from my behavior—the language I used at school, the music I listened to, the hairstyle I preferred, and now getting into drugs—I was seriously considering murdering my dad. I had now lost my claim to the promise of long life and other promises of God, and could expect to be cursed and punished. It was the height of hypocrisy to pretend to live one life at church and a fundamentally different one elsewhere, but that's what I was doing.

---

24. Exodus 20:12
25. Ephesians 6:2

The Continuing Story of Bungalow Bill

There was also turmoil in the WCG in the '70s. It's time to cover the basics of the origins and history of the WCG, which began in the late 1920's in Oregon's Willamette Valley, when members of the Oregon Conference of the Church of God, Seventh Day, convinced Herbert W. Armstrong's wife, Loma, that God demanded Sabbath observance. Herbert W. Armstrong, known to followers and detractors alike as HWA, tried to prove her wrong, but instead proved to himself that she was right. He had no choice but to start keeping the Sabbath himself.

He made many other discoveries, and being a successful advertising man, wrote these down in compelling articles and booklets. He broke away from the Church of God, Seventh Day, to launch *The World Tomorrow* radio program and the *Plain Truth* magazine, and establish the Radio Church of God. Growth was rapid and by the time of Loma's death in 1967, it was a growing media powerhouse, with three college campuses, numerous churches, offices, and Feast sites around the world. In 1972 HWA broke ground on what would become the stunning Ambassador Auditorium, with a gold leaf ceiling and a massive, rose onyx-covered entryway. The Ambassador International Cultural Foundation (AICF) hosted an expensive, top-quality concert series after the dedication of the Auditorium in the spring of 1974. AICF began to support and launch humanitarian and cultural projects around the world, opening doors for HWA to meet influential people, world leaders, and monarchs. These meetings gave HWA a global podium from which to preach the Gospel of the Kingdom to the world as a witness, in fulfillment of a key prophecy.[26] HWA made the most of these open doors, and devoted himself to his expanded global mission, buying airplanes and traveling constantly.

In creating this big money machine, HWA also unknowingly elevated insincere flatterers to key positions, with access to the rapidly growing wealth and power at the top. He was largely absent from day-to-day operations, leaving his son, Garner Ted, aka GTA, in charge of the church and its U.S. media activities. GTA leveraged the success of his radio and TV presence to become a minor celebrity. At the peak of his popularity, he visited Alaska and ended up in the news for illegally shooting a moose. Next there were allegations of sexual

---

26. Matthew 24:14

improprieties with co-eds and HWA disfellowshiped, or rather excommunicated, his son. My own marginally schizophrenic, good and bad behavior seemed not so abnormal in this situation, and was reflective of the life of many WCG teens in the '70s.

But local churches in remote and conservative locations like Alaska were strong communities focused on the mission. We kept the Feast at the fabulous Captain Cook Hotel in downtown Anchorage. During the Feast and on combined Holy Days, I hung out with Steve, a church kid a year younger than me, who lived in Soldotna, four hours south of Anchorage. We were a kind of yin-yang of teenage boys. Steve would have been a popular student if he hadn't been an underachiever intellectually, or a jock, if the church hadn't prevented him from participating on Saturday. I was more of a brooding, dark, and dangerous bad-boy type, who might have been able to capitalize on those qualities in high school if I hadn't been so short. In any case, together, we not only had each other as friends, but we balanced each other out, and felt much more successful in our social interactions when we were together than when we were apart.

Friendships with Steve and a couple of other church kids made life as an outsider, viewing the world as living in rebellion to God, bearable. And this stance justified my own rebellion against school and society. My outsider stance even extended to authority in the church, bolstered by HWA's public proclamations not to trust him, but to trust what God said in the Bible. His pope-like status inside the WCG blurred the distinction between him and God, but this statement was a get-out-of-jail-free card. I used it liberally to navigate hypocrisy or logical fallacies in the teachings, especially as I was no longer easily cowed into submission by human beings.

She Came in Through the Bathroom Window

In 1974 the WCG changed their ruling on divorce and remarriage, based on a scripture allowing a believer to remarry if the unbeliever departs.[27] I was now fifteen, the age at which Mom met Dad, and I was probably more miserable than she had been at my age. But I didn't drop out of school; I was

---

27.   1 Corinthians 7

spending tenth grade exploring the delights of marijuana and LSD, while Dad was looking for a new woman. Neither of us knew what the other was up to, but Dad's newfound freedom was probably behind his decision to send me to Sweden during the summer of my sixteenth year. I was excited to return to a place filled with memories of a happier time. To look back favorably on my years as a child in Sweden highlighted how miserable I was. Mom had gotten drunk on the last international flight I had been on, and now I was smuggling acid onto the plane so I could trip out on the trip over. I had a scare at the airport in Denmark when, disoriented, I felt like I was going to be trapped there forever. But I somehow managed to make my connecting flight, and soon I was refreshing my Swedish, which I found still came easily.

It was wonderful to see Farfar, Farmor, my aunts, uncles, and cousins. Swedish society, like most countries in Europe, accommodates generous vacation schedules, so my ten weeks there were filled with swimming, boating, fishing, and other excursions. I also stayed several weeks with my grandparents on their farm, helping bring in the hay, hanging out at the lake, spending my evenings reading and listening to new and interesting music on the European radio stations. The only unpleasant reminder of home was a puzzling letter from a church member who wrote how exciting it must be for me, "with a trip to Sweden and your dad getting married and all…" It didn't make sense, so I didn't think much about it.

The change did me good, and I had grown over the summer, so that finally, at age sixteen, I cleared the five foot hurdle. In keeping with '70's fashion, Aunt Ingrid bought me a pair of Abba-style platform shoes, and I felt pretty good about going back to Alaska and facing my junior year. When I arrived at Anchorage International Airport, Dad was there accompanied by two girls I had never seen—a twelve-year-old blonde and a fourteen-year-old redhead, named Julie and Tobi. A few weeks later I met their mother and her other two children, fifteen-year-old Mark and seventeen-year-old Minda, a week before they became my stepfamily. Dad wasn't big on involving anyone else in his decisions.

The wedding was scheduled to take place at the Feast, which came about a month later, at the Alaska state fairgrounds in Palmer, forty miles northeast of Anchorage. This was just down the road from where Sarah Palin was entering sixth grade, as were both my younger sister and my stepsister-to-be, Julie. The last few years we had enjoyed luxurious hotel rooms in resort areas, but this year God placed His name at a campground, with tents and trailers on an open field, centered around the meeting hall.

I felt humiliated at being forced to be Dad's best man in a very public wedding, attended by people we didn't even know, at the end of the first Holy Day of the Feast. It was as much a charade as the article that had been written about our reunion with our mother. Afterward, Dad and his new bride, Elinor, rushed off to Anchorage on a three-day mini-honeymoon. This was not exactly kosher, but even Mr. Gordon, who was anything but liberal, made an exception for a couple prevented for years from marrying by an overturned doctrine. They left a volatile Brady Bunch of inventive and unsupervised teens behind, excited at being on their own at a Feast. I spent my time with Jan, the daughter of a leading minister sent to the Feast site from Tennessee. It felt like true love, and we determined to stay in touch after the Feast.

While I was chasing Jan, my new stepbrother, Mark, was fulfilling the commandment to rejoice before God "with wine and strong drink."[28] At the Feasts in Alaska this commandment was obeyed with gusto. An alternate translation of Feast of Tabernacles is "Feast of Booths," which many Alaskan and other members jokingly mispronounced "Feast of Booze." In keeping with the spirit, Mark broke into the Oktoberfest hall to fill a five-gallon water jug with beer. This was enough for a relatively large number of church youth to get drunk, and Mark was discovered making out in a trailer with one of the more attractive local girls he had just met. One of my dad's famous sound bites was "After the honeymoon, then what?" We were about to find out.

The newlyweds were told to get their family under control or be suspended from church until they did. Dad had rented a large house forty-five minutes outside Anchorage in a tiny little power-plant-based community, nestled up against the foothills. On our first day together there as a family Dad took each of the six kids on a walk down a forest path, starting with me. He carried a skinny branch in his hand, somewhere between a walking stick and the famous willow switch used on little bottoms, and his breath formed small cloud puffs in the chill Alaskan air as he obnoxiously smacked the stick on the ground

---

28. Deuteronomy 14:26

to emphasize key points of his lecture. The only item lacking to complete the caricature this brought to mind was a pair of hobnail boots.

He was applying the rod of iron method, telling me to obey the rules or find a new home, in keeping with the message of the church. A key scripture was "I set before you life and death—therefore choose life." If the choice was not made properly, one could expect suffering, heartache, and death. Within a month, Mark left to live with his dad, while Minda stuck it out until high school graduation and a free ticket to Ambassador College.

Misery

Dad might have considered the impact of choosing not to involve any of us in the decision and planning of his marriage. He might have reflected on what it was like to hear from a third party while visiting a former surrogate family that you had a stepfamily of strangers. He might have considered that forcing a momentous change on all of us and demanding abject submission to his cold authoritarianism bordered on emotional brutality. In my case, he had broken a very specific promise made before my trip to Sweden that I would be able to finish high school without moving yet again. But Dad didn't apologize for or even acknowledge these things.

It was a tough year financially for the family. God's tithe and the Holy Day tithe were already twenty percent of gross income, not to mention the generous offerings expected at Holy Days. But a third tithe was sent to the church every third year, for supporting widows and orphans. In the Bible this three-year cycle was tied to a land Sabbath every seventh year. The land, the source of increase, was to rest, and debts were forgiven as part of a broader system that spanned seven times seven, or forty-nine years. Year fifty was the Jubilee year of release when land that may have been sold was returned to the original families, for whom it was an inheritance throughout their generations.[29]

Since Dad had been baptized five years earlier at a Feast, his sixth and therefore his second third-tithe year, had begun. With a new wife, four new kids, and thirty percent of his gross income allocated to the WCG, Dad probably viewed having chased Mark and Minda away as a financial blessing from God.

---

29. Leviticus 25

For those of us who had nowhere else to go, things went from bad to worse. I tried to hold Dad to his promise about not having to change schools again. He would drop me off at school on his way to work in Anchorage, at about 6:30 a.m., where I would wait at the library until school started. After school it was the library again until he picked me up at about 5:30 p.m. Counting the forty-five-minute drive each way, my days were over twelve hours long. But it was the torture of sitting in the car with Dad back and forth that was unbearable. I lasted about six weeks, at which time something even worse happened.

Arriving home one evening, I learned that Mom had died of a brain aneurysm, at age thirty-five. Dad and Elinor told me together about Mom's death in a hallway conversation in our big rented house. Elinor awkwardly reached out to embrace me, mechanically reciting that although she couldn't replace my mother she would try. Coming on the heels of several tension-filled "parents vs. kids" months in which I had been told to "shape up or ship out," this sounded not only completely insincere, it came from a woman I already viewed as an enemy. I stood like a statue, numb, not saying a word, not shedding a tear.

Carol, Mom's younger sister, shared with me that she had received a series of drunken phone calls in Mom's final months. Mom would accuse her of not caring, and she would plead with Mom to move back to Canada where her family could help, but, of course, Mom wouldn't. In tears, Carol would hang up, and not answer when Mom called back. Her recollections reminded me of one of my own. During the time WCG doctrine held that Dad was not free to remarry, he had flown Mom up to Alaska in a hollow effort to reconcile. It was a short, painful visit which Mom presumably agreed to in order to see me and my younger sister.

My memories of this visit are vague, but I remember Dad tragically attempting to woo her while she was drunk the whole time. A humiliating scene at a bowling alley on that visit is my final memory of Mom. The net effect of her visit was a sickening realization that I was stuck in an unhappy hell with no one on the planet to turn to. My connection to Mom was broken by alcohol addiction upon our return to the U.S. years ago. Her near-forgotten visit was obviously blocked out as too painful; though the emotional energy it generated was channeled into the intense hatred I had for Dad at age fourteen and fifteen. The power of these emotions was already draining when Mom had her aneurysm and died.

There was no talk about going to Mom's funeral. It was out of the question due to finances, even if Dad would have countenanced such shallow "emotionality." After all, we knew about the resurrection. At the time, it didn't matter to me anyway. The only emotion that came through was anger. The main focal point of my anger was Dad, who had yet again placed me in a powerless and humiliating situation. I was also angry at Elinor, for thinking she meant anything to me, and angry at myself for not telling them to go to hell and running away. But that hadn't worked before and now my fantasy about another place to go was gone. While Mom was alive I had still longed for her. No more. I was emotionally sealed off and nothing could touch me now.

Completely beaten and hopeless, I enrolled at Palmer High to avoid the horrible commute to Anchorage with Dad. It was less than two years until graduation and freedom. Once the decision was made to stop fighting and go with the flow, I began to sense a light at the end of the tunnel.

Students at Palmer High, whose mascot was the Moose, were friendly enough, and I quickly made a new friend. She was a tenth grader with a Swedish background named Lila and she seemed intrigued by mine. She was stunningly attractive, but down to earth, and I thoroughly enjoyed her sunny, sharp wit and positive outlook. I bought her a bracelet for Christmas and she gave me the book of Mormon in exchange, explaining that her religion was near and dear to her heart. I knew she was offering to develop a closer relationship if I would express interest in her religion. It felt hypocritical to do so, since in my view they did not properly understand the Bible. I did, however, learn that the Mormons placed a strong emphasis on families, and was impressed by the open warmth that Lila and her older sister, a senior, showed me as I transitioned into the school in November.

Another highlight that got me through this period in my life was a creative writing class taught by Doug Carney. He invited, encouraged, and inspired me to try my hand at poetry, short stories, song lyrics, and anything else that interested me. He wrote in my yearbook that I should keep writing because I would find solace.

But instead of being able to build on friendships and relationships developed in my partial year at Palmer High, Dad had another surprise up his sleeve. As my junior year was ending, he bought a piece of land outside Palmer, two miles up a dirt road from the fairgrounds where we had celebrated the Feast. He also bought a trailer for him and Elinor and pup tents for the three sisters still at home and me. We moved onto the property where we spent the summer clearing trees and preparing to build a house. There was no water, electricity or phones, just billions of mosquitoes.

By the time school started, much of the work on the land had been completed, with my dad enlisting the four of us to chop and haul wood, dig a drainage pit, and move rocks to prepare a building site on virgin Alaskan land, on the edge of the wilderness. We had a two-mile walk down to the bus stop, and I had the unfortunate distinction of entering my senior year of high school as a boy living in a tent in the woods. During the ten months I lived in a tent in Alaska, the mercury dropped to twenty below zero Fahrenheit. As the temperature dropped, my sisters squeezed into the trailer and the outsider stigma that had plagued me since third grade reached its zenith.

By this time I had traded my two-man, pup-tent summer home for an eight-man tent from the Army Surplus store, which is a lot smaller than it sounds. Still, it had an asbestos-ringed stovepipe opening, and I had an old, rusty barrel stove for heat. The problems with this poorly constructed stove, literally made from a metal barrel, was a large interior, thin metal, and leaks which sucked in outside air, turning the fire into a roaring blaze. Within a day or so, the pipe got so hot that the asbestos-covered tent material was smoking. I then tied the tent flaps wide open and moved the stove into the doorway, with three-quarters of the stove inside and the pipe just outside the open door.

In going in and out of the tent, around the stove, it was impossible to avoid brushing against the doorway, often bringing snow on the tent cascading down around the back of my neck, adding freezing insult to injury. At times it was so cold I couldn't get the fire lit inside the barrel stove before my fingers were numb and screaming with pain. I solved this by having a can of gasoline handy to splash on a small pile of twigs and paper in the middle of the stove, providing quick heat while I fumbled around inside, with my thawing hands, to get a real fire started.

The nadir of my tent experience came one evening after school when I spent forty-five minutes in my freezing tent unsuccessfully trying to get a fire started with wet and snowy twigs and bark for kindling. Sitting cross-legged and hunched in front of the square opening, positioned about fourteen inches off the ground in what was probably my fifth or sixth attempt to get the fire going, I had no more paper or other easily ignitable kindling material left. I angrily poured what probably was about a pint of gasoline over the firewood that had still failed to ignite. The sound of the gas sizzling and simmering on the hot smoldering material at the bottom of the barrel, as I reached over to my right to pick up the matches, gave me hope that this time I'd get the infernal fire going. I swiveled back to my upright, cross-legged position, and leaned toward the opening to strike and flip a match inside.

There was a mini explosion and a roaring sound as the barrel stove turned into a flame-thrower, sending a searing stream of flame directly into my face. I fell backwards and rolled over. Within seconds my surprise and shock turned to fear and horror, as it registered that my face felt like it was on fire. As the stove-turned-flamethrower ran out of fuel, I scrambled to my knees and crawled out of the tent onto the cold, wet, slushy undergrowth. The realization that I had seriously burned my face was sinking in as I staggered to my feet and ran the one hundred yards or so to the trailer, bursting in without knocking. Inside the door was the toilet and shower, where we kept a water supply in a big plastic trashcan. Swinging open the door to the bathroom, I shoved my head into the cold water. After a few minutes of trying unsuccessfully to stop the pain, and as the cold water was giving me a terrible headache, I looked in the mirror and saw that my face was red and raw, my lips were white, and I had no eyebrows or eyelashes left. Thankfully my cap had been pulled down tight due to the cold, covering almost all of my hair. The only serious burns were a couple of small spots on the left side of my head where the hair sticking out had caught fire.

I lay down in agony on the couch, and asked Elinor to get snow for my face. She did, but not without first making me get up to put plastic underneath me to protect the couch from getting wet. As I lay there, applying the snow to my throbbing face, a growing puddle of melted snow on the plastic soaked me to the bone. Already chilled from trying to light the fire, followed by submerging my head in the icy water in the bathroom, I was soon shaking uncontrollably and virtually delirious, approaching hypothermia.

One of the names of God in the Bible is YHWH Ropheka—"God your healer"[30], so reliance on doctors, hospitals, and medical treatment was considered a lack of faith by the WCG. Divine healing was available in the form of ministerial anointing with oil.[31] Elinor called Mr. Gordon, and during the forty-five-minute drive into Anchorage, my throbbing pain subsided somewhat. After Mr. Gordon applied a drop of oil to my forehead, he placed his hands on my head and said a short prayer, asking God to intervene and heal me. Then Mrs. Gordon insisted I stay at their house that night.

The brief but intense exposure to fire had caused a flash burn, which only destroyed one or two layers of skin. I managed to sleep, but woke up with my eyes and mouth sealed shut with dried pus. After a gentle, warm-water wash and another night at the minister's house, I returned to the tent and to school. I looked like Frankenstein for a couple of weeks, which was good for more attention and sympathy than I wanted, but there was no lasting damage. There was a minor bright point here. Steve, my church friend from Soldotna, four hours to the south, had started working part time, and sent me some cash in a letter, with which I bought batteries for my tape deck and candles. The Youth Opportunities United (YOU—the WCG youth program) group from his area bought me Aerosmith's *Toys in the Attic* and a couple of other cassettes as get-well gifts. These small gestures went a long way during the darkest days of winter, in which the sun rose and set during school hours, and I was living in a dark, cold, lonely tent.

I've Just Seen a Face

As the second semester of my senior year of high school began, I took PE first period to get a daily shower before government class, the final requirement needed to graduate. The intense pleasure of a hot shower was diminished by the sad reality that confronted me afterward; my clothes smelled of smoke and camping. I would put them back on and walk into government class feeling like a homeless person. This short, early schedule enabled me to land a full-time, forty-hour-per-week job in Anchorage with the Teamsters, walking a picket line

30. Exodus fifteen:26
31. Matthew 8:4 & James 5:14

for the baker's union against Safeway. A commute to Anchorage and an eight-hour shift walking outside in the winter was better than sitting broke at home in a dark tent. My transportation was a beat-up old '66 Chevy pickup Dad let me use as long as I paid for the insurance and gas.

With the inflow of cash, I bought clothes, music, and drugs. I had been into David Bowie since hearing "Sorrow" on the Radio in 1973, and added *Hunky Dory* to my collection. The song "Quicksand" and the inspiring lyric "Don't believe in yourself, don't deceive with belief, knowledge comes with death's release" was one of the tracks. Mom's footsteps seemed the ones I would most likely follow, and I wallowed in dark and extreme thinking. Somehow, though everyone knew I was a rebellious teenager, I hid the specifics from Dad, Elinor, and everybody else.

On the picket line was an intelligent young man named Dave, whose dad had been fairly high up in the military. He was well-educated, but extremely angry and bitter. He held his dad responsible for his own very unsuccessful life, in which he, at thirty, was paid to walk a picket line outside a grocery store, in Alaska, in the dead of winter. Dave and I spent hours talking while shuffling back and forth in the cold. Dave invited me to smoke some dope at his tiny little efficiency apartment. Sitting on his bed in the kitchen he told me that when he had saved up enough money he planned to go back home and kill his father. I could see he was serious, so I challenged him on it, and on his logic, sharing that I had considered doing the same thing as an immature fifteen-year-old. Now that I was seventeen, all I wanted was to get as far away from my father as possible. Dave was adamant that he would never be free until he had killed his dad.

I contrasted my situation with Dave's. I was two years past thinking that killing my Dad held any sort of answer and I had my relationship to God and His law to thank for that. Even though I was far from a model citizen, I was basically obeying the Ten Commandments as I understood them at the time and believed that "you shall know the truth, and the truth shall make you free."[32] I knew that obedience to God was the way out, the path to escape—to become free and not end up like Dave.

By March of my senior year, the house we were building was still open to the elements, but had a roof, walls, and electricity from a generator. The inside

---

32. I John 8:32 NKJV

was clean, dry, and a lot more spacious than the tent, so I moved in and enjoyed the ability to be able to stand up and walk around. But what most helped me get through my last semester of school was a freshman named Emily. Her home life was almost as troubled as my own, and she lived just a couple of miles from our lot. She was often left alone while her dad, a truck driver, was on the road. It was easy to spend a lot of time together, which we began to do.

I guess most boys that age are obsessed with sex, and that was a large part of the attraction. Yet I fought and resisted that desire, as the biggest draw was the longing for intimacy, which I knew would be ruined by a focus on the physical. Elton John had an album cover out at the time featuring the painted heads of alligators and other animals on the naked bodies of women, which was how I felt about the mixture of attraction and danger inherent in my desire. But I had no clue whatsoever how to develop a real relationship, and Emily and I really only had our troubles in common. There was an intense physical attraction and a kind of doomed, star-crossed feeling to our bond. My tendency to deal with emotional situations through song lyrics led me to use Bowie's "Heroes" and its bittersweet grasping to be lovers "just for one day" as a metaphor for what I was feeling.

At the same time, I was afraid. My mother's abandonment had instilled a distrust of women in me, and in Emily I had probably chosen someone that I knew would fulfill that fear. My ambivalence can best be expressed by Robyn Hitchcock's song "One Long Pair of Eyes" and the line "She snuffs you out like silk, and pours you out like milk." These fears may have been appropriate, because from the vantage point of where I sit today, I can see how eerily close this was to the relationship Dad had developed with Mom. I was on the verge of repeating the same mistakes, and only my desire to obey God kept me from making them.

By late April, as our house neared completion, I was able to turn the garage into my room, and had claimed my stepfamily's very old and very bad record player console. Still, I was glad to have something with bigger speakers than my little cassette player, and I spent all of my time at home in the garage listening to my growing record collection. I found Bowie's early, heavy LP, *The Man Who Sold the World* in a discount bin at a department store in Anchorage. This miraculous find quickly became my favorite record, the title track which seemed to me to be about Satan. I marveled that Bowie was singing a song about having "passed him on the stair" with the refrain "you're face to face with the man who sold the world." It also included "All the Madmen," with the lyric "Here I stand, foot in hand, talking to my wall, I'm not quite right at all, am I?" and the chorus "I'd rather stay here, with all the madmen, for I'm quite content they're all as sane as me." I played this record so much on that old system with its heavy needle arm, that I literally wore it out.

A terrifying incident in government class sums up my life at this point. Sitting in the back, high on some particularly potent grass, I began to hallucinate. Satan and God were at war, and my head was their battleground. I was no longer in control of my mind and could only watch as their argument grew louder and more heated. Satan made accusations against me, which were unfortunately true, thereby gaining the upper hand. God receded as Satan slowly turned to face me in my head, his face growing ever larger and closer, engulfing my entire being as he laughed maniacally. My fingers gripped the edges of my chair, as I tried to keep myself from obeying the voice that screamed "RUN, GET OUT OF THIS ROOM, NOW!" Every ounce of self-control I had somehow kept me riveted to that seat, though every fiber of my being was telling me to jump up and run out screaming. I sat, immobile and like stone, through the remainder of the class, hoping I would not have to interact with the teacher or the students, since I was no longer one of them. I was a lost soul whose mind was under the control of Satan the devil, and I was afraid of what I might do.

Pot-induced LSD flashback or not, in retrospect this was a hallucinogenic mash-up of the nightmare from my first Feast and the time I spent in that seventh grade Earth Science class for four-year-olds, questioning my sanity. It was also a grim awakening to the fact that I had so wasted the last five years of my life that whereas in seventh grade I had been significantly ahead of my peers, now I was falling seriously behind. By the time the class ended and I was able to leave, this particular hallucination had passed, and I had already determined that I was going to get clean and get right with God. The spirit was willing, but the flesh was weak, as temptation and circumstances kept me involved with drugs, to a degree, for another year or so. But this incident, even more than the stove-turned-flamethrower incident, helped me realize I had to stop playing with fire before it consumed me.

Mr. Moonlight

My senior prom was good and bad. Emily and I left early because she wanted me to take her to a keg party by the Butte. There she promptly disappeared, and spent over an hour talking to an old flame. After a brief fight we were able to get away and spend several romantic hours in a canoe on a lake. Of the two aspects of our relationship, the jealousy and the closeness, the jealousy was the dominant one. Part of me knew the relationship was doomed from the start, while part of me hoped that we could make it work. Despite my attachment to Emily, the minute my high school diploma hit my hand, I headed in to Anchorage, where I rented a house with a couple of older guys from church. When I got home, I loaded up the '66 Chevy pickup and moved out.

I was still working on the picket line, and got a second job at McDonald's to pick up a free meal each shift and fund the purchase of a Yamaha 100 motorcycle for transportation. Within a couple of weeks a motherly baker on the strike told me about a new Safeway store opening up across town and encouraged me to cross the picket line and apply. I was hired to man a checkout register, making a decent hourly wage with union benefits, and said goodbye to her and Dave.

As fall approached and the weather got worse, I asked Dad if he would co-sign a loan for a new Honda Civic, the most economical transportation available in 1977. Dad refused, citing a scripture that advised against providing surety for another. I didn't feel the scripture should apply to one's son at the point in time when he is trying to stand on his own two feet. In recent months I had been auto-depositing twenty percent of my gross pay into an account for first and second tithe, but had not yet sent the first tithe money in to the church. Upset that Dad refused to co-sign the loan, I felt justified in spending the $1,200 I had saved up on a used, air-cooled, two-cylinder predecessor of the Honda Civic, called the Honda 600 Coupe—Honda's first attempt at producing an automobile.

Each year since my first Feast in Minehead, I looked forward to the fun and the spiritual boost that could help me survive each dark winter. This year I would have to fund it on my own, and I had just spent my tithe money on a car. I planned to keep part of the Feast with Ron, one of my closest church friends, by driving together to Soldotna to hook up with Steve at the Feast, in pursuit of at least a couple of days of good times. We were drinking and not paying attention, and missed a turnoff. Fifty miles of increasing angst over our gas supply came to an abrupt end as a wooden sign blocked the entrance to a small bridge. I was driving too fast, slammed on the brakes, and lost control. We skidded to a stop and got out to see how perilously close we had come to sliding off the bridge.

We had no choice but to turn around and run out of gas retracing our steps. This was Alaskan wilderness territory, in the middle of the night, and we hadn't seen another car in a couple of hours from either direction. While we discussed what to do, a man ran out from the sparse, spindly, permafrost-stunted trees on the right, waving his arms. We were startled, looked at each other, and quickly agreed we should go ahead and stop. As he approached the car we saw that he was in his twenties, and was disheveled and wild-eyed. Through the open window he said he came from a party and needed a ride home. We couldn't imagine a party in the woods, in the wilderness, in the middle of the night—but decided to give him a ride.

He guided us to a small side road and then to a small house with a truck outside. He disappeared, then returned from somewhere with a twenty-five-foot garden hose to siphon the gas from his brother's truck. Gas fumes render a potent "high" followed by considerable nausea and discomfort. Inhalation of gasoline in very small amounts can cause death. Ron and I pushed that limit taking turns, inhaling horrific amounts of noxious fumes, to the point where we could hardly stand up. But we couldn't get the gasoline to flow. We asked if we could cut the hose, but he refused. One final, near-desperate "go for broke" sucking session resulted in me inhaling not only the fumes, but a large mouthful of gas, some of which I ended up swallowing. I violently coughed, then spit and dropped to my knees to keep from falling. Rolling onto my back, the world whirled around my head like a multicolored mirror, while Ron tended the now flowing hose. I managed to sit up about the time Ron finished, as the man asked us for five dollars for his brother's gas. Ron gave him a five as I clawed my way into the driver's seat to start the car before the price of gas went up.

Miraculously, we found Soldotna by 5:30 a.m., hung over and nauseous from the alcohol and gas fumes. After a few minutes of fitful sleep, cramped in the tiny car, we attended the church service that morning. Feeling very out of place at the Feast, we headed back to Anchorage after church, taking Steve with us, as he had some business in Anchorage. His business seemed to be an obsession to find something, anything, to get high on, while Ron and I, after our recent escapade, wanted nothing to do with his experimentation. For the first time in my life, I had come away from a Feast discouraged.

Help

On the job front things were more encouraging. I had been successful as a cashier, and was well-liked by management at Safeway. I was offered a spot on the night crew, stocking shelves, which meant more hours, higher pay, and nighttime premiums. It was too good to pass up. But the combination of my lifestyle, bad diet, and lack of sleep took its toll. First I had a problem with my eye that started as irritation and quickly got much worse. Within a couple of days, light hitting my eye felt like a nail being driven through my eye into my brain. As the condition worsened I couldn't work, and finally went to see an eye doctor, despite my WCG-influenced aversion. An acute eye infection called iritis was causing the iris to cramp on contact with light. The doctor gave me one medication to relax the iris and a second to fight the infection. The whole ordeal lasted a month, during which I exhausted both my sick days and vacation days.

With no savings, I swallowed my pride at the peak of the eye infection to ask Dad if I could move back home. I was not received like the prodigal son, who is welcomed back with open, loving arms by his father, despite living a lifestyle of which his father hadn't approved. I was met with humiliation, as Dad rubbed in that "it's tough out there" and welcomed the chance to "straighten me out" by laying down the laws of the house.

Before the iritis ended, I started experiencing debilitating hip and lower back pain that continued after the iritis cleared up. This meant more missed work and trips to a chiropractor, a method of treatment accepted by the WCG. The chiropractor prescribed daily visits for two weeks, twice weekly visits for four, then weekly, and finally bi-weekly visits over the course of three or four months. Though the pain began to subside over time, my improvement didn't seem related to the chiropractic treatment. It became clear, after a few weeks, that the entire treatment approach was a racket, designed to keep the money flowing to the chiropractor.

The time I had to live with my parents' dragged on due to more missed paychecks and chiropractic bills. Then the engine on the Honda 600 Coupe blew up. I left it parked on the side of the road for two days, and some rowdies tipped it over, totaling one side. With a blown engine and a seriously damaged body, it was virtually worthless. And in typical loser fashion, on top of the health problems and having to move back home, and the loss of my car, Emily broke up with me. She ended this doomed-from-the-start relationship when I told her about a couple of girls I had met in Anchorage, in an immature, tit-for-tat move because she kept mentioning other guys. This gave her an excuse to end what wasn't working for either of us anyway. This was the first but not the last time I would reflect on the book of Job, which featured a man who suffered enormous setbacks while trying to please God. The differences, of course, between me and Job were many, not the least of which is that Job was held up as a symbol of righteousness.

I was certain that God had removed His blessing due to my misappropriation of His tithes. A key scripture in Malachi, at the tail end of the Old Testament illustrated this: "Bring ye all the tithes into the storehouse, that there may be meat in mine house, and prove me now herewith, saith the LORD of hosts, if I will not open you the windows of heaven, and pour you out a blessing, that there shall not be room enough to receive it."[33] That scripture and an admonition a chapter later to remember the law of Moses[34], virtually the last words in the Old Testament, made a compelling case for my belief.

God was making me an offer I couldn't refuse. I had used tithe money to buy the car that blew up and was tipped over. As painful as it was to experience such failure, I was grateful He had made it so clear. He was allowing these events to help me turn my life around before it was too late. I responded by repenting of my sins and seeking baptism. I sought out the new minister in Alaska, Earl Roemer, for counseling. After a few sessions during which he covered the basics and asked me to read some related passages, I was fully immersed in water in a horse trough in his garage. Afterward, he placed his hands on my head and

---

33. Malachi 3:10
34. Malachi 4:4

prayed that God would grant me the gift of the Holy Spirit. Then he shook my hand and said, "Congratulations, it's all over but the growing."

The decision to be baptized was not a hard one for me. I had wanted to be right with God from age eleven, when I first read the Bible Story volumes. Subsequent events made it hard to commit to a path I wasn't sure I could live up to. In the shadow of my father and his authoritarian, rod-of-iron approach, it had been even more difficult to decide to go down this path. As an adolescent I hadn't felt worthy, but now at age nineteen, I was ready and willing.

I was very conscious of taking this step in spite of Dad, not because of him, or to please him. So I didn't tell him about it, and felt a smug satisfaction when he learned about it second hand.

4

Here Comes the Sun

Some of these days, and it won't be long,
gonna drive back down where you once belonged
In the back of a dream car twenty foot long,
don't cry my sweet, don't break my heart
Doing all right, but you gotta get smart, wish upon,
wish upon, day upon day
I believe oh lord. I believe all the way

—DAVID BOWIE: GOLDEN YEARS—

Health-related financial trouble had forced me to move back home, and subsequent setbacks and weaknesses had driven me to repentance and baptism. Seeking God's help seemed to work, as Safeway management worked with me through the health issues and actually promoted me to assistant manager of the frozen food department. I had better hours with some shifts from 5:00 a.m. to 1:00 p.m. vs. 11:00 p.m. to 7:00 a.m. every night, on my way to the Journeyman level on the union pay scale. Living at home, I spent my money on cars, including a used but top-of-the-line Firebird—a Trans-Am without the trim.

The car boosted my self-image, and I showed it off picking up my stepsister Julie from school, taking it out cruising, and generally acting like most young guys do when their car is the best thing they have going for them. Julie and I had grown close during the tent period, and now that the house was finished, we hung out on the weekends. Julie liked the additional freedom, and I enjoyed time spent with her and her cute friends.

Drive My Car

Though I was out of the tent, I wasn't out of the woods. My drug days were all but over now that it was legal to drink. I was savvy enough to mostly avoid drinking and driving, but had a problem with speed limits, stoplights, and stop signs, and had racked up a number of tickets. The associated points against my driver's license were a ticking time bomb.

In the spring of 1979, I headed out of Palmer at 10:15 p.m., late for work as usual, but there was no traffic at night so I could make up the time on my way to Anchorage. I hit the freeway and settled in for the drive, but rounding a corner saw something disturbing. Ahead on a gravel strip, connecting the dual lanes on either side of the divided highway, sat a stationary police car. He was obviously pointing his radar gun straight at me. I glanced down at my speedometer and winced at the dial that was pointing at 100 mph.

Three facts instantly raced through my mind.

Any speeding ticket would cost me my license.

He had already clocked me at 35 mph over the limit.

He couldn't pull out onto the road until I passed by.

In the next instant I felt the floorboard under my foot and I blew by him doing 120 mph.

Once I decided to run, the adrenaline rush ended and my mind became calm. Accelerating to 130 mph, I considered my options. You can't outrun a radio, so losing him meant getting off the highway. There was another corner up ahead, and once I was around it, he couldn't see me. I turned off my lights to make myself less visible as my mind and the engine raced. Taking the next exit would let me disappear and head back to Palmer before he called in reinforcements. Calling in sick was better than losing my license.

The exit was unfamiliar and I immediately faced two choices, lit by a metal streetlamp two to three hundred yards ahead: Keep right and end up back on the road I had just exited, or head under the highway. Getting back on the freeway would shrink my head start, leaving me only one option. I hit the brakes and turned my lights back on for the turn. The stone walls of the narrow underpass materialized seventy-five yards in front of me and the image of my car slamming into the far wall at sixty mph changed my mind. I tried to veer back to the right while still traveling 80 mph but my nanoseconds of indecision had cost me too much ground. It was impossible to make it back over to the freeway on-ramp from here. In my frantic back-and-forth maneuvers, I didn't really know what was straight ahead. I slammed on the brakes hoping for the best.

There was a strange white noise as my car hurtled over an embankment at about 60 mph, dropping a good four-to-six feet into snow. The front end of the Firebird dug in and snow piled up under the undercarriage, forcing its way into the engine compartment and bringing the car to a stop within fifty yards of leaving the roadway.

I was shocked but not hurt and quickly formed an escape plan. Jumping out of the car I headed up to hide by the brush near the freeway, hoping the cop would head straight long enough for me to cross the freeway and hitchhike a ride back to Palmer and report my car stolen. I ran forty feet through knee-deep snow before realizing my jacket was on the passenger seat. I turned around to see a large cloud of steam rising into the air from the snow packed against the engine, signaling the location of my car. Still, I had no choice but to head back to the car to retrieve my jacket. The clock was ticking as I grabbed the coat, slammed the door, and tried a second time to retrace my steps to avoid providing clear evidence in the snow of what was happening.

I was forty feet away again when the squad car came down the ramp that I had failed to negotiate back to the highway. As it came to a stop a spotlight lit up my car and came to life, tracing my steps like a bloodhound, from the car to where I was crouching in the snow. A large cop jumped out on the far side of the squad car and leaned over the hood to level a gun in my direction. He yelled "Get your mother-fucking hands in the air and your goddamn ass back on the road before I blow your fucking head off."

This was the second time in my life I'd heard a threat like this. At five years old I had panicked, and run out into traffic. This time, I raised my hands, walked up to his car, and was thrown to the ground and handcuffed. He barked at me to stand up, and then slammed me up against the car. After aggressively frisking me, I was shoved into the back seat and hauled off to jail. On the way he lectured me about how he risked his life for goddamn punks like me, but I did get him to radio in a message to call my shift supervisor that I wouldn't be coming in for work.

Upon arrival, I was booked and fingerprinted but was told that because I was under twenty-one, I could get out with parental supervision. Once I learned of this option, I reluctantly called my dad. To me, all I had done was drive a little too fast and make a stupid decision, but I knew how it looked. With an hour to wait for my dad to arrive, I had more to worry about than his reaction upon arrival. There was also the risk of losing my job, not so much because of missing one shift, but because I would not have a driver's license. Then there was the cost to get my car towed and, presumably, fixed.

Still, with all these things to fret about, it was the embarrassment of having to reach out to Dad for help that bothered me most, knowing how condescending and arrogant he would be. Sure enough, as he drove me to work he seemed happy to share that he would have preferred to have left me in the slammer, but didn't want me to lose my job.

My supervisor was surprised to see me show up, but I made light of the incident, completed what was left of my shift, and got someone to drive me back home. The next day I got my towed car out of impound and found it completely undamaged, aside from needing a front end alignment. I stopped on my way home to look at the scene of the accident. The car had been towed out from the front, leaving the tracks untouched, and it was easy to see exactly what had happened. But something didn't compute.

Not a second time

The tire tracks on the road told the story of someone slamming on his brakes and stopping inches before impacting the steel base of a light pole. Yet behind the pole was the embankment drop-off, with tire tracks in the snow at the bottom, forming a straight line with those in front of the pole. The pole was dead center between the two sets of tracks, but somehow the car had not struck the pole. The impression it made was like that of a fake arrow hat that invisibly bends the shaft around someone's head, creating the illusion of going straight through. But this was no magic trick. It hadn't been staged. I stood for a long time staring at the black and white evidence - the tire tracks on the pavement and in the snow - of an undeniable miracle.

Why was my life supernaturally spared while attempting to outrun the police in a high-speed chase? Wasn't the theme of the Bible obey and be protected? Disobey and suffer?

I realized, at a profound level, that my view of God was too simple, too conservative, and too human. God was more complex than I had imagined, and more loving and merciful than the one-dimensional Bible stories the Old Testament had taught me. I began to get a glimpse of God as a caring, loving being. It registered that God had treated me like the prodigal son of the New Testament, whose father ran out to meet him while he was yet a long way off, despite his profligate ways—not the way Dad treated me when I had to move back home due to illness.

This was a real turning point. As I stood there and pondered the clear evidence—the tracks on the road and in the snow—a realization sunk deeply into my inner being. It dawned on me that with extended absences from my father, the failed relationship of my parents, years in a foreign country with my aunt and uncle, my mother's alcoholism, the temporary orphanage, and the death of my mother when I was sixteen, I was a spiritual orphan. Baptism brings us into a father/child relationship with God, and I had a vivid impression of being literally adopted by my Heavenly Father. God was honoring my baptism by literally rescuing me from death, claiming my life as His in the process. It didn't matter who my dad was, or how he did or didn't treat me; God was my real Father.

Yet coming on the heels of baptism into the WCG, my understanding of a God who teaches by reward and punishment wasn't weakened, it was reinforced. I don't want to over-emphasize the contrast, because even the Old Testament stories, as understood by the WCG, showcase that God's nature is love and mercy. A toddler has to learn about "NO!" to be protected from danger and destructive behaviors, from, ahem, running into the street, eating poisonous substances, or poking baby brother's eye out. As teenagers we need to understand cause and effect and the potential consequences of careless or reckless driving before being given the car keys. As bad as my life had been, and though it might not seem to be the case, the training I had received from the WCG had protected me from falling completely into the destructive, amoral whirlpool that I had been flirting with throughout my rebellious teen years. Again, though it might not seem to be the case, there had already been many times in my life where the biblical education I had received had held me back from even worse behavior than what I've shared here.

There was a glimmer of awareness that an over-emphasis on a behavioral approach of using reward and punishment to train mankind obscures the fact that God's love is unconditional. At a subconscious and emotional level, the message of undeserved protection from certain death in a car crash was more powerful than the message about law and obedience, rewards and punishment that I had assimilated. God was showing me He would be with me, despite who I was, and that He had future plans for me, as His son. God may have built cause and effect into His creation, a universal behaviorist classroom that teaches and enforces law. But at His core He is love and mercy.

I'll Be Back

My awakening happened not long after HWA had suffered his own near death experience, and perhaps is a good time to explain what had been going on at the top of the WCG. Political troubles and a grueling schedule of over 300 days per year on the road were taking a toll on HWA, who kept moving, full-throttle, until he suffered a heart attack on August 16, 1977—ironically the same day that Elvis, half of HWA's age of eighty-five, died of one. As HWA struggled to regain his grip on the strategy and operations of the church, his reputation was tarnished by a marriage to a much younger woman, officiated by his son, GTA, who had been reinstated.

In 1978 GTA was again disfellowshiped, and loyalists and other dissatisfied executives collaborated with the State of California on complaints of financial impropriety. An investigation by the State resulted in a court-appointed receiver with extensive authority over the operations of the church. While still recovering from his health crisis, HWA relied heavily on his chief legal counsel and trusted advisor, Stanley Rader, to fight the legal battle. They established a legal entity in another state and directed members to send tithes and offerings to the new organization. With financial resources back under his control, HWA staged an effective battle against the State of California and ousted the evil receiver. Stanley Rader published *Against the Gates of Hell*, his account of how the church had withstood a satanic attack by the combined forces of dissidents and earthly government. For this, HWA ordained him an evangelist. A minister named Joseph Tkach also came to prominence for having coordinated tactical resistance at headquarters. He, too, was elevated to the rank of evangelist, and given responsibility over the global ministry as head of ministerial services. Fear helped HWA regain control, as he "marked and disfellowshiped" a number of leaders, including, surprisingly, Stanley Rader. Those marked were considered to be especially evil, and were to be avoided by the membership at all costs.

What was the spiritual fate of people who fought God's Church? Despite the title of Mr. Rader's book, the WCG did not believe in Hell. God is not a God of torture. The WCG taught that heaven, hell, and the immortal souls that supposedly populate them, were human inventions. The lake of fire referenced in the Bible and elsewhere[35] simply burns you up, ending your existence. Proof-texts from Ezekiel cemented this belief: "Behold, all souls are mine; … the soul that sinneth, it shall die."[36] This is repeated a few verses later[37], providing an exclamation point on the discussion, should anyone challenge the point. While not nearly as gruesome or sadistic as never-ending torture in Hell, the lake of fire was more real for WCG members than Hell is for most Christians. Those disfellowshiped could repent and come crawling back to the church, or face extinction, which helped people "get in line and stay there."

HWA, whose official title was Pastor General, now assumed a new title, "God's Apostle," and he worked tirelessly to reinvigorate the church. He deployed

---

35. Revelation chapters 19 & 20, and title of a Meat Puppets song covered by Nirvana
36. Ezekiel 18:4
37. Ezekiel 18:20

a fast-talking, animated, and entertaining evangelist, Gerald Waterhouse, to travel around the world and refocus the troops on the Great Commission to preach the gospel to the world as a witness, so that the end might come. Mr. Waterhouse embarked on an endless series of world tours, speaking to every single church, emphasizing that during his "heart failure" Mr. Armstrong had been "clinically dead for over a minute" before God brought him back from the dead to get the church back on track. Mr. Waterhouse's sermons at times exceeded four hours, and Dad borrowed liberally from his colorful phrases and anecdotes, including, "Get in line and stay there."

While the WCG was regaining its zeal, my own personal miracle in the high-speed chase and the deep realization that God was personally looking out for me, motivated me to turn my life around. My battle with drugs, alcohol, and sexual desires had to be won with a decisive victory. I had to put distance between the profane and the holy, and I took action. While working through the reckless driving charges and licensing issues with the court, I enrolled in church activities like Spokesman Club (a WCG version of the Toastmasters program, with a manual featuring Wolverton drawings) and the church choir. As I drew closer to God and His church through these activities, I felt the influence of the Holy Spirit increase and the pull of Satan decrease.

Fear of the lake of fire was actually not my primary motivation. In some ways I longed for extinction, and from time to time flirted with the idea of ending it all. But one of the benefits of the WCG was to help me feel better, if not good, about being different from others. I related to the church's emphasis on separating oneself from the world, as highlighted by the striking scripture "And I heard another voice from heaven, saying, come out of her, my people, that ye be not partakers of her sins, and that ye receive not of her plagues."[38] This perspective had been a positive force for me, and despite the stories I've told here, it kept me from drowning completely in the negative and destructive behaviors that I otherwise found so attractive. Now it helped fuel my motivation to change.

The icebreaker speech in the all-male, baptized-member-only Spokesman Club was to introduce yourself and share your goals. It was embarrassing to tell the older and wiser men of the church that my only ambitions were music, hot cars, drugs, and chasing girls, minus the drugs. Applying to Ambassador

---

38.   Revelation 18:4

College (AC) seemed like the right goal to have, so I proclaimed it as mine. Then I had to apply in order to rehabilitate the lie, if not my hypocrisy.

The spirit was a tad willing, but the flesh was still very weak. I had not been challenged intellectually since sixth grade in Sweden, and had coasted through high school on a B-average. I didn't care, because no one around me cared. I had grown intellectually lazy after five years chasing sex, drugs, and Rock & Roll. My interests and influences pulled me away from education and scholastic competence, not to mention Dad's and the WCG's anti-intellectual bias, which helped me dismiss college as a place where people went to avoid having to work. My stepsister Minda and my church friend Susan made AC seem no different. Minda had dropped out to get married, while Susan tried to make AC sound appealing by telling me stories about how wild it was, which backfired.

As laughable as it seems now, at the time I prided myself on advancing in my career at Safeway, having progressed up the pay scale to within an inch of Journeyman-food-clerk status, with its higher pay and benefits. The money was enough to support myself, afford my exorbitant auto insurance rate, and pay off debt. My newfound material success masked my ultra-low self-esteem and near-systemic hypocrisy.

Why Don't We Do It In The Road?

I had been living a double life for years, pretending to be morally upright, while spending most of my mental energy and free time in pursuits that tended toward the lowest common denominator and outright illegal activities. I was usually careful or lucky enough, or protected by God, to avoid reaping what I was sowing, but at times my behavior caught up with me. One Friday night Tony, a friend on the periphery of the WCG, and I were drinking tequila and decided to go cruising in a car I bought for winter driving, a white '68 Chrysler New Yorker. I christened this car the White Whale, in honor of the book *Fear and Loathing in Las Vegas*, by Hunter S. Thompson, about his crazy, debauched, drug and firearm-fueled trip to Las Vegas, which I and some of my friends had read, and found very, very, cool. This book was much later made into a movie, starring Johnny Depp as Hunter S. Thompson.

We drove up East Northern Lights Boulevard into Anchorage, one of two, broad, one-way roads on each side of long blocks of popular establishments—the cruise-strip. At a red light, two guys in the car next to me shouted something. I rolled the window down and heard "No one flips me off and *lives*" while a half-full beer can hurtled through the open window. It hit the far door and soaked Tony's pants. The light turned green and I gunned the 440 engine, putting distance between us before backing off the accelerator at twenty over the speed limit.

They were catching up as I squeezed through a yellow light a good 200 yards ahead of them. When they brazenly ran the red, I realized that it might get ugly quick, and considered my options as we approached the end of the strip. Heading out of town, Northern Lights joins Benson Boulevard to form a two-way and I tried to make a quick illegal U-turn. But the New Yorker was too big to turn in one maneuver, and their two-seater made the turn quicker. They were riding my tail toward a red light, but the Denny's parking entrance on my right offered a getaway route.

This was another example of a stupid snap decision in a car chase. Traveling about twenty miles per hour, I hit a large patch of ice. The two-ton Chrysler New Yorker barreled straight ahead and the driver's side front corner slammed into the side of Denny's Restaurant. I said "Tony, lock your door" but Tony had been smoking a hash pipe on the way in to town, on top of the tequila, and just sat there. The smaller, lighter car behind us saw us hit the ice, steered left to avoid it, and wedged us in.

As I tried to inch my way back in order to clear the building, Tony's door flew open, and the driver of the other car crawled in over Tony, swinging for me. He hit a small glass fishing globe I had hanging from the rear-view mirror in fishnet, low enough to bump up harmlessly against the padded dashboard during the accident. But the force of a swinging fist sent it smashing into the windshield, exploding and sending shards of glass flying.

Climbing out, I was grabbed around the chest and arms from behind by the other passenger, who was easily a foot taller and 100 pounds heavier than me. He dragged me back as the driver crawled through my car and pounded me in the face. Then he grabbed my hair and pulled my head down to slam his right knee into my nose, once, then twice. He stumbled on his third attempt and I broke loose, pushing past people coming out of Denny's in response to the crash.

Inside, I asked for a phone, just as the driver came running in, screaming that he was going to kill me. For good measure he hurled a few epithets at some of the customers staring in disbelief, witty things such as "WTF are you staring at?," only he didn't use the acronym as this was years before cell phones would make texting all the rage. Someone yelled "I'll call the police," while the attacker, realizing he shouldn't try to kill me right then and there, headed back out the door.

A bloody mess stared back at me from the bathroom mirror. Aside from bruises, open sores around my eyes, cracked lips, and blood splotches all over my face, the area from my nose down to my belt was soaked in blood. I cleaned up as best I could while waiting for the police to arrive.

When they did, Tony and I spent twenty minutes in the police car, filling out a report. As we finished, the other car drove back down the street, too curious to stay away. "That's them!" I said, and participated in yet another car chase, this time on the right side of the law. When they were pulled over, the officer instructed me on how to perform a citizen's arrest. Driving home in my beat-up car I argued with Tony about how useless he'd been, while he blamed me for putting him at risk of being caught with drugs. After showering off the blood, I crawled into bed.

Like a good hypocrite, I attended church services the next day. My face looked as bad as it had after the gasoline and barrel stove incident, but this time there was no sympathy, not that I wanted any. These events seemed par for the course at that time, and I took them in stride. I was both grateful that God's wrath was not any worse, and determined yet again to change. It was a mini-version of the serial disobedience, punishment, and forgiveness outlined in the pages of Wolverton's *Bible Story*.

Nowhere Man

There are many other stories showcasing how my friends and I were going nowhere. We laughed off our own bruises, pointing to others behaving even more stupidly and suffering worse consequences. There was the high school friend who, with one of his friends, beat a drunken Eskimo to death with hockey sticks in an alley on their way home from hockey practice. There was a closer friend, Sid, who broke his jaw rolling his car, then acted like it was cool to have his mouth wired shut for six weeks. After a couple of very close calls, once while using, once while selling, I had finally stopped using drugs, but was still drinking. And since breaking up with Emily, I hooked up opportunistically with any girl that caught my eye and was willing.

But I was out of get-out-of-jail-free cards, and wanted to regain God's blessing, protection, and guidance. It was time to apply to AC, even if my feelings were still mixed, knowing they would turn me down. Given this fear, I had put off contacting the AC admissions office until the deadline to request applications was almost past. When the application arrived, I sat on it until there was hardly time to take the SAT. Playing it straight on the essay for the application wasn't too hard. A newly baptized guy wanted to attend AC to get a stronger grounding in the essentials of his faith. The personal questions were a bit trickier. They wanted specifics on illegal drug use; if, what, how much, and how often? I considered lying, but lying to God's college seemed like a bad idea. So I wrote it all down—alcohol, marijuana, LSD, speed, and cocaine. I didn't state that my desire to extend my experience beyond these drugs had been frustrated by the lack of availability and opportunity. Then I amended my essay to discuss my desire to enter a healthier environment to put more distance between my bad habits and me. This confession was not likely to win me any supporters on the admissions committee.

Though he was not applying for AC, Ron took the SAT test with me, and we showed up, hung over, without having studied. Against all odds, my score was not only respectable, it was pretty good—no doubt a latent carryover from my head start in Sweden coupled with being fully bilingual. But in comparison to Ron, who had Swiss parents, and was also bilingual due to their speaking Swiss-German at home, I was a lightweight. He was younger and not only beat my score, but a year later retook the SAT and was recognized for having the highest SAT score ever recorded in Alaska. I knew he was smart, but this was impressive!

Another requirement of the application process was an interview with the local minister, Earl Roemer, whom I had avoided since my baptism. He only asked one question; "Given rumors about you, your cars, and the police, I'm wondering if you are applying to Ambassador to escape from the law up here?" My jaw dropped. But technically the law was not what I was fleeing from, so I was able to truthfully answer "No!" Still, only if it could be scientifically proven that the hot place was freezing over, would I be accepted to Ambassador College.

Passover had arrived, and I was now baptized and could attend. Passover celebrated Israel's protection from the death angel, let loose on the firstborn children of Egypt and Pharaoh, after a series of plagues failed to secure their freedom. The Israelites were to kill a lamb and strike the doorposts of their house with its blood as the death angel "passed over" in search of unprotected houses.[39]

Christ is the New Covenant Passover Lamb, the One slain from the foundation of the world.[40] Given that, the WCG celebration of Passover might on the surface appear to be a point of common interest, if not agreement, with those who celebrate Easter. But nothing could be further from the truth. Whereas the Feast of Tabernacles was different from orthodox Christian experience, it did not contrast, conflict or overlap with any Christian holidays. But the WCG understanding of Passover was very much at odds with Easter.

The book of Matthew states, "Then certain of the scribes and of the Pharisees answered, saying, Master, we would see a sign from thee. But he answered and said unto them, An evil and adulterous generation seeketh after a sign; and there shall no sign be given to it, but the sign of the prophet Jonas: For as Jonas was three days and three nights in the whale's belly; so shall the Son of man be three days and three nights in the heart of the earth.[41]

A Day in the Life

The WCG booklet *Pagan holidays vs. God's Holy Days* has a chart illustrating Christianity's dilemma. A miracle equal to Christ's resurrection seems necessary to squeeze three days and three nights into the time between Friday evening and Sunday morning. The basic math function of arithmetic renders two nights and one day. Scholarly representations claiming an hour of day on the front and

---

39. Exodus 12
40. Revelation 13:8
41. Matthew 12:38-40

back end and contextual and linguistic nuance seemed no match for the clear, blunt logic of HWA.

This is not a trivial matter. Christ gave one and only proof of who He was, along with "An evil and adulterous generation seeketh after a sign." This two-edged sword cuts those who wanted a sign in the first place, and those who fail to accept the sign He offered. Both Christianity and Judaism are cut backwards and forwards, for wanting and either rejecting it outright or adopting a theology and doctrine that implicitly rejects it.

This aspect of the Sign, as in *The People of the Sign,* identifies Christ as Israel's Messiah and God. But this was not emphasized in the WCG. The Sign of the Sabbath was the primary emphasis, cementing the WCG's claim to uniqueness. Why this matters will become clearer later, but here is the shorthand version. Orthodox Christianity misses the boat exactly because it failed to acknowledge the importance of the weekly and annual Sabbaths. A verse from the Gospel of John illustrates the point: "The Jews therefore, because it was the preparation, that the bodies should not remain upon the cross on the sabbath day (for that sabbath day was an high day), besought Pilate that their legs might be broken, and that they might be taken away."[42]

The statement "that sabbath was a high day" refers to an annual Holy Day, not the weekly Sabbath. The WCG booklet places that Holy Day on a Thursday that year. This meant Christ was crucified Wednesday, died and was buried late Wednesday afternoon/evening, and was resurrected Saturday evening, not Sunday morning. The WCG further explained the falsification of the actual dates to be part of a Satanic plot, implemented through the Catholic Church and the Papacy, to "change times and seasons" away from the true Hebrew calendar of events, replacing Sabbath with Sunday. The masses were deceived, with no possibility of wearing the badge that identified them as God's people, and no corresponding ability to identify the true God.

The WCG explanation also supported using the Sabbath and Holy Days as test commandments critical to receiving greater understanding. Understanding the annual and weekly Sabbaths enabled us to recognize the Sign that Christ gave, three days and three nights, while the rest of the world either didn't care at all (non-Christians) or were hopelessly deceived (Christians). So the Sign of the Sabbath dovetails with the Sign Christ gave. For Israel the Sabbath identified

---

42. John 19:31

God to them, and when He sent His Son, it was a failure to pay close attention to the Sabbath that led to most of Christianity failing to acknowledge the Sign He offered.

Chapters could be written on all the ins and outs and ramifications of these connections, which would bore all but the most theologically inclined. One point is critically important here. The Sign Christ offered the Jewish leaders, which I referred to as a two-edged sword, only addressed half of the Sign God offered Israel through the Sabbath. The Sign of Jonah identified Christ, but how are His people identified? This leads back to my first WCG Passover service.

In John 13 Christ instituted an important component of the Passover service: foot-washing. He washed the feet of His disciples, prompting Peter's indignant response that Christ would never wash *his* feet. The dirty job of washing sandal-shod feet that had traveled on dusty dirty roads and paths was done by the lowliest of the low. "Jesus answered him, if I wash thee not, thou hast no part with me."[43] This section is in close proximity to the Sign of Jonah that Christ gave to identify Him as the Promised One, the Messiah. The foot-washing is an illustration of the other side of the Sign, how to identify His people, though it was not clear to me at the time, nor to the WCG at large. What was clear was that the WCG was serious about the Word of God compared to the rest of Christianity. Before taking the symbols of the suffering and death of Jesus—unleavened bread and red wine—WCG members participated in a foot-washing ceremony.

Filing out by rows, men and women into separate rooms, we alternated between sitting on a chair and kneeling down in front of the seated person to wash each other's feet in a little basin filled with water, and gently dry the feet with a towel. This was done in silence and reverence in an attitude of humility and service. It was a fitting addition to the Passover, which typified the atoning sacrifice of Christ, whose blood washes us clean from all sins. The washing of the feet, per the symbolism and the words of Christ, was also symbolic of the cleansing of sins. This annual object lesson taught us that humility and love can cover sin, or perhaps even repair the damage of sin.[44]

My life may have been a hypocritical mess, but at the Passover service my beliefs and my actions were brought into beautiful, inspiring harmony through

43. John 13:8
44. Proverbs 10:12 and I Peter 4:8

the active symbolism of the foot-washing. At my first Passover, I experienced a profound spiritual power in adhering to scriptural guidance in worship vs. following religious tradition. As the Feast had always—with one recent notable exception—left me feeling spiritually energized and ready to weather a long winter in which spiritual encouragement was sparse, the Passover left me feeling relieved, free, exonerated, forgiven. It was a fresh start, a clean slate, and I walked out of the door ready to tackle and overcome my problems.

Sadly, I didn't know how to implement these feelings. I had no plan, program, or meaningful goals to apply myself to and soon found myself back in my own skin. I struggled under the weight of my history and the negative influences of my music choices, my friends, and alcohol—things that appealed to my negative tendencies. Like strong rubber bands wrapped around my arms and legs, they pulled me back into old habits and ways of thinking as I tried to move forward and change. I needed new friends and new interests in order to break the hold of this powerful negative inertia. I had to put distance between myself and these familiar sources of temptation. Going to AC seemed an easy way to get cleaned up and straightened out. Any place would likely be better than Alaska and California was looking more attractive every day. When the response came from AC, I was nervous. I couldn't have possibly gotten in, could I?

It was a letter informing me that my application was incomplete without the application fee. My nervousness vanished and was replaced by anger. How dare they use a technicality to deny me an answer? It also felt fishy, since I was certain I had included the application fee. Anger gave me an excuse to do nothing for a week or so, but in reality, I was afraid of rejection. The more I wanted to go, the steeper the odds seemed against getting in. I had to know, so I sent in the supposedly missing money. But it was too late; I had missed a deadline, and my application could not be considered.

I was furious. How dare an organization calling itself God's Church behave like this? I was a tithe-paying member, and a "missing" twenty-dollar application fee kept me out? To me, AC would make up just about any excuse to avoid telling me the truth, which is that I just wasn't good enough!

Love me do

I consoled myself that I had my driver's license back, a hot car, and enough money to buy whatever I needed or wanted at the time. Also, I ran into Lila, the girl I had a crush on at Palmer High School, before I became tent-boy; she had gone on to become Miss Alaska. I asked her out, and she said yes. I was ecstatic and very nervous, so I tried to impress her with my recent material success. At a fancy restaurant dinner Lila invited me to accompany her to one of her public appearances. Perhaps life in Alaska had an upside and maybe there were some things worth living, working, and hoping for after all.

In preparation for the big day, I washed and polished my car inside and out, and fretted like a schoolgirl over what to wear. But the event turned out to be a big disappointment. I was out of my league, and felt awkward and nervous being a celebrity escort. My effort to portray myself as successful crumbled under the weight of reality. Having achieved the exalted pay-grade of a journeyman food clerk was not exactly impressive, nor was I able to keep up conversationally with people who had real lives. Lila seemed embarrassed to have me there, and the evening felt like a failed attempt to fake my way into a society in which I didn't belong. It left me feeling even worse about myself.

At least there was an upcoming Feast and I wanted to make up for my cavalier approach during the last couple of years. My second tithe account was more than healthy; I made plans to keep the Feast on Paradise Island in the Bahamas, and threw in an eight-day cruise on the back end for good measure. To round off the journey to warmer climates, I planned a trip to Tennessee to visit my friend Jan, the minister's daughter from the Feast at the Alaskan fairgrounds. We had exchanged lots of letters and phone calls for about a year after the Palmer Feast, but had not been in touch as of late. She sounded interested in the visit, and I looked forward to seeing her again.

I called Steve, who had graduated that spring and moved to Seattle, and invited him to join me, but he was afraid he wouldn't have enough money. This was a chance to return, in a big way, his gesture of sending me money in the tent era. If he could save a certain amount, I would cover the rest. He agreed. When I arrived in Seattle, Steve had failed to save anything and he didn't even have a passport. These warning signs were ignored, as I agreed to cover his travel costs, and initiated a frantic scramble to get a passport. Then Steve had to go clothes shopping for the trip, virtually forcing me to pick up a couple of items as well. He paid for this puzzling shopping spree with a credit card that I later found out was his mother's, and he blamed the expenses on me.

With me footing the entire pre-paid bill for travel and accommodations, I looked at my remaining funds. Even without any contribution from Steve, I could still cover food, ground transport, incidentals, and buy the one thing for myself I really wanted, the new Olympus OM10 camera. I planned to pick it up tax-free on our way out of the country en route to Nassau for the Feast, but a delay in getting to the airport in Miami, followed by a rush to make the connecting flight, kept me from buying it. I couldn't find one in the Bahamas, and put it off until our return to Miami for the cruise. From the moment the plane touched down in the balmy island paradise, it was a great Feast. Paradise Island was just the place to celebrate a tropical foretaste of The World Tomorrow, with scuba diving, water-skiing, dinner parties, and lots of drinking.

All the fun and games were costing me twice as much as planned, so tension was building between Steve and me. Steve's negligence in saving second tithe was the main reason, but there were other issues. I hit it off with a very attractive sixteen-year-old girl at the Feast, but backed away from getting physical, which seemed like a wrong thing to do. A day later she and Steve had hooked up, and I knew Steve was just playing around with this younger girl.

It was two years since HWA's "resurrection from the dead." The sermons at the Feast were pointed and motivating and there was an obvious spirit of unity and happiness among the attendees. Toward the middle of the Feast, I began to regret booking the flight to Miami on the last day. It was not only a Saturday, i.e., a Sabbath, but was an annual Sabbath, a "High Holy Day"—in fact the summit of Holy Days, the Last Great Day![45]

Travel on the Sabbath was greatly discouraged, but practicality had won out when I hadn't seen any other way to arrive in time for the cruise. But that was before my sense of spiritual duty and enthusiasm to follow God fully had been heightened by the spiritual force of the Feast. Now I realized that to get to the airport in time for the flight meant missing the morning service and

---

45. John 7:37

the offering that was collected. We were commanded, three times per year, to appear before God, and not to appear empty.[46]

I made the difficult decision to change these plans. We would stay with a local church family for two days, then fly first to Miami and then to Puerto Rico, to catch up with the cruise at its first port of call. This added hundreds of dollars to our travel costs, with me picking up the bill. I didn't care. I was pumped up by the spiritual energy of the Feast, and felt my faith and understanding was increasing the more I took steps to obey God. I was determined to draw closer to God, to obey His will, His commandments, and experience the blessings and guidance that I knew would follow obedience. Money was material, and therefore not material to a spiritual equation.

As the Feast came to an end, I was in a completely different place than I had been just eight days earlier. I was very introspective about my newfound dedication to God and His will, and was extremely taken by the warm love of the native Bahamian family that had agreed to take us in for a couple of days. The husband and wife were full of love for each other, and their two children, a boy and a girl in their pre-teens, took a liking to Steve and I. The family did everything they could to keep us happy, including taking us on tours of the island, cooking for us, and spending time just relaxing and having fun together. This was an ideal expression of our faith and belief system, an outpouring of genuine love and appreciation transcending racial, cultural, and age boundaries. I was on a spiritual high as we left for the airport to fly to Miami and on to Puerto Rico.

The cruise was a complete letdown after the spiritual richness of the Feast and the genuineness of our host family. The attractiveness of the facilities and entertainment, the abundance of food, and the alcohol-induced joviality of the passengers, all seemed shallow and hollow to me. But there was plenty to do on the huge ship, and during the island stops along the way, which included St. Maartens, and St. Thomas/Virgin Islands. While I was content to just relax on the ship and work on my tan, Steve was in party mode, and was busy meeting new friends and having a good time. He quickly hooked up with a girl on the ship. Even in the bright tropical sunlight, the strain on my relationship with my best friend for the past five years hung over me like a dark cloud.

---

46.   Deuteronomy 16:16 and others

When Steve bought his new fling a gold necklace at one of the ports of call, it was the last straw for me. He wasn't serious about her, and I was tired of funding the Don Juan of Alaska. And due to all the additional expense, I had to pass on the Olympus OM10 camera I had been wanting for months. There would be no big photo album of my long anticipated trip.

We were not on the best of terms as we left for the next leg of the journey, the stop to visit Jan and her family. It was nice to see her again, but there was no spark, she was just disappointingly polite. The most memorable part of the trip was her dad, a regional pastor who was related by marriage to GTA. He had a relatively high level of responsibility within the church ministry, and he was in disagreement with what was coming out of WCG headquarters. We were visiting his family shortly before they would publicly announce their alignment with the faction opposed to HWA. They would all shortly be marked and disfellowshiped.

He and his family were being very cordial to us, going out of their way to make us feel welcome, which was appreciated, but they were also trying to convince us of the rightness of their position on the topical issues facing the WCG. Steve seemed very open to hear the dirt being dished out against WCG leadership, but I was put off by the approach. I was enthused and excited about my positive experience at a Feast in which none of these issues and concerns had been raised, and people were not being slandered behind their backs. Given my personal history, I was sensitive to being manipulated or used and was certain that their hospitality toward us was more a desire for us to follow them than a genuine interest in us.

Steve and I parted ways in Seattle, and I knew I had lost one of my best friends. We were heading in different directions at that time, and I was quite upset with Steve for having taken advantage of my friendship. I'm not writing this to condemn him, and feel it important to state that in hindsight I can see my own immaturity and self-centeredness. Issues and resentments from my volatile past lurked just beneath the surface, making me a difficult person to be friends with. At that time, though, I did not possess that degree of self-awareness, and was quite judgmental toward Steve. I was determined to move forward spiritually and that caused a rift with people who had a different focus.

Please Mr. Postman

As usual, however, at home I slipped back into old habits. I was now listening to new wave and punk music, attracted to the anger, bitterness, and potency of the artist's emotional expression. Elvis Costello was a favorite, but the record I could not take off my turntable was Graham Parker and the Rumour's *Squeezing out Sparks*, which opened with a searing anthem about disassociation and dislocation, "Discovering Japan," followed by songs of anger, disgust, and disillusionment. There was not a song on the album I didn't like, with my personal favorite being "Love Gets You Twisted." Graham spit out the lyrics instead of singing them, and the chorus simply repeated the title, "Love gets you twisted" and "screw yourself up." Throw in heavy doses of the Talking Heads' paranoid masterpiece *Fear of Music* and you've got a good summary of my personal demons at that time.

My memories of that late fall and winter, upon returning from the Feast in the Bahamas, are of alcohol and emptiness. It was depressing to come home from such an awesome Feast, with insights on how to align my life with the coming Kingdom of God and the motivation to do so (such as delaying the flight to the cruise) only to have it dissipate as the daily grind took its toll. When I learned that Ambassador College was accepting a limited number of students mid-year over the winter break, I immediately sent in the fee to reactivate my application. As the realization grew that staying in Alaska over the winter would be a slow death in spiritual quicksand, I began to pin my hopes on getting accepted.

November turned into December, and I had not heard anything about my application. By now I was honest with myself, and I was not trying to pretend I didn't care about AC. I didn't let the gnawing feeling that I wasn't worthy, that I did not have a chance at getting in, deceive me into performing some act of self-sabotage on which to blame my failure. I needed an answer, so I called up the admissions office, and they let me know that my application was still in a "maybe" pile.

I called again, a week later, and was told that I was on an alternate's list but that a number of people would have to drop out for me to be accepted.

I was devastated.

I was a twenty-year-old Journeyman Food Clerk/Assistant Manager. The money was good for a young single guy, but if this was as good as life was going to get, it wasn't anywhere near good enough for me. Alcohol was always nearby, and as December wore on my drinking was beginning to become an embarrassment. One night I took a thermos full of Tequila Sunrise to work and ended up inducing vomiting in the toilet in the back room, halfway through my shift in a thankfully successful rescue maneuver to make it through the night without getting fired. My life was peaking; it was all downhill from here. It had already been a long, cold winter, and it wasn't even January.

I don't recall the exact circumstances, but less than a week before the start of spring semester I got word that if I could make it to Pasadena before classes started, they could fit me in. I was elated. I left my Firebird with Ron to sell, and packed up things like my music collection to store at my parents' house. Then I boarded a flight for Los Angeles on Jan. 4, 1980, arriving at Ambassador College just in time to register and attend orientation.

5

Getting Better

There she stood in the doorway; I heard the mission bell
And I was thinking to myself, "this could be heaven or this could be hell"
Then she lit up a candle and she showed me the way
—THE EAGLES: HOTEL CALIFORNIA—

In my short twenty years on earth I had been forced down paths determined by others. This new path was one I had chosen. I was now five feet, five inches tall, still quite short, but no longer tiny, and I felt grown up in other ways. More importantly, I was fully committed to my decision to attend AC, which was a good thing, since my arrival on campus was underwhelming and confusing. Pasadena is cold and rainy in the winter, but the unexpectedly dreary weather was only one part of a cold and wet reception. AC had delayed my acceptance until the last minute, failed to provide the information I needed, and was now finding ways to penalize me for not knowing what it hadn't told me.

Blue Jay Way

AC's Student Financial Advisor, Arthur Suckling, seemed to relish being perceived as an unimaginative little tightwad from England. He insisted on tuition payment in full for the first semester, and room and board prior to registering. Two thirds in cash with the rest easily covered by selling my car was not enough for him to let me proceed through the line. The little time I had to get organized for school was wasted pursuing an unnecessary, if not cruel; request to secure funds in some other manner.

My dorm assignment was a room with three other guys, two of whom were away for winter break. I hadn't known to pack sheets, and without being registered, no blankets or pillows could be issued. I tried fitfully to sleep on a bare bed, without sheets or blankets, while ventilation blew cold air around the room. Toward the end of orientation, with everyone else registered, I managed to produce the title and blue-book value of my car, enabling Arthur Suckling to finally do the math. With campus employment, I would have enough by the end of the summer to pay for my entire second year in advance. Once he belatedly approved me on a standard student payment plan, Mark Kaplan, who I instantly liked, was assigned as my academic advisor. He was courteous, down to earth, and helpful. I would later learn of his Jewish background and status as a scholar within AC and the WCG.

This was the beginning of the "back on the track" phase of AC and the WCG as a whole. A thriving college had been closed in the spring of 1978 and reopened in the fall, offering only a one-year Bible Diploma program. Now in its second year of restructuring, only one degree was offered, a Bachelor of Arts with a major in Theology. Due to the financial snafu, I was the very last of the new students to register. All the classes I wanted to take, and some I needed, were already full.

Mr. Kaplan helped cobble together a schedule, including mandatory freshman Bible, a class that would count toward my Theology major, Latin Literature in Translation to fulfill half of a literature requirement, and geography, a class taught by Mr. Kaplan. Latin Literature was a senior-level course, but Mr. Kaplan felt this was a class I'd be able to handle. The fact that we were having a hard time finding any open classes might have factored into his enthusiasm as well. Now that I was fully enrolled, I was eligible for an on-campus job to meet the payment plan requirement. Of course all the good jobs were taken, so I had to join the janitorial crew.

The campus was beautiful, for sure, but the rain continued and I still didn't have sheets or blankets. That, and having just agreed to clean toilets at minimum wage to pay for classes I didn't really want but had been forced to select, started to get under my skin. The accumulation of challenges and setbacks was really beginning to irritate me. As a graduate of the tent, I could handle what AC was throwing at me, but expecting me to be happy and cooperative with such a flawed institution didn't sit well with my rebel nature. Like Israel in the desert, I began missing Egypt. I gave my old friend Susan an earful about my negative experiences during orientation.

Susan was now in the middle of her junior year and had adapted to the new, back-on-track AC. She was no longer describing it as wild and fun. She explained that the openings for spring semester were due to student expulsions during the fall semester for a variety of infractions including abuse of alcohol or drugs, poor academic performance, pairing up romantically, or just a general bad attitude. My last minute acceptance was due to additional students who had messed up and been reported by various ministers over the winter break. She told me I wouldn't last a month.

This was actually a good thing to tell a religiously zealous rebel like me. A determination to prove her wrong kicked in and kept me moving forward for a day or two. But my disillusionment came to a head a few days later while running back to the dorm in the rain without an umbrella. I saw Norman Zimmerman, whom I had met at the SEP in Minnesota in 1973, raking leaves, a campus job one rung up on the pecking order from mine. Rain poured down around a floppy rain hat onto oversized rain clothes provided by the landscaping department. Rake in one hand, he waved with the other and smiling, yelled "Howdy Wade!" as I rushed by. I managed a weak smile and a half-hearted wave, as I hurried up the steps to the dorm. Once inside, I thought, "What a moron!" By the time I got to the second floor and sat down on my bare bed, I was taking stock of my situation.

There was a spirit at work here that I didn't like. The students were lulled into thinking it was a great privilege to be here, when in fact, it was more like the army. Had some mysterious mass lobotomy been administered? Everybody was happy happy happy, without reason to be. Reflecting on my life back home, my car, the music, my fat paychecks, and the freedom these things represented, the ending of the Eagles "Hotel California" went through my head: "Last thing I remember, I was running for the door. I had to find the passage back to the place I was before. 'Relax,' said the night man, 'We are programmed to receive. You can check out any time you like, but you can never leave!'

What the hell I was doing here? Bolting up from the bare mattress I started packing, shoving clothes into my suitcase. I didn't want to belong here, and the sooner I got out, the better.

After two minutes of frenzied packing, I stopped.

Two weeks ago I was desperate to get to AC and straighten myself out. I came here to change, and now I wanted nothing more than to run away from the place because I was afraid it would change me. Susan's words also came back to haunt me. I couldn't let her be right about me "not being able to make it" here. But the most important part of my epiphany was that it was the spirit at work in me that I didn't like. It wasn't that these people were out of touch with reality; I didn't know how to be happy.

If my first application had been accepted I would have been a casualty of the first semester purges, but God had ensured that I was committed to going. Of course it wouldn't be easy; there was a lot of hard work ahead of me. But I would buckle down and accomplish what I came here for. Become a different person. I began to "get with the program," to quote another sound bite from dear old Dad, and learned about the history of the WCG and its mission, also known as "The Work."

Because

The Satanic attack by the State of California against the WCG was a wake-up call from the liberal years. The Gates of Hell had not prevailed against God's One True Church. HWA was firmly in command, having marked and disfellowshiped the unfaithful, and was leading us through a wide open door to preach the gospel of the Kingdom of God to the world as a witness, so that the end might come. "The end" meant the collapse of human society and the return of Jesus Christ. Our job was to prepare the way for His arrival. That was

The Work. But God's Apostle took time from visiting world leaders, writing, TV and radio broadcasts, and directing the activities of the Worldwide Work of God to speak to the Pasadena congregation and the student body at Sabbath Services, Bible Studies, and AC Forums. He had personal dinners with AC seniors in groups of twelve at a time.

HWA used the Garden of Eden story of the two trees to focus us on the "trunk of the tree" instead of the twigs and branches. According to HWA, the tree of the knowledge of good and evil represented man "taking to himself" the prerogative to choose between right and wrong. Eating its fruit brought death because "There is a way that seems right unto man, but the end thereof is the way of death"[47]—a point the Bible made twice, for emphasis. But eating of the Tree of Life was the path to eternal life.

When man chose the wrong fruit, an angel was placed in front of the Tree of Life, barring access, as vividly illustrated in *The Bible Story*. God grants access to the Tree of Life through a special calling to understand the truth. An understanding of the truth leads people to the One True Church, which is busy preparing the way for Christ's return. Once you had partaken of the fruit of the Tree of Life, symbolized by full immersion baptism, and the receipt of the Holy Spirit by the laying on of hands by a true representative of God, such as could only be found in the WCG, you were under God's Government, administered by duly ordained authority, which resided in God's One True Church.

As fantastic as all of this may sound, this message of authority and control was acceptable to those who through HWA's and the WCG's teaching and preaching now had access to hidden biblical secrets. Without access to the fruit of the tree, you didn't have eternal life, and in practical terms, the understanding you needed to gain access was only available through HWA and the WCG.

Most of humanity was denied this access and was not being judged spiritually. The fate of others was simply death. At a later resurrection, a choice between life and death would be made clear to them.

But those few of us already enlightened, whose eyes and ears were opened, were being judged now.[48] If we turned away, we faced the lake of fire, which would destroy both body and soul—a complete extermination.[49] It bears repeating that

---

47. Proverbs 14:12 & 16:25
48. I Peter 4:17
49. Matthew 10:28 and Revelation 19, 20 & 21

while this teaching is more humane than the classic Dante inspired vision of an ever-burning place of eternal torture, the immediacy of the teaching of the exclusivity of the WCG, coupled with the zeal and sincerity of its membership, meant that we were all on a very tight leash.

In presenting this theology, HWA leveraged his marketing background. The two trees represented two ways of life: Give and Get—an ingenious way to make these unique theological interpretations both simple and palatable to a variety of religious beliefs. HWA had a unique ability to find middle ground despite doctrinal rigidity and a tendency to enforce orthodoxy to a strict interpretation of the Bible. This is not to say that once he had an audience HWA didn't tackle the confused, syncretistic inventions of classical Christianity on many foundational topics, including: heaven, hell, Christmas, Easter, church submission to the Bible, the connection between the old and new testaments (Covenants), infant baptism, confessions, celibacy, and the abolition of the priesthood.

HWA was not always fully correct in his attacks on all of these topics, but was usually closer to the text of the Bible than Christianity as a whole. Regardless of Biblical accuracy or not, HWA and the WCG rejected the doctrine of the Trinity, which alone, without even considering all the other differences, placed us squarely outside mainstream Christianity. In fact, we were officially a cult in the eyes of many Christian watchdog groups. In terms of orthodoxy or heresy, we were definitely on the wrong side of just about any creed used to determine such things, including the Nicean Creed dating back to 325.

On the important topic of the Sign of three days and three nights that Christ gave, the Nicean Creed (and subsequently the creed from the first council of Constantinople in 381) fails to mention the time in the grave by simply including "He suffered, and the third day he rose again, ascended into heaven" whereby Sunday morning counts as the "third day" after the crucifixion on Friday. This was of primary importance to the WCG, since even if one were to allow such anorexic days, this creed neatly avoids the problem of the missing third night.

For HWA a relationship with one's Creator required a childlike acceptance of the revealed word of God, the Bible. The "Plain Truth" of God's Word was more important than fitting in with conventions and fashionable religious beliefs. For parsing through teachings of mainstream Christianity, answering the "big questions," and a sincere effort to disseminate truth in the face of much opposition, the average member granted HWA and the WCG the status of true representatives of God. And the theology of "government from the top down" administered on earth by "God's Apostle" granted HWA, his lieutenants, and the entire ministry and administration authority, backed up by God Himself and His Son, Jesus Christ, the spiritual "Head of the Church."

Along with Trunk of the Tree doctrines, which HWA emphasized, the branches and twigs not essential for salvation were fascinating to students. The Student Leaders of AC, seniors with responsibilities, some of whom had been sent out as ministerial trainees after their junior year, tended to talk about these topics in late night bull sessions. Two charismatic student leaders, Ron Guizado and Dan Samson, impressed me in my first semester. These seniors had experienced the turmoil of the liberal years, and had seen God's mighty hand turn AC and the whole WCG around. They spoke articulately and passionately about the history and future of the Work and church.

Ron and Dan were role models for a major shift in my outlook and approach. It would not be an exaggeration to say that I was acquiring a new identity. Dan was a few years older and wiser, and had experienced such a shift himself, working his way through the Jehovah's Witnesses, the Church of Christ, the Seventh Day Adventists and an obscure offshoot from the WCG on his way to AC. He got me interested in prophetic interpretation.

Do You Want to Know a Secret?

HWA's position was that fully one third of the Bible is prophetic in nature, and much of this was understood. This prophetic framework was documented in a variety of booklets and articles, complete with charts and illustrations, and featured prominently in media efforts. We lived in the end time and watched the Middle East carefully, as the recent history of the nation of Israel clearly fulfilled end time prophecy. The unification of Europe was the final fulfillment of prophecies dating back 2550 years, traced through the great empires of Alexander, Rome, and Napoleon, as revealed in Daniel, Revelation, and elsewhere.

HWA had accurately predicted a United States of Europe would emerge from the ashes of WWII. Events in the Middle East would force it to become the end-time Beast power. In response, the Catholic Church (the great whore of Revelation 17-19) would ride this Beast, forming the end-time Babylon as the world plunged into World War III—nuclear Armageddon. At the conclusion of all these events, with about ten percent of mankind left alive, Christ would return to prevent the extinction of mankind. The called out ones, the true church of God, The People of the Sign, would work with Him to establish The World Tomorrow, the millennium, 1,000 years of peace under Christ's rule.

Scripture clearly showed we could not know the day or hour, but Christ also said we could know when the time was near. So we speculated. We weren't obsessed with prophecy, but our discussions opened up the tantalizing prospect that if one was diligent enough in study, sincere enough in prayer, and attentive enough to the guidance of God, it was possible to crack the code and discover specifics that others hadn't yet uncovered in the word of God. Key areas of prophetic scripture included whole chapters in the book of Daniel, which the Seventh Day Adventists had used to arrive at 1844 as the year Christ was to return.

HWA highlighted a natural 19 year cycle of our solar system. A century of nineteen year time cycles had passed since Christ's crucifixion and the Jewish Diaspora, and he flirted with 1972 as a possible date. This was HWA's 1844 moment, a narrowly dodged bullet, in which he came close to setting a date for Christ's return. But the WCG stayed just shy of being dogmatic about 1972 and backed off a few years prior to its arrival when key prophetic indicators were not yet fully in place.

Was the miscalculation about Christ's return related to the mysterious 100 year period in Isaiah[50] which WCG theology placed at the end of the Millennium? If it were at the beginning, might it cover the period between 1844, clearly indicated by Daniel, and WWII and the Holocaust? How close were we now? Five years? A decade? WCG media efforts constantly emphasized that we were but ten to fifteen years away, providing a minimal buffer while focusing squarely on a time period close enough to ignite plenty of fear to cause people to take action and get serious about getting right with God.

---

50.   Isaiah 65:20

This was in keeping with WCG understanding about the purpose and intent of prophecy in the first place. God's reason for revealing prophecy was twofold. First, to provide insight to the righteous, who were made wise by the understanding that came from obedience. Secondly, to assist the spiritual spokespersons, the prophets, messengers, and disciples sent by God to warn others of impending calamity, to motivate them toward becoming righteous and wise.

Righteousness in the WCG was not based on comparing oneself to others, which was clearly unwise[51]. It had everything to do with the blessing of understanding God's Word, including prophecy. Dan shared an observation that was to color my AC career and beyond. After my rocky first couple of weeks, I was eager and very earnest in trying to adapt and change, hanging onto every rule and principle taught in classes, assemblies, the Ambassador Clubs (modeled after Toastmasters) by faculty and ministers grooming the student body at the West Point of God's Work. I was more earnest than most of my peers, and shared with Dan that in my zeal for self-improvement I had been warned not to commit the sin of Job, which was self-righteousness. Dan turned this around by pointing out that many people are so afraid of being called self-righteous that they never approach righteousness. For better or worse, this encouraged me to dig even more fervently in the "AC goldmine" in search of the relationship with God so tantalizingly offered in Wolverton's *Bible Story.*

Within a few weeks of my arrival at AC, HWA sent a letter to all members and donors highlighting the exciting progress of the Work, and specifically calling out that "More needs to be done in Great Britain and Scandinavia." I looked around and realized I was the only student with any direct connection to Scandinavia. The impact of this was electrifying. I found out who was responsible for international areas of the Work, Mr. Rod Matthews, and made an appointment. Mr. Matthews was a pleasant, short Australian, and I spoke freely about my Swedish background, asking for advice on how to be of use to the Work. He basically patted me on the head and said, "Focus on your studies."

---

51. 2 Corinthians 10:12

I Should Have Known Better

Prior to AC, my strong sense of right and wrong was all twisted up in personal hurts and deeply buried emotions and feelings stemming from loss of love and disillusionment. Intellectual and moral laziness had led to compromises with law and discipline, making me my own worst enemy and my choices self-destructive. A binary logic of everything being completely good or completely evil, of God or of Satan, was a welcome solution to my past fuzzyheaded subjective perspective, which had taken me where I didn't want to be. AC was helping me dig my way out of a pit by allowing me to embrace a worldwide movement to rescue the planet. It was just the motivation I needed. Issues I had with AC being parochial or limiting took a back seat to the realization that it was a stepping stone, not an end in itself. The culture of AC was preparing a new crowd of young ministers (and wives) to support the growth the church was experiencing as it warned the world with renewed urgency.

While immensely motivated by the prospect of getting directly involved in this global movement, I was still recovering from five years of coasting through school, having anesthetized myself with a variety of legal and illegal concoctions and two years in a job that was not intellectually challenging. At AC I was a sponge in class and a good reader, so tests were easy, but college-level research papers were a challenge, especially in my Latin Literature class. The professor, Kyriacos Stavrinides, was Greek and had a distinguished educational pedigree. Having covered the Greek Classics he was now taking his second semester students on an animated romp through the Roman period, and I had been thrown into the deep end.

Not all the students who had been around in the prior much more intellectually diverse version of AC were happy that HWA had turned AC back into a Bible school. Dr. Stav, as he was known, was a hero to these students. He had real academic credentials but had been deemed loyal or important enough to survive the purge. He avoided the overly simplistic black and white approach in vogue, encouraging open discussion that ran counter to the AC experience. The class appealed to me intellectually, and I rose to the challenge of the underlying logic of the class discourse. I also enjoyed Dr. Stav's warm humor and gentle personable style, but couldn't embrace him completely. His approach was at odds with the Maoist Style Cultural Revolution underway at the newly back on track AC, which I was swallowing hook line and sinker. I got a D on my term paper.

While struggling with Dr. Stav's class, I was stewing over having been patronized by Rod Matthews during my visit with him about my Swedish connection. Cleaning up my act and getting my hair cut gave me confidence to try again to get this man's attention, this time with HWA's letter about Scandinavia in hand. He agreed to facilitate a hands-on introduction to doing the Work adding fuel to my arrogant view that I was destined to play a role in the Work of God. I became more cavalier with the difficult material and assignments that Dr. Stav, in his defense, was assigning to challenge his students. He had graciously allowed me to re-write my term paper, and I responded with a manifesto titled "Latin Literature as it Relates to the 'Garbage Can Principle'." I posited a garbage can in which, amongst the refuse, one could find the occasional kernel of whole corn. The result was an F on the paper, an F in the class, and academic probation, with one semester to turn the situation around. This was an embarrassing scholastic and intellectual wake-up call.

This setback was in contrast to being appointed an officer in Outreach, a community service group in which I had been tutoring local children who were wards of the state with histories and situations similar to mine. I was also an officer in an Ambassador Club where I consistently won a cup for each assignment. These responsibilities, awards, and good grades in my other classes, gave me the confidence that I could turn my academic situation around. And as the semester was winding down I learned something else encouraging, which my so-called financial advisor, Arthur Suckling, had missed. I was eligible for a social security benefit as a student with a deceased parent. I had missed an entire semester of this benefit, which would end when I turned twenty-two, but now there would be a small monthly check for the next twenty-four months. With the sale of my car and my wages as a custodian, my school bill was covered, with enough left over for some exciting summer opportunities.

While I was happy to be financially secure, I had also developed a strong aversion to materialism at AC, where the negative impact of greed and obsession with physical things—on us, our families, our children and our society—came into focus. Making money, driving flashy cars, and impressing people with material success were now distasteful. The Old Testament modeled a society based on universal land ownership and a 50 year cycle of debt forgiveness culminating in the year of Jubilee[52]; a 4,000 year old solution to today's economic problems. The WCG somewhat glibly stated that Christ's return would sort out the problems of the world, but the Bible did provide divine insight to humanity on how to fix things rather than waiting for Christ to do so supernaturally. We were literally being trained to help Christ implement a new civilization.

With a Swedish background and Rod Matthews' help, this lowly academic-probation-hampered-single-semester freshman now had an unprecedented opportunity to make a difference. As the semester drew to a close, Mr. Matthews worked with Frank Brown, regional Director of Great Britain, Scandinavia and West Africa, and the business manager, Francis Bergin, to draft plans for me to participate in an exciting summer opportunity.

I'll Follow the Sun

Each spring, announcements were made about Student Leadership Opportunities, for ministerial trainees, and service projects to various parts of the world, under the auspices of the WCG, AC or the Ambassador International Cultural Foundation (AICF). My name was not announced, since my tailor-made opportunity was not sponsored by the college, but my under-the-radar program seemed more exciting and vital than the publicized college sponsored activities.

I worked in the British office assisting the man directly responsible for Scandinavia and West Africa, Peter Nathan. Peter and his young family were from New Zealand and their warmth and his zeal and vision were impressive. He encouraged me about my future in the Work. It was exciting to visit family in Sweden in this context and brush up on my Swedish.

I spent two weeks with Farfar, who had lived in a little apartment since the death of Farmor three years earlier. He was over ninety years of age and was still fairly independent. He did receive help from his daughters, who took turns delivering frozen meals and doing laundry, and also received a bi-weekly social services visit. But he seemed cautious and leery about the intention behind my visit, as though fearing that I wanted something other than just to spend time

---

52. Leviticus 25

with him. Aside from wanting to honor and help him, there *was* something I wanted—a better connection to family. Was it perhaps my religion that kept us apart? Or were love and affection still things he was just not equipped or able to give? In any case, the palpable distance and barriers between us cast a shadow over an otherwise wonderful visit.

To wrap the summer up, I served as college faculty at the SEP program in Scotland, sharing a tent during camp set-up with a somewhat flamboyant character named Jay Brothers. We were about the same age, both having graduated from high school in 1977. We were also of similar build, height (since I had now passed five feet, six inches in height), hair color, and demeanor. Jay had gone straight to AC, but had since moved on to pursue a degree in International Business, and we had both heard about each other before SEP, due to people confusing me with Jay. He had been to SEP Scotland a year earlier and on his second tour of duty he was tanned from participation in "The Dig"—Ambassador's involvement in a prestigious archeological expedition in conjunction with Hebrew University at the City of David in Jerusalem. Jay was a minor cult hero at the camp, with his cavalier attitude and pop-star/bad boy image. Given people's proclivity to get us mixed up, his little entourage of giddy young teenage girls labeled me "Mr. Brother's Brother" making camp the icing on my summer cake. Jay and I shared lengthy conversations and a friendship was formed that would arc across musical interests to find me talking him into returning to AC.

My pedestrian role at camp was head of Campus Improvement, managing the campers' most hated activities: cleaning the latrines, picking up sheep dung from the field, managing the inevitable mud, and other sanitary and maintenance functions. My focus was to make the tasks interesting and purposeful, while actually improving the camp, which the director, Paul Suckling, Arthur's brother, appreciated. In the late evenings and early mornings I spent time a few meters offshore on my prayer rock. God's presence felt real in those moments as I thanked him for rescuing me from my personal Egypt and asked for clarity of direction.

In the desert on the way to the Promised Land, God revealed Himself to Israel in the form of a cloudy pillar by day, to guide and shade, and a fiery pillar by night, providing warmth and light. From my perch on that rock, with the lapping of the waves and the moonlight on the water, I poured my heart out to God. I contemplated a future in His Work; the preparing of humanity for the return of His Son to earth, to establish the Government of God across the entire planet. It was important to be of a different Spirit—like Caleb[53], so I asked God to purge me of wrong motives and desires, to show me the heart of the Gospel, and align me with His will. And I dedicated my entire life, heart and soul, to His Work.

SEP in Scotland was populated with hundreds of young people from all over Europe, with interesting backgrounds and unique perspectives. The camp was like a dream come true with daily activities that were fun and challenging. Any remaining disillusionment was completely replaced by excitement and enthusiasm about the future. God was guiding my path and the possibilities and sense of purpose were palpable. Energized by the summer's activities, I couldn't wait to get back to AC. For the first time in my life I was happy and confident about where I was headed.

Roll Over Beethoven

Two co-eds from England had been at SEP, and I was looking forward to getting to know them better. Dating at AC was required, but "pairing up" was forbidden. Underclassmen were not allowed to go steady. Dates were light social affairs, non-physical, and the student body all dated by accompanying each other to the many college and church activities and functions. Some students bristled at this level of micromanaged social engineering, but it was a healthy situation for me. My troubled background had led to an intense desire for close relationships, without the maturity or skills to handle them. The relationships I had with girls and young women in my teen years and up to the time I entered AC were frustrating experiences in which any reciprocation of interest on the part of the girl I liked, led to physical involvement without a basis for mutual respect, much less true friendship. For someone as emotionally immature as me, the AC policy was a blessing, allowing me to catch up on how to handle basic boy/girl relationships.

---

53. Numbers 14:24

One example of this was an AC movie night in the luxurious Ambassador Auditorium late in my first semester. The chosen movie was *The Sound of Music*; a ridiculously anachronistic choice of movie for a college audience. But for me, the experience was cathartic. I remember sitting in that beautiful setting, surrounded by wholesome young people from around the planet, watching a movie unsullied by the tawdrier aspects of popular culture, and I was overwhelmed by this surreal experience. It seemed I had been transported through time and space to a parallel universe quite different from the chaotic nihilistic one I had known, to a world of beauty, purity, and hope. I had not cried since about age thirteen, not even at hearing the news about my mother's death. What was frozen for years began to thaw, bringing water to my eyes. I sat silently, hoping to God that no one would see the tears rolling down my cheeks.

The impact of culture was also making itself felt. Ambassador Auditorium was home to a globally respected concert series, with some of the most celebrated classical musicians and a variety of other cultural events. I interviewed and was hired as a member of the house staff, performing ushering and other duties under the tutelage and mentoring of Roman Borek. Roman took a sincere interest in the students and his approach managed to be both down-to-earth and snooty at the same time. He helped us acquire an air of sophistication that began to rub off on us from the outside in, enabling us to present ourselves in a dignified and cultured way that changed the way others reacted to us. I took to his approach and this cultural conditioning like a duck to water. With the aid of my international and bilingual background, in this environment I pulled off a transformation that moved me light-years away from the image of the boy who had lived in a tent and embarrassed Miss Alaska.

Aside from Ambassador Club, all freshmen took public speaking, with more advanced speech classes offered as students moved through the four year Liberal Arts program. Richard Ames, a stern but well-liked and somewhat fatherly minister and faculty member, taught freshman speech. Assignments in speech class stretched us beyond our comfort zone, and my personal history often bled into the topic. It was therapeutic to process personal demons, as in an Alcoholics Anonymous meeting, but some students felt uncomfortable with the airing of dirty laundry in public. During an evaluation, a female co-ed[54]

---

54. Connie Deily

remarked that perhaps I had a root of bitterness[55], a spiritual problem even worse than self-righteousness.

Misunderstood or not, I took the criticism and reflected over the course of AC on whether I was working things out, or wallowing in the past. Her comment, however, makes the point that, although AC felt like home and I fully embraced it, it didn't fully embrace me. A rebel doesn't suddenly get along with everyone and many resented the judgmental attitude that accompanied my zeal for change. Throw in anger, resentment, a lingering sense of being a victim, and it's not surprising I was not always accepted.

One memorable speech assignment was to deliver a story as a radio announcer. I chose the story of Elijah and the Prophets of Baal on Mount Carmel[56], with its dramatic confrontation and the triumphant victory of the hero. Elijah called fire down from Heaven to demonstrate not only the power of God, but his alignment with it, inspiring The People of the Sign to wipe out the prophets of evil. I had become an iconoclast, willing to tackle anyone and anything, in the pursuit of righteousness and truth. A 'take no prisoners' approach was very appealing to me, but while the WCG seemed to endorse such an approach, the reality was that being uncompromising was not favored by leadership who wanted more pliant, cooperative individuals under them. You had to be politically savvy to know when to act on principle and when to bend to authority. I did not possess this talent.

Jay, my friend from SEP Scotland, had obtained a position as the butler to Dr. Roth, a pioneer in laser eye surgery, while pursuing a degree in international business. Roth Manor was just a few blocks from AC, off Orange Grove Boulevard, and Dr. Roth's son, David, was the celebrated lead singer of the massively popular group Van Halen. Their legendary hits "Running with the Devil," "You Really Got Me" and "Jamie's Cryin'" had been part of the soundtrack to my Alaskan life. David lived at home and Jay gave me a tour of the mansion while Van Halen was out on tour. Van Halen's practice room downstairs was a mess, with mattresses, trash and who knows what else on the floor. Jay explained that Van Halen wanted an atmosphere of filth to create their music. My recollections of David's room include the original draft lyrics of "Jamie's Cryin'" written on the wall. Another lyric in progress on a white paper

---

55. Hebrews 12:15
56. I Kings 18

was tacked to the wall with a hunting knife, to the right of his bed; an unmade mattress on the floor, covered with a tangle of blankets, sheets and Playboy magazines. Aside from this and a large set of shelves for shoes, the room was pretty bare.

David's day began around noon, and Jay had befriended him by cooking him breakfast, replacing the cookies and beer David was prone to start his day with if left unattended. Once they became friends, David had confided a number of things to Jay in their talks, including conversations he had with "his friends in the attic." That comment, and the overall visit, including the stone gargoyles on the grounds confirmed my new viewpoint, which was that the Devil really was behind much of popular music.

Distance from my life in Alaska, coupled with the lily-white environment I was in, and the many weekly messages about any number of right vs. wrong related topics, led me to reflect on why I had been involved in drugs and other illegal or immoral activities. I came to blame the music I had been listening to, as being Satanic in its inspiration, given the drugs and debauched lifestyles of many of those producing it. Direct insight into the life of David Lee Roth prompted me to call and ask my pleasantly surprised dad to destroy my prized music collection, with specific instructions, not to sell it, or give it to my younger sisters. This action was discussed by students and faculty to evaluate whether it was good or even appropriate to emulate, and the consensus was that if this was done for reasons of conscience it was certainly a good thing. No one at the time felt it was a recommended example for anyone else to follow, but I was only slightly ahead of the curve.

A couple months later, on December 8, 1980, John Lennon was shot and killed outside his apartment building in New York. The massive outpouring of global anguish prompted HWA to write one of his periodic topical pieces to the church. He lamented that the world would follow anyone who would lead them in the wrong direction, as he felt the Beatles had done. For HWA's generation they would always be the longhaired rock musicians who had ushered in the decadence of the 60s. Despite my love of the Beatles and their music, I was inclined to agree with him at the time.

Perhaps inspired by his article, or just because of my attachment to it, rock music became the topic of my research paper in English class that spring. I did further research into music in general, making a connection to the work of a noted expert on brainwashing[57], and wrote a withering indictment against the music of my generation entitled "This Ain't Rock 'n Roll, This is Genocide"—a nod to David Bowie's decadent *Diamond Dogs* LP. In contrast to my *Garbage Can* paper for Dr. Stav., this one was destined to be very well received at AC. It was later noticed by Joseph Tkach, head of Ministerial Services and used to support a brief but powerful anti-rock and roll wave throughout the church.

Glass Onion

Spring brought Passover and the Days of Unleavened Bread, symbolizing Israel's rescue from Egypt.. I took these annual rituals very seriously, and was increasingly looking to God for guidance in some of the minutest details of my life. In hindsight, this may have been more superstition than spiritual openness and included a minor interest in numerology. I looked for number patterns that reinforced my belief that God had a specific purpose in mind for me. Writing this today seems borderline scary, and although it heightened my sense of self-importance, the same technique sometimes encouraged humility. Foot washing at Passover in 1981 is a good example.

Pasadena was the epicenter of the Work of God. God's Apostle, many evangelists and executives with overall global responsibility would all be in attendance at Passover services. Which important feet might I randomly end up washing, I wondered? Instead, standing in front of me was a single gentleman visiting from Alaska, who, without knowing him, struck me as a goofy hillbilly type. I was immediately disappointed having gone into the ceremony with a silly idea about meeting someone important. Already aware of the crass nature of my attitude at this most solemn and selfless spiritual ceremony of the entire year, I had scolded myself for my thoughts. What was driven home by this encounter was the inherent putdown of anyone I did not consider important, and the grim nature of this line of thinking. I had to acknowledge my fundamental lack of respect for others, based on an immature, superficially judgmental attitude toward my brothers and sisters, coupled with recognition of an equally disgusting desire to be important in some way.

---

57. William Sargant: *Battle for the mind: a physiology of conversion and brainwashing.*

This is how Passover was supposed to work, imparting insight into our nature and the need for humility in our relations with God and man. It also reflected a fabulous sense of humor and perfect comic timing on God's part. Why do I, even today, feel that something so subjective had God's involvement? It's not just the astronomical odds of hooking up with someone from Alaska, while focused on the thought of washing more important Pasadena feet. The man's name was David, who for any WCG trained person is a clear indication of a man after God's own heart. But it wasn't his first name that was the key. It was his family name—Foote. This is but one example of how I perceived gentle parental guidance from my adopted Father, throughout my days at AC, where I was making up for what I had never had as a child.

Despite personal growth and early success at AC, mine was not a 'Joe AC' personality. Living according to the Law of God is essential for human happiness, but resentment of military style respect for hierarchical authority made me, at heart, an independent rebel, a James Dean style bad boy, even though I was trying hard not to be that bad boy any longer. I was hyper-alert to hypocrisy in those who wielded authority because of how those in authority had failed me, lied to me, and manipulated me all my life. Having been a huge hypocrite for years, my bullshit radar was fine-tuned. I was not afraid to hold the ministry and other authority figures accountable for what we stood for, and speak my mind about things that needed correcting. Understandably, others were equally critical of me and pegged me as this or that kind of a person. I was a walking contradiction and someone others had a hard time understanding.

During my first three semesters at AC, my friends were mostly international students. They were cultural outsiders with a more nuanced view, and could relate to not wanting to be judged by the mono-cultural view prevalent among the U.S. ministry and faculty. The accents and interesting ways of the British, French, and French Canadian girls were also intriguing. These students influenced my decision to take French to fulfill my literature requirement. My negative experience with Latin Literature and the fact that I was bilingual also weighed heavily into the decision.

Not being accepted by those in power didn't bother me, and I took pride in not seeking political approval. Living according to the Law... with "Living according to the Law of God is essential for human happiness, but resentment of military style respect for hierarchical authority made me, at heart, a James

Dean style independent rebel, even though I was trying hard not to be. The teachings and doctrines of the church heavily influenced my view of what God did or didn't want, but the Bible was the final word. HWA publicly thumped his Bible, telling us to "blow the dust off" it and "don't believe me, believe God." In practice he may not have tolerated disagreement with his interpretations, but I was not close enough to him to be concerned about that. The scripture "Let God be true, but every man a liar"[58] allowed me to draw my own conclusions. As a survivor in a world of people who lied and abused trust I was not afraid to disagree with anyone; if necessary, even God's own Apostle.

The two trees, for example, seemed to represent that God's greatest gift to man was freedom to choose. He gave the answers, but He allowed and respected our choices. It wasn't yet clear that some behind the pulpit preferred a claim to divine authority over having to humbly proving their case from the Word of God. It would be my junior year before the beginnings of disillusionment with the oversimplification, opulence, and the arrogance of those in positions at "HQ" would surface. But from the beginning, I held those assuming the mantle of authority to the highest possible standard.

HWA spoke of his intended but never used first cover of *The Plain Truth* —which was an illustration of a classroom where a teacher poured ready-made propaganda from a pitcher into the open brains of students. He declared AC to be different, but it wasn't, and the irony of this was not lost on me. The AC Bible Correspondence Course used the exact method that HWA called out with this vivid image. It was clearly expected of us to accept authority without questioning it, and resistance to such cognitive dissonance was part of a long love-hate relationship with the leadership of the WCG and its offshoots. Competing desires to be righteous, worthy, competent, important, and successful, contrasted with a desire to remain humble, meek, lowly, and submissive to God were destined to govern my thinking over the remainder of my college career and beyond.

If I Fell

As my second AC summer approached, academic probation was behind me and I had earned several distinctions, such as being among 70 students (there's

---

58. Romans 3:4

that numerology again) selected to transfer to the newly reopened Big Sandy campus, which would now offer two-year associate degrees. HWA personally spoke at an assembly to encourage us to re-establish this sister campus of God's College and teach the incoming freshmen God's way. I was also selected to be an Ambassador Club President, establishing me as an early student leader, despite some of my less well received qualities.

Then there was the prestigious Dig—the archaeological excavation at Jerusalem's City of David. Richard Paige managed AC's entire involvement in this project: the logistics, travel, selection, training, and oversight of the students who participated. I applied, but recurring back pain, hearkening back to health problems after high school, almost kept me from being accepted. As spring progressed, my condition improved and Mr. Paige waived his concerns, enabling me to plan another customized summer program. It included a trip to Sweden and travel through Europe before meeting the group in Athens. From there, we embarked on a boat ride to Haifa, where my first view of the Holy Land was Mount Carmel, the location of the spiritual battle between Elijah and the prophets of Baal.

As our ship approached the harbor we eagerly looked over the bow, taking in a golden Mosque-like structure on the side of Mount Carmel. Mr. Paige explained it was the center of the Baha'i faith and that its location on the mountain held prophetic significance he couldn't explain. Such was the mystery of Israel. It is hard to convey, in writing, the power of visiting the biblical sites our reading had invested with spiritual significance. The archaeological site, the City of David, just outside the old city of Jerusalem, was one of enormous importance to biblical archaeology. Our visit to the Sinai Desert, in open-air British Army vehicles, was also utterly unique. We ascended Mount Sinai early in the morning to watch the sunrise; we stood on Masada, we visited Jericho, and on and on it went.

In Israel I began to conceive of faith as a blindfolded walk down a pirate's gangplank, above a sea swimming with sharks. Only after stepping off the end would our faith be rewarded by the appearance of a platform to land on and explore, before being faced with the next gangplank. This was similar to the analogy of following the guidance of the cloud/fire pillar, but addressed the issue of our fear and/or unwillingness to follow it. One of the components of the analogy I liked was the idea that even though God wanted us, at all times and in all ways, to speedily progress through the trials and tests of faith that would lead us to greater and greater platforms of awareness, we typically refused to walk down a gangplank until there was a knife at our back, and we saw no other option available to us. God would not force us to choose the tree of life. We have a tendency to move forward only when our exploration of the tree of good and evil brings such painful results that we see no other choice. But I was no longer an angry young man fighting teachers who wanted to fill me up with rules; I now eagerly embraced God as my teacher.

During the summer, my stepsister Julie, inspired by stories of my world travels, had pushed to graduate from high school a year early. She and my friend Ron had both been accepted to attend AC in Pasadena. In this light, my decision to apply to go to Big Sandy felt a bit like a voluntary walk down the gangplank. Pasadena had been very good to me and it was difficult to leave it behind, even for a year. My goal was to move forward, in faith, despite the feeling that I was leaving the Promised Land of Pasadena for the deserted wasteland of East Texas.

6

With A Little Help From My Friends!

Electric guitar is brought in to a court of law.
The judge and the jury, twelve members of the jury
All listening to records. Is this a crime against the state?
This is the verdict they reach.
Never listen to electric guitar

—Talking Heads: Electric Guitar—

Things were different in Big Sandy, and not in a good way. We were tucked away in the middle of nowhere, a hundred miles from anything that could be called a city, and light years from the center of the Work of God in Pasadena. The freshmen were also a bit raw, if you will. Many were disinterested in AC or had been deemed unworthy for Pasadena. Average age and SAT scores seemed a bit below the average for the freshman class in Pasadena. And where were the International students? The administration cited Visa issues, but that was probably only half the reason.

You Can't Do That

I don't make these comments lightly, given the inherent disrespect, but they reflect my attitude at the time. If Big Sandy had been open when I had applied I would have landed there, and wouldn't have been transformed by a global vision of what God was doing. Big Sandy was a problem needing to be fixed. AC had enabled me to turn my life around and I was critical of those who resisted its influence and the efforts of those sent from Pasadena to establish its culture in this remote outpost.

A number of the sophomores who had started in Pasadena had a similar perspective. This quickly set up a maturity and attitude divide between the freshmen & sophomores, as all but the wildest among the sophomores were now on the conservative side of the equation. Being a bit older than average with three semesters of AC and two summers doing the Work of God under my belt, I was one of the worst offenders in terms of looking down my nose at the incoming class. My arrogance applied not only to students, but also to certain faculty members. Not surprisingly, as the sophomore class worked to support the party line coming from Pasadena, faculty not from Pasadena resisted our approach.

Ron Kelly was Dean of Students and directed the Ambassador Club of which I was president. We got along well enough despite obvious differences in style, tone, and approach, typified by his insistence that students drop the standard "Mr." in Club in favor of a first-name basis. Paul Schnee, the younger son of Regional Director Frank Schnee (who had arranged for my dad and his three kids to travel to our first Feast in England) was also in the club. Paul had been pretty wild since his graduation from German school at age sixteen, and at eighteen he was still not ready to adapt to the rules and regulations of AC. The fact that his father was an important leader in the church emboldened him to openly resist any and all authority that didn't suit him. He took every opportunity to challenge me during our weekly meetings.

That year I tackled my eighth assignment, the Attack Speech. This was a chance to express moral outrage, righteous indignation, and rip the subject apart with logic, passion, and genuine, controlled anger. I chose rock music, leveraging material from my research paper the year before, and gave what some considered one of the most powerful and dramatic attack speeches on record, pun intended. At the end, as the intensity mounted, I moved from behind the lectern to wave an offending piece of vinyl, and smashed it against my knee, sending shards flying into the stunned audience. But not everyone was stunned. Paul and two of his buddies had smirks of opposition on their faces. They enjoyed being a countercultural force amongst the self-righteous sophomores.

The difference between righteousness and self-righteousness still bothered me, and I determined to fast once a week to deepen my humility and pursue true spirituality. One of the Holy Days Israel was commanded to observe was Yom Kippur, the Day of Atonement—a fast, not a feast. WCG members abstained from food and water from sunset to sunset to focus on spirituality, humility, and drawing nearer to God. The idea to apply this on a weekly basis was partly due to HWA's autobiography, in which he discussed his "72 hour cure"—three days and nights of fasting, with alternating prayer, Bible study, and meditation for an hour at a time, in rotation. WCG theology held that Job suffered tremendously as God worked to cure him of the sin of self-righteousness, so to exchange the curse of self-righteousness for true righteousness, I combined my weekly regimen of fasting with a study of Job.

Not surprisingly, many students and faculty in Big Sandy viewed me as a pompous, self-righteous, wanna-be minister. Two events helped transform that image. To promote the speech program several students were selected to deliver speeches to the student body and I was asked to deliver a "My Life" speech, a confessional personal triumph story. The audience sat spellbound as they listened to the story of my childhood. Many students told me that their impression of me was changed by that speech.

And Your Bird Can Sing

The second event related to my struggle with music during my anti-rock phase. Wanting to approach music in a more positive way, I joined the choir.

Second semester I also took piano, which was my first attempt ever to play an instrument. I was an absolute beginner surrounded by students who had been playing since they were toddlers. The other beginner in the class was a semester ahead, so I was a bungling incompetent, even in comparison to her. My insecurities had led me to avoid such situations like the plague, but now, toward the end of the year, everyone in the class had to perform in a recital. I was assigned two pieces: a Czechoslovakian children's ditty and a duet with the teacher, Mrs. Bryant. During the duet, I would simply be playing loud staccato chords that would support her sprightly melody.

Dress was semi-formal and surrounding dignitaries were invited to this East Texas cultural highlight. Dressed up, everyone was displaying their snootiest behavior, which for the WCG, and especially AC, is saying a lot. A number of accomplished performers had played to an enthusiastic audience when I confidently walked on stage to announce my two pieces. I took care to articulate the correct pronunciation of the title of the Czechoslovakian tune, translating it as "Dance," and announced that for my second number I would play a duet with Mrs. Bryant. I sat down and managed my way through "Dance," while the audience looked puzzled and exchanged confused, then knowing, glances.

Mrs. Bryant then joined me on the stool, and I paused before aggressively and dramatically banging out three alternating chords, in an 8-beat rhythm. Mrs. Bryant commenced her light, lively melody on the upper keys, and I smiled, as the effect was pleasant and actually entertaining. On my second attempt I missed one of the chords, badly, resulting in a loud and clearly discordant noise followed by a repressed laugh from Dominick Furlano in row two. Having let the first laugh go, he could not stop himself from continuing. As his muffled giggles grew louder, it was time for my third round of chords. The same wrong chord rang out loudly above the expanding laughter, as others failed in their desperate effort not to join Dominick. After I vigorously banged out the wrong chord for the fourth time, the entire audience was in hysterics.

Mrs. Bryant, seated between the audience and me, recognized a hopeless situation and stood to bow. I grabbed her left sleeve with my right hand, and pulled her down on the seat, determined to finish the song. The audience howled, uncontrollably, as I massacred my part a fifth time. Poor, sweet, demure Mrs. Bryant could no longer contain herself and her hands left the keyboard to cover her mouth. In contrast to Dominick and most of the audience, she was able to politely hold her laughter inside, but her petite body jiggled like Jell-O on the piano bench next to me, betraying her.

By now Dominick had literally fallen off his chair into the aisle, and someone stood up to lead the audience in applause to put an end to my merciless humiliation. I had succeeded in bringing an entire audience to hysterical laughter, not with me, but at me. Anyone not laughing was in shock at what they assumed might be permanent damage to my tender ego.

Even as we took our bows and left the stage, the laughter still overpowered the applause, and intermission was called to allow the audience to compose itself. Rather than being crushed, the effect on me was liberating. Having a large audience brought to tears, in laughter, at my incompetence, was cathartic. The distance between me and others would never again be quite as great. The overall effect of my year in Big Sandy was to break down some of the defenses I had built to protect myself, and become just a little bit more human as a result. Along with barriers coming down, I began to worry less about self-justification and self-righteousness and began to realize that the person in front of me was more important than whatever was going on inside my head.

The 70 students in the sophomore class in Big Sandy grew close, and we worked together to organize two events to end the year, a variety show and a burn-out bash. The highlight of the variety show was a three-tiered scaffold on the stage, with nine students sitting in an amazing replica of "Hollywood Squares" renamed "Faculty Squares." When the curtain opened and the lights went up the audience exploded with laughter and applause at the amazing set that filled center stage top to bottom. I was a contestant asking questions of students delivering spot-on impersonations lampooning faculty, administration, and Gerald Waterhouse. The skit brought the house down, but some of the laughter was nervous, as not everyone could take the pointed humor directed at faculty and ministry who were normally accorded intense respect and deference.

The Waterhouse impersonation was the most problematic. He had no role in the College, which gave anyone offended a way to criticize the effort without appearing unable to laugh at themselves. To further add to what we didn't yet realize was a bad reputation for our class, the end-of-the year burn-out bash slide show featured me and another student, arms outstretched, riding the sacred *Swans in Flight* sculpture that graced the entrance to the campus. This was a David Wynn sister sculpture to the iconic sculpture depicting soaring egrets ascending from the reflecting pool in front of Ambassador Auditorium in Pasadena. These events contributed to a backlash in Pasadena toward the Big Sandy Campus, which some were now calling Ambassador High School.

As summer approached, I was out of the loop on potential opportunities in the Work, since Big Sandy was far removed from the hub of activity of Pasadena, the headquarters of the church. When Richard Paige visited Big Sandy to interview candidates for the Jerusalem dig, he asked if I would return for another season to assist. I was flattered and wanted to go, but felt it unwise to spend the money and time on a "been there, done that" activity, even a prestigious one. I was turning twenty-two, bringing an end to the social security checks, and anticipated finishing my sophomore year just under $2,000 in debt. In addition, I had bent the rule about pairing up, and was serious about a freshmen girl, which affected my thinking about my financial situation.

In Big Sandy I had worked on the electrical crew, and this experience opened up an opportunity to work in Alaska for the summer as an electrician's assistant. Earning the money to pay off my college debt seemed the best course of action. As the year came to a close, I was called into Ron Kelly's office to learn that an anonymous member of the Big Sandy congregation donated the money to pay off my student debt. I was floored. Three or four members of the local congregation came to mind, but I couldn't imagine any of them having done this. Working on this book, it became clear who that donor was, and I would like to offer public thanks, while maintaining anonymity.

The outcome of my fasting and study in Big Sandy was to conclude that the book of Job was not about self-righteousness at all. Job was clearly righteous, and his suffering at the hand of Satan was quite unjust. Job was typical of Christ and through his suffering he was granted understanding and compassion beyond a righteousness based on obedience to law. To arrive at conclusions different from or beyond those being taught officially within the WCG was a big deal.

I don't know which particular one of the many changes I experienced was most responsible, but at Big Sandy I began to actually feel good about who I was for the first time since I had landed in Sweden at age 9. I saw myself on the path to success, and for the first time in years I actually thought about my mother. If Mom were around I knew that she would be proud of me, and it brought tears to my eyes. I had cried once since her death, at the *The Sound of Music* screening, but now I cried because she was gone, and she didn't know that I was turning out ok.

Think For Yourself

While working in Alaska I also obtained a low-interest state student loan and returned to Pasadena flush with cash. Julie and Ron transferred to Big Sandy, where a big summer clampdown revoked student driving rights, so Ron left his car with me in Pasadena, where things were even tighter. Jay had re-enrolled while I was in Big Sandy, and we were roommates in a dorm with a monitor known as a "Resident Assistant," or RA for short. Silly and unnecessary rules encouraged overzealous RAs to intrude on student freedom and autonomy. They served more as informants than assistants, and I began to refer to them as "two-thirds rat." Rumors from Big Sandy further tarnished the reputation of anyone who had been there. Having money, a car, and a girlfriend in Big Sandy automatically put me at odds with faculty and student leaders trying to micro-manage the spirituality of students. And my relationship with the girl from Big Sandy was not going well.

I had invited this lovely girl to spend the Feast in Alaska with me and my family, but it was clear Dad didn't approve. Her mother had an illness, which he said was a warning sign. I was floored, and fired back that if girls followed his advice to review my family background, I would spend the rest of my life single. Regardless, I wasn't mature enough for a serious relationship and by the end of the Feast this one was over. Returning to AC, I wondered if my desire for a close romantic relationship had distracted me from returning to Israel and had gotten me off the path laid down by the cloud/fire pillar. Was I now beginning to wander around aimlessly in the desert, spiritually?

But being a sinner viewed with suspicion by the righteous also pushed my buttons as a rebel. It was clear that the more controlling approach I had longed for at the beginning of my Big Sandy year was counter-productive authoritarianism. Comparisons between Moses and HWA were rampant. Moses' father-in-law had advised him to establish a pyramid authority structure to manage the affairs of the people[59] and Aaron the High Priest "held up the hands of Moses" to give the people victory. Israel's criticism of Moses' leadership and God's clear backing of Moses was constantly cited by HWA's lieutenants to back the authority of WCG's "government from the top down." HWA was God's Apostle "in the seat of Moses"[60] as Christ referred to the authority of the Pharisees.

The reference to the Pharisees was not exactly a ringing endorsement and in becoming more familiar with the structure, approach, and content of the Bible, my understanding and use of scripture helped me move past an overly simplistic black-and-white approach to the texts. Richard Paige's Ancient Israel class helped in this, as it expanded numerous brief accounts in scripture into relevant examples of how Israel had actually practiced their religion. The daughters of Zelophehad, for example, came to Moses because they were not eligible for inheritance. A practical exception was made, showing God to be reasonable, flexible, and one who honored the claims and needs of women as well as men—even in the Old Testament.[61] This and other practical examples indicated God did not want us to blindly accept the status quo. We should follow Jacob's example and wrestle with God.[62] The result would be the blessing of a more mature understanding as was the case with Job. This perspective helped me get through my junior year.

I'm Only Sleeping

Wanting to get spiritually centered again, I entered into a competition with George, one of my friends from Big Sandy. The challenge was that whoever got up more often at 5:30 in the morning to pray would be treated to dinner by the other one. This was done under the auspices of iron sharpening iron[63] and HWA's recommendation to spend 90 minutes daily alternating between prayer,

59. Exodus 17 and 18
60. Matthew 23:2
61. Numbers 27 and 36
62. Genesis 32:24-30
63. Proverbs 27:17

Bible study, and meditation. This was very hard for members, including busy students, but I was determined to put my spiritual life first, and everything else second. Perhaps this commitment paid off, because I was soon asked to interview for the choice student position of assistant to David Hulme. David, an intelligent and articulate Englishman, had studied Philosophy at the University of Edinborough before transferring to AC. After a recent promotion by HWA to handle global print advertising and public relations, he carried the title of Director of Communications and Public Affairs. He was a rising star, with a high degree of political prominence, and his position directly aligned with my main interest, the publication of the Gospel to the world as a witness or, simply, the Work.

He interviewed seven students for the position, including key student leaders and sons of prominent ministers. I was none of these, but against all odds, I landed the job, temporarily vaporizing self-doubt and feelings of being disconnected from God's Work. My office on the fourth floor of the Hall of Administration even sported its very own mint-dish, supplied by the secretaries from the adjacent suite of offices that housed HWA and his top deputies. The position gave me direct insight into WCG media efforts and a sense of privilege and excitement at being on the inside.

Along with this success came fear. This sudden rise to prominence made me nervous and uncomfortable; I was waiting for the other shoe to drop. At the time I didn't understand the nature and mechanics of these feelings. It would be some time before I would gain deeper insight into exactly how I was my own worst enemy, and how a profound level of psychological self-sabotage had become systemic. Initially what heightened my anxiety was a comment from David that I often seemed tired, which was an understatement.

I was burning the candle at both ends, adding German to my French minor and Theology major, clubs, work, dating, and getting up every morning at 5:30 to pray. My new role as David Hulme's assistant was proof I was tracking toward ever more exciting opportunities to serve God and His Work, unaware of the overall toll this was taking on my health. As the year drew to a close, George and I tallied up our results, and he had beaten me in the prayer contest. After cashing in on the dinner, he admitted to taking his pillow into the prayer closet to sleep. Who cheats to win a prayer contest?

I'd fallen behind some of my peers in French while in Big Sandy, but my prior immersion into Swedish helped me to dive into AC's grueling program in a fearless manner and excel. I was on par with many third year students in my pronunciation and ability to communicate, even if grammar and vocabulary were still somewhat lacking. I looked forward to yet another trip to Europe, with a visit to Sweden, eight weeks in France for the French language summer immersion program, and a return to Scotland for SEP, where I was to be a counselor. As the last week of school arrived with the announcements of student leadership positions for the following year, I was named a resident assistant. I again headed to Europe, for the first time feeling fully respected by the powers that be in the AC government of God hierarchy. There were other feelings of reconciliation as well.

Since arriving at AC I had worked to bury resentment and obey the commandment to honor your father and your mother[64] and past humiliations were fading from memory. Julie was accepted to the Jerusalem dig and we arranged a cheap flight to Frankfurt, Germany, followed by sixteen hours of train travel up to Stockholm to meet our parents in Sweden, where Dad planned a visit to pick up a new Volvo and introduce his second wife to the family.

These travels weren't all fun and glamour. Arriving from L.A. and relying on my one semester of jet-lagged German, we boarded an airport train heading in the wrong direction and missed our connection to Stockholm. We had a bleary-eyed great time wandering around the massive Frankfurt train station grazing on hazelnuts and bananas for six hours, then traveled through the night. Our sleep was interrupted by the constant harassment of doors being slammed open, lights thrown on, and authoritative voices calling out "Passkontroll!" at the frequent borders. The train was then loaded onto a ferry by running it back and forth for an hour, delivering a massive jolt each time another car was disconnected. We had the same experience again, for another hour, on the other side. In Sweden we worried about sleeping through our stop, so Julie washed her hair in the wee sink of the train and we arrived in Småland exhausted, with Julie looking like a drowned rat.

We were picked up by our parents and driven to the Sten Stuga, the little red summer cottage formerly part of my grandparent's farm, but now owned by

---

64. Exodus 20:12 and elsewhere

Uncle Ingemar. We embarked on a tour, playing unfamiliar roles as participants in the happy Fransson family, visiting uncles, aunts and cousins.

Being for the Benefit of Mr. Kite

The WCG had recently decided to focus efforts on Norwegian as the most accessible language within Scandinavia. A Norwegian *Plain Truth* and a number of booklets were now available. I had presented David Hulme with population statistics, demographics, and personal anecdotes about how Norwegians understood Swedish, while the opposite did not hold true, supporting my biased opinion that Swedish was a wiser choice. I was confident God would guide us to find a better way to advance the Work in Sweden than the current ineffective efforts to promote Norwegian literature through print ads in the Swedish *Reader's Digest*. I was also confident I had a role to play.

At Sabbath services in Stockholm we met interesting, if somewhat eccentric, Swedes who had embraced the WCG. One member, Göran Bring, had an important media connection; he had been in a youth choir with Lennart Swahn, an enormously influential media personality in Sweden. To Swedes, Lennart Swahn was the equivalent of Walter Cronkite, Larry King, and Johnny Carson, all rolled up into one. He had been Sweden's reporter at the Nobel Prize Celebrations, had hosted several top rated TV shows on Sweden's state controlled television channels, and was repeatedly voted Sweden's favorite radio and television personality. He was a powerful insider in Sweden's closed, government controlled media. Göran had mentioned his connection numerous times before, but no one of importance had taken an interest.

David Hulme had said "keep your ear to the ground" in Scandinavia, so I took an interest, only to find Göran reluctant to contact Lennart Swahn. He admitted he hadn't spoken to Lennart in decades, and wasn't sure he would be remembered. After talking about this for years, he was afraid to come up empty-handed. I argued that my direct connection to David Hulme was his best chance to finally get Pasadena's attention. Perhaps due to the recent decision to promote Norwegian and the chance to bypass Frank Brown, who had ignored him in the past, he finally picked up the phone and dialed the number.

While this was happening, I tried to reach David, who was traveling in the Caribbean. This was before mobile phones and the Internet, and it was hard to connect. In my next attempt to reach David I left the number to Aunt Ingrid, our next stop. Göran excitedly contacted me saying Lennart Swahn wanted to talk. Lennart was at his summer cottage so Göran gave Lennart Ingrid's phone number as well. Ingrid got two phone calls from David while we were out and was not pleased at having had to fumble unintelligently with extremely limited English, unable to even tell David he had gotten the right number. Her frustration about the drama of it all was exceeded by her skepticism that *the* Lennart Swahn would call her house asking for me.

She was stunned to pick up the phone late one evening, hoping to finally connect me with that Englishman in America, and find Lennart Swahn on the other end. Lennart was amazed that my Swedish was fluent and authentic, even if I still used sixth grade and teenage expressions a Swede my age would have outgrown. Göran had told him about my kidnapping and my time in Sweden and it was all a bit intriguing to him. Against all odds, he invited me to meet with him in Stockholm to discuss programming ideas for Sweden's TV2. He gave me his address, the code to ring his penthouse apartment in Stockholm's old city, and a time to meet.

Dad, whose name was also Lennart, but at the time was still sporting the added "h," was nervous and proud as he dropped me off on the street in front of Lennart's building. I was just nervous. I took a deep breath and punched in the code. The buzzer sounded, and I walked up the stairs to Lennart's apartment, where he met me at the door and welcomed me in. He was dressed in a suit, as was I, customary attire for evening meetings in Sweden. He invited me to sit down in a large sitting room, with a piano and numerous autographed pictures and awards from his illustrious career. He excused himself to retrieve a silver tea service and cake, apologizing for not preparing anything special, having just returned from his summer home.

My unease and nervousness quickly evaporated as Lennart deployed his legendary ability as a conversationalist. He shared that he had taken Göran's call because Göran had once ridiculed him when they were boys. Göran had told Lennart that he didn't have a singing voice, which Lennart admitted had a grain of truth to it, and that he would never amount to anything, which had not proved to be prophetic. We chuckled at Göran's expense, though Göran was no slouch either, as a Professor at Sweden's prestigious Uppsala University. Still, Lennart had a definite edge in the amount-to-something department.

More interesting than this little revelation was that Lennart's mother had been a Seventh Day Adventist, and he had kept the Sabbath as a boy. Although he did not feel any compulsion to do so today, he respected Sabbath keepers and wanted to learn about the WCG and our connection to the Adventists, and the Jews, etc. He spoke fondly of his mother and her faith, admitting to occasional nostalgia for the feelings he had as a child regarding his mother's beliefs and related activities. People of the Sign had amazingly affected Lennart's life, as they had Lennarth's and mine.

As the evening drew to a close, Lennart assured me that he would help get our programs on the air. He had enjoyed the evening and genuinely wanted to help in the unusual and somewhat bold expression of faith that had led me to his doorstep. He seemed amused with the prospect that his success and prominence might benefit a religious group similar to the one that he had known as a child. I assured him David Hulme would contact him and exchanged a warm goodbye handshake. I descended the stairs in a daze, amazed and grateful for what had just happened, attributing glory to God for having opened a door to begin the process of bringing the Swedish people a message of hope. Sweden learning about the Kingdom of God would bring us one step closer to the return of Jesus Christ to usher in 1,000 years of global peace and prosperity.

My immediate goal was to get in touch with David, but of course Göran wanted to know the outcome of my meeting with Lennart. I shared what had happened, but asked him to keep it to himself. It seemed proper to handle this confidentially to avoid unnecessary discussions and rumors. My intuition was correct, as Göran was unfortunately not able to keep such good news quiet, and there would be repercussions.

Here, There and Everywhere

From Sweden we headed to Bonn, Germany which was Frank Schnee's territory. He oversaw the operations of the church and Work in Germany, Austria, Switzerland and large parts of Eastern Europe, at the time still behind the Iron Curtain. He had continued to work tirelessly to expand the reach and operations of the Work in his region, and he was eager to meet students with an international perspective, who were viewed as a source of potential manpower to support the growth taking place. He had worked with Richard Paige to arrange for the Jerusalem Dig group to start their European tour with a visit to the Bonn office.

In Bonn I finally connected with David Hulme by phone, sharing the highlights and following up with a telex report with the details and contact information for Lennart Swahn. Then we joined the Dig tour through German speaking Europe. The students were chauffeured in an ornate yellow bus, driven by a young member of the Swiss congregation, along with his attractive and sharply dressed girlfriend following behind in a red convertible sports car. Dad and Elinor brought up the rear in our new Volvo, with me standing up and filming through the sunroof. We enjoyed German white wine on the Rhine River, toured Hitler's stadium and Dachau, the Munich Beer Halls, Salzburg (featured in *The Sound of Music*), and much, much more. This glorious adventure ended in Lucerne with Julie and the group heading south while I wistfully pondered having passed up a second trip to Israel a year earlier. Then I headed north to meet up with students arriving in Paris for the French Summer Program.

The French program consisted of successive two-week immersion visits with three families in different regions of France. The participating student helped the families with work, chores or projects in exchange for room and board. My first stay was with an amazing family of six, a delightful educated couple who had chosen to live on a small farm to experience country life. Their 18-year-old boy, Thierry, was a talented and witty musician, and in his footsteps followed Eric, age thirteen, and darling eight-year-old twin girls, Caroline and Christine. They loved hearing me mangle the French language, providing humorous opportunity to learn and practice. My project was to build a pigeon coop with wood and wire, for which my gracious host family expressed delight and admiration.

Next came two weeks as a bricklayer for a family of Italian descent with a shy daughter who was intrigued by this college boy. They were wonderful, but the days were long and hot for someone unaccustomed to physical labor. My next stop was another small farm supporting a family of four, who were extremely quiet and reserved. They lived in a very old stone and thatched roof house which was under reconstruction. The situation reminded me of my tent days in a number of ways.

My job was manually cutting, loading, hauling, and storing hay in the barn. On the second day the dust irritated my nose, which started bleeding and wouldn't stop for hours, followed by a low-grade fever and exhaustion. I'm no slacker, but on the third day I felt terrible and was visibly miserable with the work. When my nose started bleeding again, the family had to once more interrupt the work and return me to their house, delaying the project. The remainder of my time was spent resting on a mattress on the floor of a large open room. The husband had an impenetrable dialect, and communication was near impossible even before this turn of events. Though I couldn't understand him because of the language barrier, his disappointment in having a laborer who was an invalid came through loud and clear. It was like I was fourteen again, in the Alaskan cold-war situation with my dad, unable to communicate while being judged a miserable failure. The remaining ten days were very uncomfortable, physically and emotionally.

When I rejoined the group in Paris for two weeks of intensive French lessons, I was still not well and struggled with the jam-packed schedule. Back-to-back tours of museums and exhibits and the all-day bike tour of the castles along the Loir River were more exhausting than fun or educational. Still, I was well enough to drive the van when our designated student leader, Eli Chiprout, was too insecure. He sat in the passenger seat using what I felt were poor map reading skills to navigate. I should have been more aware of his reactions to our petty arguments as I maneuvered us around Paris, getting us to our destinations on time, one way or another. French drivers did as they pleased and I was happy to apply the "when in Rome, do as the Romans do" principle, including breaking an occasional traffic rule or driving up on the occasional sidewalk. My combination of accomplishment and rebel spirit mirrored the French attitude, in contrast to Eli's more cautious, rule-bound personality. The tension between us was at its worst when, from time to time, Eli couldn't keep up and I stopped to grab the map.

When the French program ended I met Julie at the Paris airport. She was tanned and back from the Dig and we accompanied a group of French teenagers to SEP in Scotland. This time I knew the ropes, had lots of returning friends, and loved being a counselor. Having met many of the French campers, I was welcomed into the inner circle of a warm close-knit group who were happy to have an advocate in the English language environment. More of my childhood baggage was shed at this camp through participation with my dorm of campers in their activities and challenges, helping them connect with friends, and mentoring them. SEP was a mini-society designed to give campers an exciting and meaningful learning experience, but I was the one benefiting most from the outpouring of love targeted directly at the needs of teenagers.

Frank Brown also made an appearance. With no word back from David Hulme I did not mention anything about Sweden, nor did he. Despite the fabulous time I was having at SEP, seeing Frank Brown made me antsy to get back to Pasadena and find out how things were progressing with Lennart Swan. I had reason to be nervous.

Boys

On my first Monday back in Pasadena, bright-eyed and bushy tailed in David's office, he tilted his head in his classic make-you-nervous-way and asked, "Who are you?" I was taken aback for a second before confidently responding, "I'm that hot young punk from college." An impenetrable half-smile crossed his lips as he said, "I'm glad you said that. You've managed to make some waves but before I react, what is your side of the story?"

Caught even more off guard, I warily covered my meeting with Lennart Swahn, with less detail on the background, and more on the programming ideas we had discussed. David said, "Frank Brown asked 'Who is this Fransson punk, and why did Hulme send him over here?' and told me to 'blow you out of the water'." Into the awkward silence I nervously interjected, "Maybe he feels his toes were stepped on, but he's missed the point. This is clearly an open door!" David's response was, "We'll see, but for now consider yourself blown out of the water." I appreciated that David had listened to my account, and implicitly acknowledged that Frank Brown was out of line, but the Work walked by, not through, this open door. As a token follow-up, David's office sent some information on our standard programming, which was not what Lennart Swahn was expecting.

I tried once or twice to resurrect the idea, highlighting that we were guaranteed huge audience ratings on the more popular of Sweden's only two national channels. For a tiny fraction of the cost of U.S. airtime we could reach a totally new and important audience. With what we would save on media buying, we could afford to translate all materials into both Swedish and Danish, in addition to Norwegian. But political considerations and territorialism had taken precedence over what to me seemed like the pillar of fire lighting the way forward. While vastly discouraging, it only increased my resolve to dedicate myself to following the pillar of fire more completely, knowing that when the time was right, the Red Sea would open, Pharaoh's armies would be swallowed, and we would all triumphantly enter into the Promised Land. I was determined, more than ever, to play a role in that success.

But my health was not as strong as my enthusiasm and faith. Toward the end of the first semester of my senior year I had a relapse of the eye infection that had forced me to move back home as a teenager, and a debilitating loss of energy. Too many nights with too little sleep coupled with the weight of responsibility that I felt, had conspired to shut me down. In retrospect, being in a power position within the church structure was a contributing factor, however tiny my actual level of authority. This cause of deep-seated emotional stress was not, however, clear to me at the time.

As with my prior bout of iritis, light caused severe cramping of the iris and intense pain. But this time it was even worse. While confined to a dark room, the anti-cramping medication became ineffective and the antibiotic inflamed and irritated the lining of the eye in an allergic reaction due to prolonged use. The cramping of the iris caused increasing and prolonged pain—massive migraines originated in the eye and traveled backwards to engulf my entire head. After a couple of weeks of deterioration and missed classes, I was falling behind with school and becoming worried about my position with David Hulme. What would happen if I couldn't finish out the semester? This was serious, so I called for an anointing.

Greg Albrecht, AC's Dean of Students, was on anointing duty. He was feared, and could be cold and seemingly heartless. Many students have Albrecht horror stories; mine is relatively minor. In my freshman year he had marked a term paper down because I had used a library typewriter, which broke down halfway through the paper. I finished on a different typewriter in a different typeface and Albrecht wrote, "It's a shame, because the paper deserved a better grade." He then stubbornly refused to change my grade when I asked for the grade it deserved. But I didn't care who the anointer was, I wanted God to intervene in this eye infection gone berserk. If something didn't change soon, I would be dropping out of AC.

Albrecht applied the anointing oil, placed his hands on my head, and prayed. When he removed his hands, the pain simply vanished. It felt as though a loud oppressive drilling noise had suddenly stopped. I blurted this out and a seemingly startled Greg Albrecht dropped a wisecrack about not hitting the gym just yet, and left without further comment, almost in a rush. I didn't immediately hit the gym, but I did go off the medication. For a day or two there was temporary double vision, but my eye recovered completely.

The connection between my ongoing hip and lower back pain, frequent low grade fevers, and the iritis was still lost on me, but neither did I make a superstitious connection with Albrecht—he was just an instrument of God's favor. But it seemed that God supported the WCG "chain of authority" in requiring us to call the elders of the church for prayer and anointing [65] before honoring our faith. This reinforced a willingness to grant a degree of deference to those in command, despite knowing that they often did not fully practice what they preached. We're all just human, after all.

A Taste of Honey

As spring arrived many seniors were all but planning their weddings while I still struggled with the impact of my past on my present. One of the benefits of AC was that many faculty members were also ministers and available for counseling. One man who was feared, but whom I respected for his ability to cut to the core of an issue, was Dr. Albert, who had a Doctorate in Psychology. In a previous counseling session he had given me sound advice: "With your lack of role models of successful interpersonal behavior you should not rush into a relationship." My early experiences had not only left me lacking in basic, simple approaches to developing strong relationships, they had actually led me

---

65. James 5:14

to behave in the opposite fashion. I was constantly biting the hand that wanted to feed me, acting out of mistrust and suspicion, reading genuine expressions of interest as manipulation or as evidence of ulterior motives. Love and how to achieve it was a mystery I was ill-equipped to solve.

Dr. Albert's psychology class required us to establish a psychological hypothesis, then test it and write about it for our term paper. This assignment could help me learn more about behavioral modeling applied to relationships. Could something as transcendent as love be achieved through consistent behavior? My hypothesis said it could and I outlined a plan to test it. Citing the scriptural principle "A man *that hath* friends must shew himself friendly"[66] I outlined specific behaviors to follow in an effort to win over the girl of my dreams.

Since the Dig I'd had mild crush on her but she had been out of my league and in a couple of relationships. The timing now seemed right, but launching a concerted effort to make her like me was terrifying, since rejection would be overt if she resisted. On top of that, it seemed wrong to behave in a manner intended to motivate someone else to like me. The planned behaviors were not earth shaking, difficult, or devious. They were simple things like being attentive, considerate, offering sincere compliments and a weekly note on the Sabbath, a common campus tradition. Such a focus naturally reduced my more typical negative and selfish behaviors, such as interrupting people, dominating conversations, engaging in debate and not having the interest or patience to understand the life and perspectives of others. The results of these minimal changes were immediate and shocking. Within a matter of two or three weeks, the difference in how she treated me was undeniable. She responded to this attention much more quickly and more willingly than expected. The next logical step was a serious relationship.

This turned out to be more terrifying than rejection. Tossing aside my hypothesis, I realized love shouldn't be this easy, and it shouldn't develop as a result of a psychology experiment. I felt dirty, as though I was looking at one of my uncle's Swedish pornography books. It felt calculated and manipulative to be kind and considerate to someone hoping for the same in return. This was too new and too unexpected for me to process as natural and normal.

So I ran. I did not feel worthy of her affection, and knew I would only hurt her, which I'm sure my schizophrenic behavior managed to do, anyway.

---

66. Proverbs 18:24

This story highlights the ridiculously immature state of my emotional approach to love, even at age twenty-four. I was still a long way from being able to have close, healthy relationships, but I was learning. One thing I learned was that I wasn't ready for marriage, which helped me be more at peace with leaving AC without having found the one for me. My thoughts turned to graduation and what attracted me most, the Work of God.

As graduation approached many seniors hoped to be picked up by the Work. *The Plain Truth* Magazine had a monthly circulation of six million, which was growing rapidly and "The World Tomorrow" program would soon be the highest rated religious program on American television. There were lots of opportunities for those who wanted a career of one kind or another with the church. David Hulme's counsel was to work for an international office. He arranged an internship in mail operations in order for me to learn the mechanics of fulfilling the demand generated by the church's media machine.

It was not our responsibility to proselytize, much less convert people to Christ. Articles and sermons had forbidden us to go "door to door" because Christ told his disciples not to go "house to house" in a scripture used to proof text that concept[67]. But in rotating around the departments, a new approach to newsstand distribution caught my attention. A field minister had piloted a local program with members stocking and monitoring newsstand outlets carrying *The Plain Truth*. It was cost effective and allowed local church members to become more involved in the Work.

Imagine if the membership were truly mobilized to become a more active component of the core mission of the church! The church's responsibility was to preach the Gospel of the Kingdom of God to the world as a witness prior to Christ's return[68]. The media work (radio, television, and publications) was in fulfillment of this "Great Commission." At AC we were all pumped up and excited about getting involved in the operations and activities of the church, while in local areas people were discouraged from participating in the church's core mission. What if these resources were allowed, and even empowered, to help?

My excitement about this idea was dampened by doubts about my own future in the Work. The illness in my senior year and disappointment at not being

---

67. Luke 10:7
68. Matthew 24:14

offered a permanent position by David Hulme had provided some much needed humility, and I sought counsel with several college faculty and administration members, including Richard Ames and Greg Albrecht. Mr. Ames, in trying to help me avoid a foolish decision, bluntly said, "Don't move overseas thinking you will be picked up by the Work." Albrecht produced a negative report, filed by someone on the French language program about my "reckless driving and bad behavior" to explain why he wasn't recommending me for employment.

Despite some success and surprisingly significant contributions, I hadn't made the A-list. My tendency to make up my own mind despite clear direction from leadership might have made some in power uneasy. But this same tendency kept me from throwing in the towel. My foreign language abilities, my international experience, my connection to David Hulme, and a belief that God had called me to play a role in His Work in Europe, all gave me courage. It didn't matter if the flawed leaders of the church recognized it or not, God was guiding my efforts, and I was on a highly individualized path.

I decided I would move to Sweden to support the Work and the church and to find out what God had in store for me. The Swedish consulate would grant a work and residence permit and, once back in the country, reinstate Swedish citizenship, which I had renounced at age 16 to become a naturalized U.S. citizen. Uncle Ingemar had a small fiberglass manufacturing business and had provided a letter of invitation.

The British office offered summer work and a stipend from my buddy Frank Brown. Sarcasm aside, Frank Brown and I never spoke about the Lennart Swahn incident, so it's hard to say if he was one to forgive and forget, or if it was a political favor to David Hulme, or some combination of the two. In any case, the stipend was arranged through Francis Bergin, the British Work's colorful finance manager. Francis' unique blend of warmth and acerbic wit helped me lighten up just a bit. To cite just one example, he dared to spice up his sermons with phrases such as "A snowball's chance in the hot place" which is about as risqué as it got in the WCG.

Jay had graduated a year earlier and worked as a teacher at Imperial Schools (WCG's private K-12 school just off campus), while being groomed as a steward on the church's Gulfstream III (G3) jet, which took HWA on his global travels. That connection allowed me to ship a box of files and personal items on ahead to England. Too late, I realized my passport was in the box. A mad scramble to LA and a rush passport averted a more serious crisis. With my new passport in one hand, and a one-way ticket to Europe in the other, this twenty-four year old, five foot, six and a half inch tall college graduate left for the airport. I was still short, but no longer a runt, and despite Richard Ames warning me not to take this step, I walked down another gangplank of faith. Having done everything I could to prepare myself, I wasn't concerned—God would be with me.

Tell Me What You See

Faith is defined in two key verses in the faith chapter: Hebrews 11:1 "Now faith is the substance of things hoped for, the evidence of things not seen." And verse 6: "But without faith it is impossible to please him: for he that comes to God must believe that he is, and that he is a rewarder of them that diligently seek him." God had miraculously intervened once to save my life, then again to ease my pain. Stepping off the gangplank in the right direction and for the right reason would manifest the right results. My attitude was best expressed in the phrase "I'll see it when I believe it." What wasn't yet seen would materialize based on faith and whatever it was would be good, regardless of how it initially appeared on the surface. Simply put, God would reward me for diligently seeking Him.

This perspective became stronger and more expansive in walking the plank, leading to further direct guidance and intervention. But this was not blind faith. Experience revealed God as amazingly patient, loving, forgiving, and kind, but if we failed to act wisely, God would not bail us out. Put another way, I agreed with the cutesy quote, "Pray as if everything depends on God, work as if everything depends on you."

The summer in the British office brought valuable experience and an opportunity to deliver a short sermon, first in an outlying area, then in the St. Albans headquarters area. I somewhat ironically, if not arrogantly, contrasted classic WCG scriptures on Godly wisdom vs. what the Bible calls foolishness. A twist and a humorous ending may have saved what in hindsight was a pompous and possibly ostentatious topic for a young college graduate that was thankfully well received by gracious congregants. But my main job was organizing the SEP schedule of activities, under Paul Suckling's direction.

In my third trip to SEP Scotland I was again a counselor, but this time for the older boys' unit, mentoring boys aged sixteen to eighteen. Their activities included water skiing, wind surfing, scuba diving, and a grueling hike up three peaks, culminating in Ben Nevis, the tallest mountain in the British Isles at 4,409 feet. Julie was there again serving as counselor for the older girls, which made it easy to work together to elevate the SEP experience for these seasoned campers who welcomed the chance to push the boundaries in a positive way.

Frank Brown's younger daughter, Liz, was in Julie's dorm, and Rachel, his older daughter, was on the ski crew. I couldn't resist asking them about the "Fransson punk" quote, much to their amusement. They hadn't heard about it, but said it sounded like the kind of dust-up their dad often had and just the kind of thing he might say.

My plan to travel to Stockholm and contact BBDO (the large advertising firm that the church retained) for a better position than sweeping the floor in my uncle's factory never materialized. Julie told stories about beer and wine tours on the German immersion program and asked her contacts if they needed anybody to work in Germany until the Feast. When an offer was made to work in the office for room, board, and pocket money, it was another plank I felt good about, so I kept walking. A British classmate I'd always been fond of was also at SEP again and was accepted to SEP in South Africa in December/January, so I applied as well before traveling southeast, from Scotland to Germany.

In Germany, my rapid progress with the language and a whole-hearted support of God's Work was not lost on Frank Schnee or his office manager, John Karlson. After the Feast in Denmark, where I delivered a short sermon in Swedish, they offered me the role of assistant office manager, reporting to John. God was still a rewarder of those who diligently seek Him. I had been picked up by the Work.

7

Flying

And to the angel of the church in Philadelphia write;
These things saith he that is holy, he that is true,
he that hath the key of David, he that openeth, and no man shutteth;
and shutteth, and no man openeth; I know thy works: behold, I have set
before thee an open door, and no man can shut it: for thou hast a little
strength, and hast kept my word, and hast not denied my name.

—REVELATION 3:7-8—

South Africa pushed the number of countries I had visited to more than thirty, but this wasn't just another European country. Frank Zappa coined the term "Frozen White Wasteland" and visiting Africa was a perfect bookend to having lived in a tent in the state known as "The Last Frontier." The experience exceeded my imagination and expectations.

Octopus's Garden

In 1985 Apartheid was on its last legs. From the moment the plane touched down in Johannesburg, I got a sense of a people in transition under tremendous pressure. World opinion was hammering the country with boycotts and blockades. Paul Simon's *Graceland* was a year away, but the tension was all there, under the surface. The attitudes and the discussions about the issue of race relations was eye opening. The WCG believed in keeping the races distinct, a view derived from an interpretation of early scriptures in Genesis related to Noah being "perfect in his generations.[69]" The idea was that three races were preserved in the flood through the families of Noah's three sons. The WCG insisted that it was God's will that the races not intermarry, while not seeking to establish any other separation and absolutely considering all men to be equal.

Many, if not most, would call this perspective racist in itself, but in the WCG I did not personally experience any overt discussions about racial superiority or inferiority. Any such comparisons were based on culture and behavior, as distinct from race. So while the policy of maintaining racial "purity" was not a policy or interpretation I found appealing, at the time it was not an approach I was personally motivated to confront. Also, on the whole, opinions and attitudes of those in the WCG, even in South Africa, seemed less negative toward other races than the attitudes and opinions of non-WCG members there, in countries such as Germany, England, the U.S., and elsewhere.

What was most appalling was the cultural and economic disparity. Systemic poverty in proximity to wealth made for a shocking contrast. Relatively wealthy educated whites constituted about twenty percent of the population, and their reasons for living in South Africa were largely not humanitarian in nature. They did not wish to sacrifice their standard of living in what they considered a futile attempt to raise the standard of living of the poor, uneducated natives who formed eighty percent of the population. Many believed, rightly or wrongly, that the natives were not culturally open to being educated in the way required for them to enjoy an equivalent standard of living, and could cite specific examples to support the opinion. The problem was enormous in its proportions.

The SEP took place in Wagendrift Nature Reserve with whites and blacks segregated by area and activities. The WCG broke apartheid law by holding

---

69. Genesis 6:9

mixed religious activities, a gesture that risked serious legal trouble to follow a higher path, supporting my positive view of the overall sincerity of the WCG. At SEP the raw energy of Africa, the feel of the heat and the difference in the skies, highlighted by the Southern Cross, were overpowering. I awoke earlier, feeling rested and alive, with a persistent feeling that dinosaurs might appear, towering over the short trees dotting the savannah and forming a striking image against the vibrant morning skies. Highlights of the camp included a multi-day survival hike in the Drakensberg Mountains, sleeping both outdoors and in a cave, and eating plants found along the way.

After camp there was an amazing visit to Hluhluwe Umfolozi game reserve park in KwaZulu Natal and to a beautiful remote sugar plantation owned by one of the church members. Proximity to such a foreign version of nature was spiritually inspiring and my sense of being close to God and aligned with His will was further heightened by the experience. I returned to Germany fully energized and expectant of furthering the Work of God.

The Bonn office helped me obtain a work and residence permit in Germany to be trained to open an office in Scandinavia. I supported a number of the small, internal departments within the German office, learning the ropes about regional marketing and mail operations, the data center, editorial and translation services, and a variety of other functions.

Frank Schnee, the Regional Director of the WCG for the German region, was born in Hagen, Westphalia April 12, 1928, the youngest of three boys. His dad, Emil Peter Schnee, immigrated with his family to Canada shortly before Hitler came to power to keep his sons out of Hitler's war machine. Emil had taught John Karlson German at AC. Mr. Schnee had recently launched an aggressive faith-filled program to dramatically increase the subscribers and co-workers in Germany, Austria, and Switzerland. He was also very focused on expanding into Eastern Europe, and was using the Feast of Tabernacles as a way to operate behind the Iron Curtain.

There were a number of members in East Germany and to help them celebrate the Feast, a site had been opened up in Czechoslovakia, a country for which they could obtain visas. The Czech government turned a blind eye to the fact that this was a religious festival and therefore against the law. As long as the church was discreet, the East Germans could unofficially attend. Arrangements were negotiated with the government controlled tourist agency, Čedok, which was interested in the tourist dollars of a large group staying for eight days or more. Cultural tours and events made the Feast site a popular destination for large numbers Westerners.

Mr. Schnee's success in enabling the Work to gain a foothold behind the Iron Curtain was of prophetic significance to the WCG, because the gospel of the Kingdom of God needed to be preached to the whole world before Christ could return.[70] Expanding on this success, in 1984 Mr. Schnee initiated negotiations with Polorbis, the Polish government tourist agency, to open up a second Iron Curtain Feast site, in Poland. I was asked to be the Feast Coordinator of the first Feast there, an exciting, flattering, and overwhelming opportunity. My boss, John Karlson, supported me as I muddled my way through the job despite mysterious and frustrating bouts of illness.

My dad and Elinor were in attendance, and given my prominent role in what was most important to Dad, i.e. the church, he treated me with what approached respect and consideration instead of his typical criticism and dissatisfaction. This was another positive step in reconciling the people of my broken past with my present experience. Despite what I would call, at best, a mediocre performance in Poland, Mr. Schnee invited me to join him on a trip to Budapest to discuss the possibility of a Feast in Hungary. His son, Paul, back from two years at AC in Big Sandy, was along for the ride as well.

Mr. Schnee had such enormous drive and vision that a joke made the rounds that "he would drive his Mercedes off the Rhine River bridge, and emerge from the water proclaiming the accident to be 'the best thing that ever happened to God's Work in the German region.'" This quote likely originated more than a decade earlier with a colorful but now disfellowshiped WCG evangelist, Charles Hunting. It was easy for detractors to take pot-shots at Frank Schnee because of his larger than life persona, but I respected him immensely.

Despite bouts of illness and self-doubt, in Germany I began to come into my own. To further support the push into the East, several of us took Russian classes in the office, and to support the youth programs I attended the Austrian Winter Educational Program (WEP), serving as an organizer and ski instructor. I became good friends with Mr. Schnee's older son, Mark, who was my age. Like his brother Paul he had also attended two years of AC. His first year had been in Big Sandy in '76, at which time it was closed, and he then transferred to

---

70. Matthew 24:14

Pasadena in 1977, to find it closing after his second year, making his experience a mirror image of mine. For me, life in Germany was like a happier, more positive parallel universe to the one I came from.

There's a Place

The German region of God's Work felt like the home I had never had, a perfect mix of comfortable cultural elements from Sweden and the U.S., bringing my fractured personality together inside the protective bubble of the WCG and the Work. Frank Schnee was like my dad in many ways. He had the background of an immigrant with humble beginnings in Canada. He was single-minded and unwavering in his support of the WCG system, zealous, hard-working, full of faith, and demanding.

Why, if they were so similar, was it easier for me to respect and get along with Frank Schnee? This was partially because of his many talents and the way that he openly displayed his passion for and dedicated his life to the very thing that was most important to me, the Work of God. But even if Dad's talents didn't lie in a direction useful to furthering the goals of the church in a big way, he made himself useful and valuable to the church locally. The bigger reason was that Mr. Schnee opened up his home, his family and even himself in a number of ways my own father had not. I'll explain in a minute, but a description of him written by Mark sets the stage.

Dad was a very enthusiastic person who cared for people and was compassionate. He greeted people energetically and with a firm handshake. His family was always greeted with a hug or a kiss. Above all, he loved God and studying His word and was constantly thinking about the Work. He spent time on his knees in prayer, in his bedroom, leading a congregation, or with people needing God's healing or intervention. There was streak of a reckless adventurer in his blood that had him crossing the East German border with hidden bibles and literature in the car trunk, when he wasn't playing volleyball with office staff, a drum solo at fun shows, shot-gunning down a ski slope in Zermatt, Switzerland, or drinking Slivovitz shot glasses with Čedok personnel in Brno, Czechoslovakia. He could meet the German president Richard von Weizsaecker in a gleaming black tux or tear up the dance floor with his wife Esther to the music of a live band playing Glenn Miller tunes.

For him the key to congregation growth in Germany was an increase in "Klar und Wahr" magazine circulation and was interested in anyone who would supply fresh and economic ways to do that.

Given Mark's last statement, that Mr. Schnee was interested in anyone who would further his main goals, it's easy to see another similarity he had to my own father, one I colored negatively earlier. It's a fair question, then, to ask why it was easier for me to treat him with respect vs. my own father. The first answer is simply that there was less emotional and historical baggage. The second is certainly that Mr. Schnee was more successful and accomplished than my dad. But the third is perhaps the most important one. Despite a similar cultural background and personality, it came easier to Mr. Schnee to show love, concern, and magnanimity to others. One of the expressions of this that was most striking to me was that Mr. Schnee trusted and encouraged others whereas Dad's tendency was to express doubt about others ahead of the eventual expression of disappointment in their failure to meet his unrealistic standards.

This illustrates at a personal level a systemic issue. Many in the WCG had a negative experience by failing to meet expectations. The many laws, rules, and standards that the WCG imposed upon its membership formed a high bar, one which many were just not well-equipped to jump over. Those who were able to attain these standards often tended toward a degree of smug self-righteousness, which contributed to the number of dead and wounded bodies the church left in its wake. Mr. Schnee was demanding, but it was clear that he believed you would succeed, not fail.

Mark had married Elaine Patapoff, a lively co-ed I had gotten to know in freshman French. She was of Russian descent, and was also in the Russian class. Elaine and Mark were central to the hub of the regional office social network, given their multi-talented combination of lively energy, a fun, youthful outlook, and their proximity to Frank and Esther Schnee, the heart and soul of the German region. They took me under their wing, showed me the ropes, helped me with my German, and treated me like family. Others in this circle were recent AC graduates Sherri Means and Norbert Schneider, who soon married each other, and Mike Benjegerdes and young people like Meinrad Eckert, recruited by Mr. Schnee to work in the office. We worked together to further the goals and mission of a worldwide enterprise in this regional outpost. I was not only happy, I had arrived, I belonged, and I fit in.

The icing on the cake was when Mark formed a band and helped me learn to play bass. Paul was the drummer in the band, and although there was some residual resentment, tension, and even a bit of animosity from the mutual dislike we had shared in Big Sandy, aside from one or two flare-ups we actually began to get along—once the worst of our mutual pissing contest had played out. We got good enough to play at church dances and activities. Performing as a musician and singer had long seemed an unattainable fantasy, but at this time in Germany any and everything seemed possible.

My respect for John Karlson, my boss, was second only to that which I had for Mr. Schnee. John was his antithesis in many ways, diminutive and retiring, avoiding the spotlight, and quite content to play second fiddle. He was the ideal second-in-command during Mr. Schnee's tenure. Elaine was Mr. Karlson's administrative assistant, and she joked that she had to delegate her work to Sherri, so that she could do Mr. Karlson's work, since he was busy doing Mr. Schnee's work. A student in Germany for the AC summer program quipped that if Sherri was doing Elaine's work, and Elaine did Mr. Karlson's work, while Mr. Karlson did Mr. Schnee's work, it must be because Mr. Schnee was so busy doing God's Work.[71] But if that is the case, she wondered, what was God doing? We all laughed, but the joke stuck with me, and added a humorous element to some painful conclusions that lay ahead.

But for now, I was accepted by the Schnee family and others in the office and church and had exciting responsibilities on the front line of God's Work. My experience with David Hulme in media and print advertising qualified me in the eyes of John Karlson and Frank Schnee to assist with regional advertising efforts. Tom Lapacka, the pastor over German-speaking Switzerland and southwest Germany had been handling this and I began to work with and develop a relationship with him. Tom had executive presence, making him a natural in this space, and he seemed initially reluctant to work with a young upstart. But after meeting him and his wife, Linda, in his home, we hit it off and enjoyed working on a few projects together before he was transferred back to the U.S. Linda was likely the driver of that decision, as she stated Americans viewing Switzerland as a slice of paradise were seeing it through tourist eyes. Linda was a bit more assertive than many WCG minister's wives.

---

71. Lisa Derstine

But what distinguished me in the eyes of Mr. Schnee was an unsolicited effort to launch newsstand distribution. Newsstands in Europe were more important than in the U.S., as people picked up magazines on the go, at bus, train and subway stations. Mr. Schnee was skeptical, due to a failed 70s program, but I took excess magazines from the print run, inserted hand-coded response cards leftover from an ad campaign, and convinced a Bonn newsstand owner to prominently feature our magazine at no cost. I cobbled together a couple of other display racks and duplicated my success. Now I had Mr. Schnee's attention and his blessing.

Working with the regional pastors, I expanded this fledgling German language newsstand program into Munich and Hannover. Then I requested an extra 10,000 magazines in the next print run, loaded them in a van, and smuggled them through East Germany into West Berlin. While there I secured distribution of 30,000 copies a month at key subways and the main train station. Within two months I expanded this to 70,000 copies, doubling German *Plain Truth* (*Klar & Wahr*) circulation. Like the new U.S. program, I had members monitor the program and the tiny West Berlin church was particularly excited about their chance to influence the growth of the Work and their own congregation. And who could resist a trip into East Berlin?

Crossing through Checkpoint Charlie was nerve-wracking. Concrete corridors, barbed wire, and automatic machine guns framed a starkly lit open expanse of no-man's land. Once across I met two East German girls at a museum who showed me around the city, introducing me to a Cuban restaurant for dinner and drinks. Here, behind the Iron Curtain, lay a parallel universe. The restaurant was reminiscent of a Mexican place I had frequented in Alaska, and my two new friends talked excitedly about their plans to vacation on Lake Balaton, in Hungary, in ways similar to what Steve and I had done in the Caribbean a few years earlier. It was also the first time I was accused of working for the CIA by a newsstand owner in West Berlin, but it would not be the last time.

Mean Mr. Mustard

What I was accomplishing was of importance to the church, making me a regional rising star. It was a personally exciting and profoundly fulfilling time. But while I was changing the world for the better, events in Pasadena were changing the lay of the land in the church, politically, doctrinally, and culturally. Herbert W. Armstrong, the founder and leader of the Worldwide Church of God, was expected to help usher in the return of Christ. Instead, he died shortly before 6:00 a.m. on January 16, 1986, at the age of 93. The implications to us were enormous, but at the time I was unfazed. It was God's church, after all, not HWA's, and if anything the prospects for growth that such a dramatic change implied were exciting.

One reason was that I had begun to see the focus on authority and power in the ministry as a kind of "cancer." It's not that things were worse in Germany than in the U.S., it's that I was getting a first-hand look at it for the first time. Success in Germany led to my being groomed for the ministry by accompanying associate pastor Alfred Hellemann, a native German who had been in the ministry for some time, on trips to perform ministerial counseling, anointing, and baptisms. Alfred shared with me that at times he had to inform those who had committed sins, or who showed moral weaknesses, or had behavioral problems, etc., that they did not possess the Holy Spirit. They would have to "bring forth fruit of repentance" and be re-baptized in order to be considered a member of the WCG. I was personally involved in one situation where a man tended toward physical abuse of his wife, and when the man was re-baptized, the situation improved. It seemed reasonable, until this same approach was applied to me.

Mr. Karlson was the pastor in Bonn, and to allow him to focus on the explosive growth of the Work, Grant Spong, originally from Australia but serving in the U.S. as an associate pastor, was brought to Germany for his first pastoral assignment. Grant was asked to continue my ministerial training, and perhaps because he was fairly close to me in age, he invited open conversations about the opportunities and challenges facing the WCG and the Work in the German region. Things changed, however, as my responsibilities within the region continued to expand.

Grant seemed to have a love/hate relationship with the government of God doctrine, perhaps viewing HWA's official title of Pastor General, and the entire church hierarchy, in military terms. This manifested itself in his inability to deal with the gray area of office employees who were members of his congregation. For example, he seemed increasingly irritated with my close relationship with his superiors. My access to the church and its resources outside of his personal management was unacceptable and he increasingly voiced sharp criticism of Mr. Karlson and Mr. Schnee, and the way that they were managing office operations, the church areas, and the Work in the German region.

At one point he was criticizing Dirk Händeler, who had maintenance responsibilities in the office and also for the ministerial fleet program. In Grant's case, because he was a minister in Bonn, Dirk was expected to wash his car. Grant was venting about how long it had taken Dirk to get it done, and so on. I defended Dirk, causing Grant to expand his critique to include other personal qualities. In my defense of Dirk I dared to suggest that Grant was the one out of line.

The next day Grant called and said he'd like to talk, leading me to speculate that perhaps he regretted the incident. He invited me to walk with him down the grassy center of the Poppelsdorfer Allee in front of the Bonn office, where he told me that my argumentative spirit was clear evidence that I did not have the Holy Spirit. Given that Grant was my pastor, and therefore a duly appointed representative of the government of God, I took his assessment seriously. Acceptance of Grant's opinion and a re-baptism was my only escape from the lake of fire.

But as I walked alongside him, it only took a moment to review the scriptural requirements for receiving the Holy Spirit. "Repent, and be baptized, and you will receive the gift of the Holy Spirit." I asked myself if my repentance and my desire for baptism had been sincere. I was able to instantly answer with a clear "Yes!" Within probably no more than 90 seconds of silence, I had processed this and turned to Grant and said, "You're wrong. I do have the Holy Spirit."

Grant looked confused, but said nothing further, then or later, but trust in Grant was irreparably damaged and I became aware of the spiritual impact of heavy-handed rulers in the church. My tendency to defend the underdog grew more pronounced and my resolve to stand up for what I believed in was strengthened. Standing up to the threat of being declared a non-member was about as bold as it got in the WCG, and so I will always be grateful to Grant for helping me over that hurdle.

The WCG had provided me with an understanding about the revealed Word of God, as a moral anchor, and its mission filled me with discipline and drive, motivation, and momentum. But this first-hand look at the WCG tendency to shoot its wounded raised doubts about its claim to being the administration of the government of God on earth, even as I became part of the machinery that had such features built into its DNA. An internal struggle was going on, including ongoing efforts to take ownership of my own life and situation, to no longer be a victim, while trying to prove myself worthy enough to become part of a system that treated others as though they were not fully autonomous. These mutually contradictory beliefs placed me in what is known as a double-bind—a "damned if you do, damned if you don't" situation, describing my conflicting, unresolved senses of responsibility.

Whether it was responsibility to myself, my family, or the church, there was always a feeling that whatever I did, it wouldn't be enough. Christ's statement that He would bring a sword, and that a man's enemies would be those of his own household, didn't help matters. True peace was elusive under such governance. There was little or no peace, love, and understanding. We were constantly monitoring our own and others' performances against incredibly high standards, and those in positions of spiritual authority tended to create the illusion that they were achieving these standards by forcing those under their authority to serve their needs, instead of the other way around. A conscious realization of this was just below the surface as I tried to emulate those in authority who I admired. This internal conflict was compounding a DNA-based autoimmune condition that was ticking like a time bomb.

The Ballad of John and Yoko

One expression of this internal conflict was the longing to have a truly close romantic relationship, which my emotional immaturity had so far kept me from being able to achieve. I had reconnected with one of my classmates in Poland, and had sought her out on a trip to the U.S. to study the U.S. newsstand program and to discuss media matters with David Hulme. In 1986 we arranged to attend the Feast together, along with my old Alaskan friend, Steve, at the Iron Curtain Feast site in Czechoslovakia. This became an emotional pressure cooker as I struggled to rebuild my relationship with Steve while trying to develop a closer relationship with my girlfriend.

They were on a European vacation and focused on fun, looking to me as an informed personal tour guide, while I was excited about my responsibilities as a coordinator, speaker, and translator. Interpreting seventy minute sermons from German to English was an amazing experience. It was thrilling to settle into a groove and channel the tone, cadence, intent, and message of some of the most animated, fast-talking, and colorful speakers before an audience of hundreds of people. But it took time to prepare and it was draining to perform under pressure. When my girlfriend had her passport stolen, it immediately became my responsibility to fix her problem in an unfamiliar city where I didn't speak the language and was already under an intense workload. But it was the emotional stress that was getting to me, caused by the tension between serving attendees, who respected my role, and Steve and my girlfriend, who seemed resentful of my responsibilities and oblivious to the impact all of this was having on me.

After the Feast, I had to get Steve to Munich, pick up my parents in Denmark, and then drive them and my girlfriend to Frankfurt for their respective flights to the U.S. This was a grueling drive through four countries, and my car broke down on the road a couple of hours outside Munich. Somehow I got the car towed, rented another one, got Steve to the airport, hooked up with my parents, and got everyone to their respective flights on time. Along the way I missed a lot of sleep, but the worst part was the physical, financial, and emotional stress of responsibility for all of these people and the competing relationships between all of us, while my girlfriend evaluated how I handled being in the middle of all this.

The stress and exhaustion from this trip and the looming decision to continue with my relationship or call it off was enough to cause another crippling bout of iritis. Within a week my eye stopped responding to the medication and the morning after a frighteningly painful weekend I waited impatiently for my eye doctor to arrive at his office at 8:00 a.m. He measured the pressure in my eye, found it high enough to permanently damage the optic nerve, and sent me directly to the hospital.

Over the course of the next twelve days, the chief doctor and seemingly every other doctor and intern took turns examining my eye for educational purposes. Cortisone shots were prescribed, which were injected into the tender inside of my bottom eyelid. These shots prevented permanent blindness, but caused the skin to deteriorate and shrivel up. The other piece of "good news" was that my condition was finally correctly diagnosed, explaining the recurring, seemingly unrelated health conditions that had afflicted me for over ten years. The bad news was that I had an autoimmune disease—a chronic, crippling condition called *Morbus Bechterew* in German, or Ankylosing Spondylitis in English.

A counselor showed me pictures of what the disease would likely do to me, explained that my case was aggressive, and would put me in a wheelchair by age forty. He rounded off the session by stating, "But you Americans have a positive view of life; I'm sure you'll come to grips with your situation." I'm still not sure if this was sincere or sarcastic. One of the reasons I fit in well in Germany was that many Germans are even more awkward in interactions with others than I was.

But times of stress often bring about real change. The shock of the diagnosis paralleled the loosening of dogmatic WCG theology in the wake of HWA's passing. One of the early changes was an effort by HWA's successor, Joseph Tkach, to help members set appropriate priorities in their lives. He himself had experienced the dark side of the WCG and was determined to change some of those things that were obviously wrong and negative. One of the negative aspects was the psychological power and control that the ministry had over the membership, a situation which had impacted Joe Tkach's own family in a very negative way.

As I understand the story, Mr. Tkach was a minister in southern California during the turbulent '70s, in which a variety of power politics games were being played by HWA, GTA, and other dominant figures in what had rapidly become a global religious powerhouse. One day, while Mr. Tkach was on the road performing ministerial visits, a couple of high ranking ministers met with his wife to convince her to side with their faction against the official church leadership. The conflicts between loyalty to God, loyalty to the established church hierarchy, loyalty to her heart, to these men, and to her husband, put an emotional strain on Mrs. Tkach that she was unable to bear. A mental breakdown resulted, from which she never recovered. I had seen her wandering aimlessly around the campus and headquarters area, in a dress that looked like a nightgown, with no care or concern for her appearance. Her situation was a sad testimony to the way in which the church was anything but a blessing to people not strong enough to weather the forces at play in such a dogmatic but compelling mix of beliefs.

Perhaps this is why Mr. Tkach immediately engaged in a world tour to personally shake every member's hand and promote the theme of family. Using a "We Are Family" slogan he traveled to the corners of the earth, not in pursuit of photo opportunities with world leaders, as HWA had been accused of doing, or even to pursue the great commission of preaching the gospel, but rather to meet and greet every single member of "God's Family," the Worldwide Church of God. HWA had been accused of vanity and wasteful spending for having met with world leaders and dignitaries. I believed he was sincere and I fully supported his focus on carrying out a worldwide Work, aligned with the church's mission to preach the gospel to the world as a witness. But I cannot imagine an approach more in alignment with where I was at, personally, emotionally, and spiritually than that which Mr. Tkach was undertaking. So for me it was very easy to see God's hand in HWA's choice of successor.

Within You, Without You

My respect for our new Pastor General increased when he issued his list of priorities. God was naturally our first priority but, instead of the church and the Work, which for HWA were synonymous and always a close second, Mr. Tkach listed health as number two. Though I had more serious health issues than the average member, and though health, healing, and the question of seeing doctors had been a major issue for many, my view of the matter was simplistic. I followed the Biblical food laws—no pork or shellfish—and HWA's guidance to "eat foods that spoil, and eat them before they do." Even before natural, healthy, and organic became popular, WCG members focused on these choices for their diets, choosing natural whole grains instead of white flour, honey instead of sugar, and avoiding doctors and medication as much as possible. Beyond that, having done my part, I washed my hands of my health and put the matter in God's hand, essentially holding Him responsible for my overall health condition.

Perhaps Mr. Tkach chose to address this so shortly after HWA's death in response to segments of the church who were shocked that HWA had openly availed himself of medical assistance. This contrasted hypocritically with his emphasis that reliance on doctors was evidence of a lack of faith. The explanations provided with Tkach's new prioritization emphasized that faith did not exclude taking prudent and wise actions, including seeking medical attention, while looking to God for both guidance and the actual healing. This was in alignment with my thinking, but prioritizing health as our number two priority was not. Now I could no longer delude myself that dedication to the Work somehow made my health God's responsibility.

Priority number three was work/career, then family, with the church way down at number five, which was very different from HWA's approach. He constantly rallied his troops to the WCG's financial, emotional, and spiritual support by announcing an endless series of crises and "gun laps" in the race to prepare for the return of Jesus Christ. We were to "hold up his hands" while the Work of God took priority over everything else, vying for dominance even with our own relationship with God.

It might seem strange that adults looked to church leadership to set their priorities, but we prided ourselves in following Christ's command to become like little children[72]. Joe Tkach's priorities were helping me come to terms with a cross section of issues hidden by my addiction to a kind of faith-filled spiritual workaholism. Now I could finally begin to reconcile my current thinking and behavior with my health, my broken past, my broken relationships, and my desire to get married. It was now clear to me that whatever the reason for being sick, the only way to health was to take full responsibility for my own healing. God would help, guide, support, and encourage, but He wanted me to wrestle with and figure out the mechanisms governing health on every level—mentally, emotionally, spiritually and physically—instead of supernaturally bailing me out.

Once out of the hospital I recovered relatively quickly from the acute flare-up and though the chronic condition was not improved, I was well enough to move forward with life. To see if our relationship could become permanent, I arranged for my girlfriend to be invited by the German office to do some work for the German region, allowing us to explore our relationship further. The unstated reason for this was that I had seen how WCG ministerial wives were essentially unhappy at being a tagalong to a husband whose mistress was the church and the Work. This dissatisfaction was worse for expatriates, especially

---

72. Matthew 19:14, Mark 10:14, Luke 18:16

in foreign language environments. Frankly, I was testing her to see if she could make it in Germany. This attitude was not a basis for a strong relationship, but it was in line with how I believed God worked with us. While slowly becoming more emotionally mature, I still had no understanding or experience with the day-to-day mechanics of how love-based relationships actually work. We hit a tear-filled low-point during a weekend ski-outing with a singles group in Switzerland; I'm fuzzy on the specifics but extremely clear on the emotional content of what happened. We were struggling through a fundamental disagreement that affected every interaction.

My relationship with God and my career were tied up with my activities in Europe and I wanted her to prove she could be happy and fulfilled in a foreign language culture, without me trying to make it seem romantic. I wanted no part in trying to keep a disappointed woman happy once the excitement of being a tourist wore off. She, on the other hand, focused on the relationship, not the external situation, and she wanted me to prove that her happiness was important to me. This, in turn, caused me to doubt that she was the right one to stand by my side in my service to God. So we butted heads over every conceivable issue, including a ridiculous dispute during the skiing trip in Switzerland. Instead of enjoying a breathtakingly gorgeous day, we fought over how to get onto a ski lift together. When the chair came up behind us, I refused to help her get on and she managed to be left behind, almost injuring herself in the process, while trying to make it seem like my fault. We were supposed to be bonding and we were behaving worse than squabbling children.

It was clear that the relationship would not work, but in a last minute tear-filled moment of mutual contrition, we patched up our differences long enough to convince ourselves that we were, after all, right for each other. We then began planning our wedding, to be held in June on the campus of Ambassador College.

Day Tripper

One other experience from around this time that bears mentioning was Gerald Waterhouse's tour through the German region. I had been a fan of his for years, captivated and fascinated by his messages which held audiences spellbound for three and even four hours as he visited each church on his sequential world tours. He was the closest thing we had to a rock star in the ministry, and when he came through Germany in 1986, if I have my year right, I was given the task of being his chauffeur and setting up the translation equipment as he traveled through southern Germany and Austria.

While on the trip I witnessed, firsthand, that the man was one hundred percent dedicated to the church, and that he had no life whatsoever outside of his role in the church. He was like George Clooney in the movie *Up in the Air* (without the affair) but instead of firing people, he was inspiring people. I not only spent hours with him in the car, but joined him on his early morning jog and ate dinner with him for several consecutive days.

We had lengthy conversations and some of my jokes and references appeared in the sermons he was delivering at the various churches in the German region. Insiders know that a favorite topic of his was HWA's book *The Wonderful World Tomorrow: what it will be like*, which pulled together scriptural references to the millennium, the coming Kingdom of God, Christ's rule on earth, and key names in the Bible associated with this future vision. HWA speculated on the structure of the government Christ would implement on His return, and the roles of individuals in it, from Abraham to the Apostles, including Job, David, Daniel, Elijah, and everyone else in between. Mr. Waterhouse took this a step further, including HWA and now, in light of his recent death, introduced a section on Mr. Tkach as Joshua, to HWA's Moses-like role. Mr. Tkach would lead us into the Promised Land, the Kingdom of God, as Joshua led Israel after Moses was only allowed to view it from afar.

On the stretch between Salzburg and Nuremberg I mustered up the courage to ask him a question I had wanted to ask since joining his never-ending world tour, "As you review, study and discuss the role all these other individuals in the government of God, do you ever wonder what role you might be asked to fill?" His response was quick and simple. "I imagine there might be a need for someone to travel around the universe and point people toward headquarters."

Gerald Waterhouse was absolutely sincere and one hundred percent dedicated.

This tour was also when I learned that the paper from my English class at AC, "This Ain't Rock 'n Roll," had come to the attention of Joe Tkach when he headed up ministerial services. Gerald Waterhouse had been inspired by related discussions to deliver a famous line about rock music: "That filth should be scraped of the face of the earth and chucked into Satan's cesspool." By this time, though, my thesis had changed. It wasn't the music itself, per se, that had been such a powerfully negative influence, but rather it was my broken spirit and confused state of mind. Fractured relationships and deep inner pain had caused me to respond powerfully to certain kinds of music. The music I listened to validated and encouraged my desire to act out, but the acting out would have occurred regardless of whether the music was there or not. Having realized this, I was about to move away from the position of my paper and back into the warm embrace of my old friend, music.

Perhaps because I was moving forward with marriage plans, the church now felt I was "ministerial material." Although my fiancée was still working in Bonn, I was sent to work with Henry Sturcke who had been brought over from the U.S. to replace Tom Lapacka in German-speaking Switzerland and southwest Germany. I lived with Henry's family in Zurich, Switzerland while training to become a minister, preparing for the wedding, and looking for an apartment on the German side of the beautiful Rhine River border area.

Henry was a "kinder, gentler" version of a WCG pastor, and was more secure in himself and his position than Grant. He was well-educated, well-rounded, and experienced. Though he was from New Jersey, his wife was from northern Germany, and they were very happy with their new assignment. Along with his two young boys, he had brought over two of three teenage girls they had recently adopted. The oldest girl had just entered her freshman year at AC. These girls were from a troubled church family and similarities to my situation were not lost on me. Henry and his family had taken on the monumental task of integrating troubled teenage girls into their family, which spoke volumes about the kind of people they were and why we were destined to get along as well as we did.

Beautiful Boy

My room also housed Henry's large music collection, which included many records I had thrown out in my freshman year of AC. Henry did not have my negative associations with this music and the family played an enormous variety of music at various times of the day and week. It was here that I was introduced to Leonard Cohen, whose lyrics grace the opening of chapter one, and I was also able to dive deeply into the music and words of Bob Dylan, something I'd wanted to do since I first heard "Tangled up in Blue" in 1974. And there was a song I hadn't heard in years, John Lennon's "Beautiful Boy," written for his younger son Sean shortly before John's murder in December, 1980.

At the time of his death, my perspective had been colored by my recent rejection of rock music, HWA's article on Lennon and the Beatles, and my research paper. Now I reconnected with the emotion and lyrics Lennon had created, and reflected on the connection to McCartney's "Hey Jude," written for John's older son Julian. Realizing how this related to what Lennon had written for Sean was heart rending. Paul had comforted John's older son Julian while Lennon himself had been at first absent, then had all but abandoned Julian when he fell for Yoko Ono and divorced Julian's mother.

In "Beautiful Boy" John was telling his five year-old son Sean that it would be different this time. He sang, "When you cross the street, take my hand, life is what happens to you when you're busy making other plans." Fate's cruel trick would be that John would abandon this son as well, with only a song to comfort him. A bullet took John away from Sean just three weeks after the release of the album that announced his plan to walk alongside Sean, making sure nothing would happen.

Once again the music of the Beatles had managed to speak to me personally and powerfully, touching my soul with the realization that music provides a universal experience. There was a mysterious quality that transcended time, space, and specific separations between people. The mass appeal of the Beatles seemed to typify this phenomenon. The Beatles had, in fact, done much to open up the world to new ways of thinking and acting that were ultimately positive. Who else could have gotten four hundred million viewers to tune into a live performance of a song titled "All You Need is Love"? I was again accepting music as a language of the heart and embracing its powerful ability to communicate with and move people as a positive force that should be encouraged, not turned into fear.

During the few months spent living with Henry's family I experienced the warmth of loving relationships and observed the best example of healthy interactions between parents and children that I had ever seen. Model behavior and a balanced approach to music, diet, and a number of other areas of life helped me begin to soften my own approach, despite the bitter experiences of my youth and the general approach within the WCG with its focus on law and obedience.

In my transition from student to teacher to ministerial representative, I considered our approach to "The Truth." We talked about finding The Truth, knowing The Truth and especially having The Truth. We had an exclusive claim on divinely revealed insight into the Bible and many other things. Having to represent and defend this led to doubts and concerns about it. I realized that no one could "have" or "own" The Truth. This started as a subtle difference in perspective, but gradually widened to a broader understanding around the arrogance of such a viewpoint.

In other words, we prided ourselves on having minds opened by God to understand the truth. But as soon as we learned "The Truth" and became a WCG member, we tended to close our mind more completely than before it had been opened. Most disturbing was that many ministers and leaders encouraged this tendency. To counteract this and encourage open-mindedness, I coined the phrase "He who knows everything can never learn anything" and sought to discover new insights and continue down the path of education and enlightenment that we supposedly all were on. This subtle shift marked the transition point in being rebranded from HWA loyalist to a liberal.

HWA had built a worldwide organization out of nothing but faith, and had defended it from internal and external attack. The membership granted him enormous respect and leeway as God's Apostle. It was easy to believe, as he so often emphasized, that it wasn't him but God working through him that accomplished these things. Basic WCG doctrine held that God would lead His church, but many biblical and contemporary examples indicated false leaders would lead people away from God. Many viewed Mr. Tkach with more than a healthy degree of skepticism.

In Joseph W. Tkach, HWA had appointed a recently tested loyalist to continue his legacy. Tkach had rallied the troops in Pasadena to barricade HQ offices and hold prayer and hymn meetings, keeping the receiver out. In light of his appointment by HWA, most believed he would continue the path and pace set by HWA for over 60 years, but doubters and skeptics abounded, since Tkach was not one of HWA's longtime insiders and was not considered particularly talented or intelligent.

Mr. Tkach's own relationship to the WCG was not entirely uncomplicated. As a Russian immigrant, he had initially adapted well to the hardline approach that had become institutionalized by the men who had spent time close to HWA and who were vested in establishing and maintaining hierarchy. But after the event that caused his wife's illness and as the scope and breadth of his authority in the church had rapidly grown, landing him at the pinnacle of power, he began to move away from a cut-and-dried military style of leadership.

He appointed his son, Joe Jr. to head Ministerial Services and relied heavily on his son's friend, Mike Feazell, for doctrinal guidance. Mike had been taken in to the Tkach home as a troubled teen and many felt he and Joe Jr. had a chip on their shoulder against the WCG. Changes began to be announced that were troubling to long-time members. People whispered about the source of these changes, daring to question Mr. Tkach's ability to manage and lead. They were concerned he was being swayed, even led around by the nose, by more talented and brighter individuals with agendas.

Initially it was easy for me to reject such concerns since I agreed with the changes. God was using him to encourage us to more fully follow the cloud and pillar in the direction God wanted us to go. But many were arriving at the exact opposite conclusion.

Hello Goodbye

By now I was gaining access to the inner workings of the WCG. Jay had become the main steward on the corporate jet, the G3, granting me inside information on the conduct of the Tkach road show and entourage. HWA had spent money representing the church to the world but now the focus was "We are Family!" it seemed wrong that some family members enjoyed luxury and privilege with funds provided by much less privileged members. My sensitivity to this inequality was increased by the tendency of those connected to the power and wealth at the top of the organization to show little regard for the financial and other sacrifices made by the members. In international regions it was worse, as the Work and the church were run on shoestring budgets like unwanted stepchildren.

I was on the ground when the Tkach road show came to Munich. They stayed at one of the most expensive hotels and did not hesitate to enjoy the conveniences, spending hundreds of dollars a day on room service and having clothes laundered at the hotel, for example. They seemed to believe God smiled on His super-elite group and was happy they lived a life of ease and luxury, given their proximity to His Apostle. My approach to personal travel and my experience with Mr. Waterhouse, who had laundered his own underwear and shirts in hotel sinks, was in stark contrast to this. And being closer to the source of the funds they were squandering, I was aware that members making significant financial sacrifices believed the tithes were being carefully managed. I was appalled.

Over a thousand members had travelled a great distance for the event and in the evening I was a guide for the inner circle as they considered their evening options. A lively discussion unfolded about which aspects of the Munich nightlife to enjoy. There seemed to be no awareness that their European excursion was at the tithe-payer's expense, even as hundreds of these tithe-payers had hoped for some community activity or at least interaction with the people at the top of the WCG heap.

They wanted to disengage from the membership as soon as possible to eat, drink, shop, dance, or do anything that might give them more satisfaction than what the members thought they were there to do. This was understandable on one level, but the hypocrisy was painfully clear. The "We Are Family Tour" to meet their global family members was a canned propaganda show. The celebrities couldn't wait to get away from their distant and tiresome family members, preferring to hit the town, which classic WCG theology labeled "The World" at best, or in the case of Europe, the actual end-time manifestation of Babylon, the Beast power that would fight Christ at His return.

As they discussed the merits of their options, I watched intently to see how Mr. Tkach would handle the matter. He became visibly disinterested and perhaps a bit perturbed. Noticing an organ grinder with a monkey on the corner, Mr. Tkach walked over, exchanged a few words, and dropped some money into the cup. Returning to the group, he asked them what they settled on. It's impossible to say what was going through his mind, but it seemed he had distanced himself from the more worldly materialistic approach of his entourage to give a brief object lesson in how easy it is, at any time, to find an opportunity to carry out a small act of compassion and kindness. I took it as evidence of sincerity; he practiced what he preached.

This perspective was corroborated by an invitation to fly back to Bonn aboard the G3, with its gold-plated belt buckles and other flashes of opulence that seemed so unnecessary and so indulgent. Mr. Tkach had not made the decision to acquire or upgrade the plane, and at least he was using it to serve and solidify the church, the Body of Christ.[73] On the plane he was personable, down to earth, and had a genuine interest in me as a person and as a member of the church. His approach to the membership was sincere; he equated us all as God's children and saw it as his role to serve and lead. This was key to my acceptance and adoption of the changes issuing forth with ever greater rapidity from Pasadena.

The view of the church as family, while prioritizing personal health and family before service to the church, and encouraging members to explore medical options and make wise choices based on God's guidance, were all major positive changes. And allowing birthday celebrations despite ministerial extrapolations on obscure Bible verses were good examples of this loosening without sacrificing truth. A reduction of ministerial intrusion into members' personal lives was a welcome move away from a Pope-like approach to doctrine and the police-like power and authority of the ministry.

In German-speaking Europe, these changes would also have to be digested and addressed without the longtime respected leadership of Mr. Schnee. He was diagnosed with Parkinson's disease and transferred back to Pasadena in 1988 and John Karlson was named Regional Director in his place. Members who had looked to Mr. Schnee were having a double dose of the change and transition that was beginning to shake the foundations of the WCG.

You've Got To Hide Your Love Away

The changes aligned with my growing perception that spiritual growth resulted from freedom of choice and not ministerial coercion. In that sense I was more liberal than Henry, my new mentor. There were several older Swiss ladies interested in attending church services, but Henry was not eager to see them join

---

73. I Corinthians 12:27 among other scriptures

us too quickly. The church had an unusually high degree of enforced doctrinal conformity and Henry had valid concerns about how the members would react and interact with people who believed differently on this or that point. He would ask my opinion and I would argue for inviting them sooner, rather than later. This wasn't about doctrinal change; it was about creating breathing room. We needed to become more flexible and skilled at bridging differences of interpretation with love, kindness, understanding, and acceptance.

A clear example of this was a woman frustrated by Henry's insistence that her idol, Albert Schweitzer, could not have had the Holy Spirit. Repentance of breaking God's law, including the Sabbath, baptism, and the laying on of hands performed according to scripture were pre-requisites he hadn't met. Henry was trying to help her accept this as evidence of her own repentance.

I was uncomfortable with a relatively young man asking an older woman to pronounce judgment on a European theologian who was universally recognized and had been awarded the Nobel Peace Prize for his philosophy of reverence for life. He practiced what he preached by famously founding and sustaining the Albert Schweitzer Hospital in Lambaréné, now in Gabon, west central Africa (then French Equatorial Africa). His works of love were recognized and valued in Switzerland, so Henry was demanding a level of personal abnegation that crossed a number of lines. My heart went out to this woman who was denied the option to follow God in the way that she felt He was leading her. It was reminiscent of the double bind placed on Mrs. Tkach, and I began to reflect on the spiritual and psychological implications of our approach. As painful as the visits to this woman were, there were many other experiences that were positive, including a pending wedding and new relationships with the wonderful people in the three churches I was serving.

Henry and I had lots of time for discussions as we traveled across south-central Europe. The open sharing of viewpoints with an educated man whom I greatly respected was instrumental in formulating biblical and spiritual perspectives in my messages at Sabbath services, Bible studies, and Holy Days. Others were pleased with the progress I was making as well. Less than a year after returning from Pasadena as a married man, John Karlson and Henry ordained me into the ministry of the WCG on the day of Pentecost, 1989.

8

Revolution

"No one can serve two masters.
Either he will hate the one and love the other, or he will be devoted to the
one and despise the other. You cannot serve both God and Money"

—Matthew 6:24—New International Version—

My first assignment as an ordained minister in the WCG was in the border region of Switzerland and southern Germany. There were many reasons to be cheerful at this very positive time in my life. I was at peace, validated by my choices and how they had turned out, while also looking forward to making a larger contribution to the Work of God on earth. At the same time, events brought flaws in doctrinal and religious theory into stark relief. Nothing brings home reality like a funeral or two.

In discussing funerals, it's important to explain that the WCG did not believe this to be the only day of salvation. Only those few specifically called by God today were offered salvation now. The bulk of humanity was not yet called and would be resurrected in the future. The idea of an immortal soul destined for heaven or hell had its roots in pagan philosophy, not divine revelation, whereas the Bible did call out a spiritual component granting us our extraordinary emotional, intellectual, creative and moral capacities. Job called this aspect the spirit in Man; "But *there is* a spirit in man: and the inspiration of the Almighty giveth them understanding"[74]. It is also referred to briefly in the book of Ecclesiastes "and man hath no pre-eminence above the beast: for all is vanity. All go unto one place: all are of the dust, and all return to dust. Who knoweth the spirit of the children of men? Doth it go upwards? and the spirit of the beasts, doth it go downwards to the earth?"[75].

The New Testament clarifies this in the resurrection chapter, I Corinthians 15. Paul outlines that all men, like Christ, will die and be resurrected. True Christians who die in faith or are alive at Christ's return receive a new spiritual body, almost infinitely more powerful. First to rise will be those "dead in Christ," followed by those still alive: "But I would not have you to be ignorant, brethren, concerning them which are asleep… For if we believe that Jesus died and rose again, even so them also which sleep in Jesus will God bring with him. For this we say unto you by the word of the Lord, that we which are alive and remain unto the coming of the Lord shall not prevent them which are asleep. For the Lord himself shall descend from heaven with a shout, with the voice of the archangel, and with the trump of God: and the dead in Christ shall rise first: Then we which are alive and remain shall be caught up together with them in the clouds, to meet the Lord in the air."[76]

This scripture gave us certainty that we once again, in yet another important area of doctrine, had a unique understanding that set us apart. In those not called today, this spirit element is dormant at death, like a seed waiting to germinate, until a future resurrection.

Eleanor Rigby

In the fall of 1989 a relatively young, well-respected Swiss member named Rosemarie died of cancer. Henry delivered the eulogy in the small chapel and

74. Job 32:8
75. Ecclesiastes 3:19-21
76. I Thessalonians 4:13-17

I presided over the graveside service. As Henry had wrestled with the issue of having to represent that Albert Schweitzer could not have been a true Christian, I struggled to adapt a scripted message that just seemed wrong. WCG's funeral sermon was short on sensitivity and long on doctrinal passages related to our beliefs about the afterlife. We felt obligated to deliver the truth that the dead sleep until a resurrection instead of ascending to heaven (or descending to hell, though not many funeral ceremonies tend to send folks there). While the intent was to share truth we found inspiring and reassuring, it came across as an annoyingly transparent and opportunistic use of death to preach our beliefs to those we believed to be deceived. The tone clearly revealed that while we recognized the audience would not see or accept the truth, the WCG minister was nonetheless going to force it down their grieving throats.

Rosemarie's large circle of non-WCG family and friends were in attendance and I was uncomfortable approaching such a personal event in such a calloused manner, but I saw no easy way out. I soldiered through as best I could, trusting that God would somehow make it right. It was a hot August day and after Henry's eulogy, attendees were unexpectedly forced to stand in direct sunlight as I mercilessly droned on. A number of older family members were sweltering in their black funeral dress.

Rosemarie's sister confronted me afterward, saying she felt no love in my funeral message. She was right, and I was horrified at what I had just done. All I could do was apologize profusely, asking for forgiveness in exchange for a promise that her direct feedback would make this the first and last time I delivered this kind of sermon. Paul didn't want us to be ignorant, but we were behaving ignorantly, and the WCG needed to fundamentally change its ways. Mr. Tkach was steering the church into new and unfamiliar waters, but in a direction that was sorely needed.

Some months later, a member asked if the spirit in man was a generic component, like a spoonful of spirit scooped from a lake and plopped into the fetus, or if it had personality components. Intrigued, I found scriptural support for the idea that God created us with unique characteristics. "And they shall be mine, saith the LORD of hosts, in that day when I make up my jewels"[77] and "To him that overcometh will I give to eat of the hidden manna, and will give him a white stone, and in the stone a new name written, which no man

---

77. Malachi 3:17

knoweth saving he that receiveth *it.*"[78]Each of us was unique and special and this uniqueness pre-dated our birth, as was clearly the case with Jeremiah about whom God said: "Before I formed thee in the belly I knew thee; and before thou camest forth out of the womb I sanctified thee, *and* I ordained thee a prophet unto the nations."[79]

On a trip to Pasadena I had a chance to discuss this idea with Dr. Hoeh, a leading evangelist considered by many in the WCG to be the primary scholar in matters of doctrine. Over an authentic Chinese lunch at one of his favorite low-budget haunts, he stated that while the idea was new to him it had considerable merit. In a sermon I used these and other scriptures to explain the idea[80], covering stories about God working through families as a further indication that in addition to creating something unique, special, and of importance to Him in each of us, certain characteristics and traits were being cultivated over a long period of time. Each of us would be amazed and delighted when God revealed to us who we really were, why we were specifically created, and how we fit in to His overall plans for the advancement of humanity and, ultimately, His goals for the universe throughout all eternity. Such respect for the individual was often lacking in the application of WCG theology and ideology, where members were herded like sheep. Such thinking led me to change the way I interacted with people in the region, beginning to treat everyone with more respect, understanding, and compassion.

This was reciprocated by the membership and one Stuttgart couple, in particular, provided significant material and emotional support. Rene Hübner was a well-to-do financial advisor who was ordained a deacon during my stay there and with his gracious wife, Beate, selflessly served us and others at every opportunity. They shared their home and financial blessings with those in our church community, providing a cultural experience otherwise unknown or inaccessible. Some took advantage of their generosity or diminished it by assuming that it was easy for them, since they were materially blessed above others. It was clear however, that what they were really sharing was an asset that we all possess in equal measure: time. They were far from alone in their approach

---

78. Revelation 2:17
79. Jeremiah 1:5
80. Isaiah 48:8, I Peter 1:2

and any love and care directed toward the membership was overwhelmingly returned in much greater measure.

Aside from sermons, counseling, weddings, funerals, and baptisms, WCG ministers visited *Plain Truth* readers, interested coworkers, and prospective members. Typically our approach was one of indifference as to whether people joined or not, as evidenced by the example of the woman who was an Albert Schweitzer fan. It was God who called and only those who clearly responded to His calling were allowed to move forward and associate with the WCG.

The WCG has been called a cult, which I'll not comment on now except to say that if it was, at least it wasn't predatory. It was the opposite. We tried to scare people away. So those who requested and received a ministerial visit were treated kindly and with respect during what amounted to an interview about how much they understood in order for us to determine whether they were approaching the Word of God with an open mind or not, as defined by us. Often they were given specific literature answering their questions and asked to study it and request another visit when done. This was to help them count the cost[81] before putting their hand to the plow[82], since there was no looking back.

Despite the example of the elderly Swiss woman, when it came to inviting people to attend church, Henry was more lenient than Tom Lapacka had been. I took this further and invited people to attend church as soon as possible to get connected to other members and experience the reality of the WCG first hand. I also invited a family of five back to church who had been asked not to attend until the parents had quit smoking. This resulted in discomfort on the part of ministers and members who had been required to make painful changes prior to being allowed to attend.

My goal was to prepare the congregation for what I hoped would be an influx of new people who should expect warmth, assistance, and acceptance, rather than a wary judgmental evaluation. Those who had already made the cut and were now part of the elite insider group—The People of the Sign—might not like it, but if the church was going to grow it needed to make this shift.

---

81. Luke 14:28
82. Luke 9:62

You Never Give Me Your Money

Political events to the east at that time caught almost everyone in the West by surprise. The stability of the Soviet Union seemed unassailable, but due to its prophetic outlook the WCG had been expecting a restructuring in Europe. Given my role in establishing and growing the newsstand program for the German *Plain Truth* magazine, I was well aware that West Berlin had by far the biggest geographic penetration of *Klar & Wahr*. At its peak, it boasted sixty thousand copies of out of a total circulation of about one hundred thirty thousand. I remember sitting in our unfurnished living room watching a tiny black and white TV given to us by a generous member, as on November 9, 1989, West Berlin was flooded with visitors from East Germany, who were now, suddenly, allowed to cross over into the west.

I literally jumped up from my chair with excitement, proclaiming to my wife that I now understood why God had so clearly opened up the doors of distribution there, of all places, in contrast to the miniscule programs in Munich and Hannover and despite the opposition within the church by ministers and others in the Bonn office who seemed jealous at my success. *Klar & Wahr* was prominently displayed at every newsstand outlet that the eager, curious, Eastern Europeans would encounter as they entered West Berlin. They would not necessarily have the means to purchase what the West had to offer, but they could pick up this free magazine at every subway station, the main train station, and even the airport, as they crossed over the border, perhaps for the first time. And they did.

Imagine my shock and disappointment when the circulation manager in Bonn, whom I liked, but who had seemed the most resentful of my prominence, had shut down the program specifically because the magazines were flying off the stands. In his view we could not afford the cost of distributing the magazine to those whose means were limited.

This was, at best, extreme short-sightedness. While I was in Bonn I had clearly shown that the relative cost of gaining newsstand readers was much less than gaining a new subscriber by advertising in other magazines. Not to mention that many subscribers responding to nebulous ads immediately found the magazine distasteful, yet we continued to mail them copies for many months.

The newsstand program allowed many more people to read before subscribing. I had previously won such arguments and had the full support of Mr. Schnee. But he was gone and Mr. Karlson, who was more timid, cautious, and careful with things like budgets, had agreed to shut the program down. Now there was nothing I could do about what I saw as a lack of the kind of faith needed to boldly go through the door God had opened. It was a repeat of my experience in Sweden.

Mr. Karlson's approach was supported by a film played at all Feast sites that covered the parable of the sower and the seed[83]. This highly professional and powerful mini-movie focused our attention on our efforts to do the Work, but was slanted to portray Mr. Tkach as a wise steward who would no longer waste the seed that was falling upon the stony ground, among the thorns, or by the wayside. He would use it on good ground. This sounded good on the surface, but it distorted the scripture for political and financial reasons. The parable didn't encourage us to worry about where the seed landed. Our job was to walk down the fields, dispersing it in a wide arc. But a bigger problem with the concept was the idea that wealthier demographics represented good ground.

Good ground had nothing to do with finance and everything to do with openness to God's message. If anything, the poor were good ground, not the rich. This new approach was based on ill-founded logic, if not a lack of faith. God would provide if we sought to reach those who would be most open to the truth, regardless of their socio-economic standing. To avoid the poor in favor of those with more money was evil. The WCG seemed suddenly willing to turn numerous clear teachings on their head in the name of good business practice.

On the bright side, the emphasis on stewardship resulted in the sale of Gulfstream III in January, 1989 for about $12.5 million, ending the worst of the extravagant lifestyles at the top of the WCG. Sadly for Mr. Tkach and the WCG, this lent weight to the opinion of some that he was purposefully distancing himself from HWA, whom they clung to with superstitious tenacity. The winds of change blowing across the WCG formed an almost eerie parallel to what was happening in the Soviet Union. In the same way that Perestroika (restructuring) and Glasnost (openness) in the Soviet Union began to result in ideological change, waves of change in teaching and approach that were spreading out like concentric ripples from Pasadena began to ripple over the edges of core

83. Matthew 13

doctrines. Germany and Europe were perhaps even more intellectually engaged in and by this process than those closer to the epicenter. This brings me back to Stuttgart, where we were grappling with issues Pasadena hadn't touched yet…

The second funeral I officiated at took place shortly after I moved to the region and affected a family that had helped me administer the newsstand program from Bonn. Wilfried Kaiser was a long-time leading member in the Stuttgart church area, an exceptionally intelligent and gifted man, who thought deeply about things. About the time I began working with Henry, Wilfried began to experience a series of inexplicable health problems that turned into a painful downward health spiral as his system lost its ability to assimilate protein.[84] With his personal health deteriorating, one of his concerns was the financial health of his family. He initiated a discussion on tithing at a time when I was regrettably not properly informed about what the Bible actually has to say about the subject. I listened sympathetically but ultimately did not grasp his objections at the time.

As Wilfried lost weight and became unable to work, he was hospitalized and underwent a variety of treatments and psychological analysis and was given psycho-pharmaceuticals. His situation became increasingly desperate and the treatments affected his thinking. Feeling pressure from every direction, ending his own life occurred to him as a possible solution. During a particularly low point, he was unfortunately successful in doing so.

Wilfried's death fueled more discussion on tithing as members felt empowered to voice open disagreement. The tragedy of what happened to the Kaiser family was but one example of the negative impact on members who, in faith, followed church teaching without receiving the expected blessings. After being ordained it was time for me to move north, closer to the Stuttgart church, which was now seen as a hotbed of dissent. My proximity to people wanting to discuss their doubts played a significant role in changing my perspective on critical church doctrines.

Initially I was resistant to the members' questions on the subject of tithing. My personal experience, informed by WCG teaching, had proven that God blessed those who faithfully tithed, and He removed His protection from those

---

84. Wilfried gave me a book called *Körper Sprache*, or *Body Language*, by a naturopath who dared to interpret the language of sickness—what our body tells us. It was critical to my healing process.

who didn't. Even if we obeyed, but grudgingly and without faith, we might fail to reap the blessings. It was a spiritual law, which is why the WCG got away with re-implementing it in a way that did not follow the letter, and if a member was not blessed, it was obviously their own fault. This was frankly my mind-set when I moved to Stuttgart, but I was not so calloused or arrogant as to refuse to at least listen to members' complaints about tithing. Ministers were to be helpers of our joy[85] and I believed it would be easy to answer questions from the Word of God and explain their error.

But just as HWA had been proved wrong by his personal study on the topic of the Sabbath, I began to understand from the Bible that the laws of tithing as applied in the WCG had no relation to God's original intent.

Taxman

In Israel tithing was a ten percent tax on agricultural increase based on a divine land grant, free and clear, providing a sustainable livelihood that completed their rescue from slavery. Self-sufficient land owners could take care of themselves and a tithe was a reasonable tax on the increase from the land they had been given. Tithing did not apply to non-farmers living in cities. Tithing was clearly not intended to be applied to wage-slaves and certainly not on what is today called gross income. Most on the planet today eke out an existence while up to their necks in debt, which did not occur in the divinely delivered fifty year economic cycle, with its forgiveness of debt.

In the fabulous wealth of the post-WWII United States the tithing system seemed to work. The U.S. economy was expanding and the average middle class family lived like kings in comparison to people in ancient Israel. Principles of moral discipline and diligence went a long way in a wealthy country with those characteristics. Perhaps most importantly, U.S. tax law allows an unlimited deduction of one hundred percent of charitable donations, and our tithes to the Church qualified, which made a big difference for those with decent incomes. So WCG members in the United States were relatively well-fed, well-clothed, and healthy compared to their international brethren. An acceptance of one's lot as a pilgrim on this earth and identification with the fruit being born by the Work

---

85. II Corinthians 1:24

of God—in terms of magazine circulation and TV program viewer growth, et cetera—masked the rest of the gap. The added benefit of being enthusiastically involved in a calling enabled most U.S. members to feel blessed compared to what they considered worldly, materialistically deceived neighbors.

But for those who were poor to start with or who lived in countries with different socio-economic factors and different tax laws, such as Germany, the true results of the tithing system became apparent more quickly and more painfully. The WCG system of paying tithes on gross income was clearly economic oppression. It created a ruling class of privileged ministers generally wealthier than the majority of those they supposedly served. These overlords were sometimes less diligent, educated, competent, or even less righteous than the sheep they were shearing at every paycheck and three times a year[86] which HWA had re-interpreted to require members to pony up generous offerings on seven annual Holy Days, on top of two or three tithes.

While still in the Bonn office, before I was ordained into the ministry, I had fought a battle with German tax authorities over claiming my second tithe expenses as business expenses. The German tax authorities stated that my employer should cover such business expenses and declined the deduction. My response quoted scripture that required me to use my own tithe money, but given the nature of the work, it was still a business expense. To the amazement of the WCG finance manager, who had recommended against the claim, the authorities accepted the argument and allowed the deduction. Only after leaving Bonn did I learn the reason for the finance manager's reluctance to support my battle. Ministers in Germany did not pay any tithes at all and their Feast expenses were covered as well. Then there was a housing and car allowance in addition. Germany was not alone. In the U.S. and elsewhere, third tithe, which publicly was believed to be for orphans and widows, was largely used to support the ministry, especially covering their Feast expenses. Only a small portion of the third tithe money collected was used to actually provide assistance to people in need.

Most in the WCG did not know that administrative rulings granted different dispensations to different countries based on socio-economic conditions and tax laws. In Sweden, the nominal tax rate for workers at times exceeded eighty percent, which the government used to eradicate poverty. You can't very

---

86. Deuteronomy 16:16

well allocate an average of twenty-three percent of your gross income to tithes under those circumstances. So dispensation was granted to Scandinavians to tithe on net instead of gross income, and third tithe was not required at all. But this was not public knowledge until Holland was granted a similar dispensation. When Stuttgart members forged relationships with some of the Dutch members through international youth volleyball tournaments, the cat was out of the bag.

Germans in the Stuttgart region were generally industrious and self-sufficient. Here WCG members struggling with the teaching on tithing came to similar conclusions and the Stuttgart church quickly got a negative reputation because of it. When the discussion and debate spilled over into the Basel and Zurich, Switzerland churches in our circuit, it was time for Henry to give a sermon on the topic. He explained that the tithing system was an exercise in faith, using the simple example of ten apples. Give one to the church and God would supernaturally make the remaining nine go further than ten. While I still agreed with tithing as a spiritual principle, I found his message offensive if not disingenuous. The WCG taught tithing as a matter of law and faith, but clearly didn't really believe it was. It was, in fact, a humanly devised oppressive religious taxation system, that could be administratively softened for members taxed way beyond their means to pay.

The fallout of Henry's sermon was another double-bind. Since the WCG was God's Church, and since He backed it up, I had to ask members to follow their conscience while keeping silent about a teaching that I increasingly did not agree with. Looking back on my own history with the topic, the plain, bizarre, and painful truth was that in a year my dad was paying an additional ten percent of his gross income to the WCG, supposedly to support orphans and widows, he himself was unwilling or unable to pay to send his children to their mother's funeral. It wasn't until writing this chapter that this sickening connection became apparent. Why?

My victimized mindset welcomed the role of martyr. It took having responsibility for others to see that people were hurting and that I was aligned with the problem, not the solution. But ultimately it took Wilfried Kaiser's death in a country where the macro-economic situation didn't mask the fact that God was, in fact, not making nine apples stretch to cover ten, to help me begin to see the WCG tithing system for what it was: a twisted misapplication of scripture resulting in oppression.

The magnitude of WCG's error was not really clear at that time because I viewed it as an honest mistake fueled by a sincere desire to help usher in the World Tomorrow—i.e. the return of Christ and global utopia. Unquestioning acceptance of the WCG's dogmatic and rigid belief systems kept us from seeing the obvious. But despite indoctrination, cracks began to appear in the impenetrable edifice of misinformed faith that let light seep through. Wilfried's death forced my eyes and ears open just as I assumed the role of a shepherd to tend and shear the sheep on behalf of the corporate body.

Ob-La-Di, Ob-La-Da

In fairness to Henry, in response to my agitation on the issue of tithing, he wrote a letter to Bonn requesting that Mr. Karlson look into the matter. Many months later the message from Bonn was that Pasadena had supported the status quo. I was more than a little disappointed; my perspective was increasingly out of sync with WCG teaching. There was a continuing emphasis on and a desire to see the rod of iron applied to a sinning and stubbornly unrepentant humanity. And in Stuttgart true believers were trying to make the law, as taught by the WCG, work for them, but it didn't. The reaction to their complaints about an obviously flawed so-called spiritual taxation system was like Pharaoh forcing Israel to make bricks without straw instead of setting them free to worship God.

Although Jesus clearly supported the laws of Moses, he lambasted religious leaders for their failure to interpret the law properly and more importantly, to apply it appropriately in a modern context. So while there is no authority for going directly against revelation, leaders have a responsibility to lead those who look to them for guidance into more mature understanding and application of the revelation, which means uncomfortable changes.

But the idea that the WCG represented the government of God, and that God would change things when He was ready, pointed in the opposite direction. We should willingly bear suffering under an old interpretation until God clarified the spiritual intent to the leaders He had chosen. As one of those leaders, with God making things clear to me, the changes our new Pastor General was introducing gave me hope and patience. Most WCG ministers seemed adamantly opposed to all the changes. In their eyes, Joseph Tkach,

HWA's authorized successor, was changing HWA's teachings and the identity of the WCG. They found themselves in the awkward position of disagreeing with the divinely authorized channel—God's Apostle.

WCG history provided an example of how to handle error at the top. God would use it as a test against those who failed to submit to God's authority as deployed in His church. The legendary example of Dr. Hoeh's disagreement with HWA over Pentecost was often cited in support of this teaching. Pentecost was a Holy Day, an annual Sabbath, and thus a test commandment. Pentecost meant "count fifty." If you count the day you started counting from as day one, like Dr. Hoeh did, you must observe Pentecost on Sunday. If you do not, like HWA and the church that followed him, you must observe Pentecost on Monday.

Dr. Hoeh was faced with an error on HWA's part that was just a hair less significant than changing the weekly Sabbath, the true test commandment for all People of the Sign. And it meant observing Pentecost on Sunday, which was anathema to the WCG, which held Saturday Sabbath observance as the primary test of a person's willingness to obey and follow God. Prior discussions on this topic and preliminary investigation had associated it with Christianity's attempt to use the Sunday morning resurrection, despite the lack of three days and three nights in the grave, as a rationale to move from Saturday to Sunday worship. You can imagine which side HWA took, and Dr. Hoeh knew better than to confront HWA on this, of all things, after HWA had declared the Sunday view to be in error.

Dr. Hoeh's solution had been to publicly keep the wrong day with the church, in support of HWA's role, while privately keeping the correct day. After doing this for years, HWA finally changed his mind and in 1974 acknowledged that Dr. Hoeh had been right. This provided proof that you could trust God to direct the leadership of His church, after first testing us on the critical issue of government. This was proof that it was our role to obey and follow, in faith.

The WCG was God's one true church, and while we might in some ways be wandering around in the desert like Israel, we needed to follow the cloud and the pillar under the direction of the leadership God had put in place. We were heading for the Promised Land and Jesus' return. The seemingly circuitous and painful route the cloud and pillar might take to get us there had purpose. Seeking to understand, in faith, would lead to spiritual growth, whereas fighting and resisting the leadership would lead in the opposite direction. Soon, very soon, we would see the return of Christ, in all His glory, and we would be transformed into a new, spiritual creation, experiencing the results of the resurrection of the dead. For us this meant an immediate transformation into Spirit, to assist Christ in ushering in a new era for mankind, beginning with 1,000 years of peace and prosperity.

Things We Said Today

With a supportive church in Stuttgart, I was asked to assist in other areas. In 1990 I was tasked by Mr. Karlson with launching and directing an SEP in Germany, which I expanded to European status by operating in multiple languages. This was the fulfillment of a dream to leverage my experience and creative ideas to improve the way the church worked with young people. I invited and recruited friends from Bonn: Mark and Elaine, Sherri, Norbert, Mike, and others, to get the program up and running. Later I traveled to AC in both Pasadena and Big Sandy to recruit students. This allowed me to connect with a number of senior college and church officials on both sides of the changes and for a while I maintained a middle-of-the-road stance, passionate about traditional core doctrine while supportive of the hierarchy and the direction of Mr. Tkach.

I travelled to France to visit Joel Meeker, a former classmate in a similar role to mine in the Alsace region, bordering on Germany, who had responsibility for the French SEP, to work together on some ideas for the camps. With college participation I added a European tour component to the SEP in Germany for AC student staff and American campers. In the last year, the camp included several non-church kids and integrated creative fundraising ideas to empower the teenagers financially. These and other innovations didn't sit well with more conservative elements of the church. One example was my decision to award camper of the session to a non-church youth, the friend of Joachim Kaiser whose father's funeral is addressed above.

This irritated Matt Fenchel, the assistant camp director, a recent AC grad ordained into the ministry shortly after I was ordained, who was adamantly opposed to the award, and increasingly complained about my unorthodox behavior. Matt was an associate pastor under Winfried Fritz, who had been moved from Austria to replace Grant Spong. Winfried had responsibility for the region's WEP, which in some ways began to take a back seat to the longer, larger, more international and more diverse SEP. This rivalry was unfortunate, as I had first met Winfried and his wife at AC the first time he had been to Pasadena, before I spoke a word of German. Matt's disapproval was causing additional friction with Winfried and negatively impacting Mr. Karlson's view on what I was doing at SEP.

As my formerly great relationship with the Fritz family deteriorated, Winfried corrected me at a ministerial conference after I had spoken out in some way in support of a kinder, gentler approach to the membership. It was clear he meant his comments to be taken seriously, from him in his role as head of Ministerial Services in the German region as opposed to being a personal observation. He said, "We don't need any Absaloms in Germany." Absalom was the rebellious but popular son of King David of Israel who used hypocrisy and flattery to undermine his father. He "stole the hearts of the people" as he worked to unseat his father from the throne.[87]

What was going on in the church with Mr. Tkach's change in direction unsettling and unnerving hard-liners, while exciting and energizing those who were forward-looking change agents, was being paralleled in the Soviet Union under the rulership of Gorbachev. In Europe, Gorby, as he was called, was enormously popular, especially with young people. Russian was in vogue, and clothing featuring Russian printed in the Cyrillic alphabet and the Russian flag were popular fashion choices. Words such as *perestroika* (restructuring) and *glasnost* (openness) were entering our vocabulary. *Klar & Wahr* literally translates to *Clear & True*. I remember joking about the trouble we'd have with a magazine called *Glasnost & Pravda*, given that the Russian word for truth, *pravda*, was clearly associated with the Russian government-controlled propaganda machine.

Back in the USSR

Those of us who had studied Russian in the Bonn office and who were involved with Feast sites behind the Iron Curtain had developed an affinity for

---

87. 2 Samuel 15

Gorbachev and the winds of change that were blowing. The fact that Mr. Tkach was of Russian background and was interested in Russia made it easy to be excited about the developments in the church and the proximity we enjoyed to this new area of focus. I had been prepared for this moment with my experience and study of Russian, and was excited that God was obviously about to open up the region for His work.

A small group of students and recent graduates were working with Radio/TV Leningrad on a project under the auspices of AICF, and I finagled an invitation to visit them and provide moral support and western supplies, in combination with a road trip to Scandinavia. My friend Joel Meeker from France, along with his wife, Marjolaine and baby daughter Fiona, accompanied us on this road trip. I had arranged for us to stay for a week on the eastern coast of Sweden in my uncle's summer house. The chance to fish during the day, eat our catch, and then play cards outside on the detached deck at the edge of the lake under the midnight sun was rejuvenating, even if Joel, who is exceptionally bright and multi-talented, regularly managed to kick my butt at cards. At least I was the one catching all the fish.

It was rewarding to deliver a sermon in Swedish in Stockholm and to see the members again, but I couldn't wait to get to Russia and practice speaking Russian. Just prior to leaving for Leningrad via Finland, we learned of a coup underway in Russia, led by hardline Communists who had abducted Gorbachev. Rather than reacting with nervousness and worry about this development, I was excited. The Spirit of God was moving dramatically, inside and outside the church. I thrived on change, and it didn't get much bigger or better than this.

Mr. Karlson got word to me to abort the trip, but I asked if the participants in the Russian project were being pulled out. He admitted that they were staying to show solidarity with the Russians that they were working with on the project. I responded with, "This is why we were inspired to take this trip." and promptly ignored his advice. God had clearly brought me to another important gangplank.

The experience of driving through Finland toward a Russian crisis was surreal. There was normally little traffic between the west and the east, even less by car along this remote stretch of road, and now there was none whatsoever. Approaching the remote wilderness border crossing, I shared an old joke told by my Swedish cousin about the Russian submarines and warships in the Baltic

Sea, which was to our right. These ships were border patrols preventing the disillusioned Western masses, oppressed by capitalism, from illegally entering the worker's paradise. But a feeling of nervousness and dread was building as we drove for hours across the eerily quiet landscape headed toward that waiting nirvana.

The tension was palpable as we crossed through the Finnish checkpoint and stopped on the Russian side. Then calm replaced fear, as I noted a similarity to a scene from *Star Wars*. Obi-Wan Kenobi used a Jedi mind trick—a small wave of his hand and the words, "You don't need to see his identification" to get past the guard at a checkpoint. The glazed eyes of the guard who waved us through had that same look. From there we headed toward Leningrad, en-route to meet our colleagues at the headquarters of Radio/TV Leningrad. What we didn't know was that the Russian military had already occupied media outlets in neighboring Latvia and Lithuania.

We also didn't know that tanks were heading toward us from the other side of the city. Somehow, using broken Russian and perhaps a degree of divine guidance, we managed to find our way through eerily empty streets to the studio and meet up with our comrades. There we learned about these developments and that the soldiers coming from Moscow had stopped a mere fifty miles outside the city. They had decided not to attack their own people. The coup was over.

As the dust was settling, we had another memorable experience when we randomly chose a restaurant for dinner that was obviously controlled by the state political apparatus. The manager came out to find out who we really were and why we were in the city, as he tried to figure out whose side we were on. I told him we worked for a western foundation but he refused us entrance. Then I explained that we were on official business with Radio/TV Leningrad and that we were, in fact, going to eat in this restaurant. He backed off, allowing us in, only to try to throw us out again moments later. I dogmatically stood my ground and he backed off, but insisted we pay the dollar prices. Again I refused, so we paid the prices listed in rubles. The multi-course meals we ordered featured salmon, champagne, and caviar, and cost about $1.20 per person. The stares we got from the few others who were eating there, along with the snippets of hushed conversations I overheard, were priceless.

What struck me most, and stuck with me longest about this trip, was an insight gained in discussions with the young Western-oriented English-speaking

Russians on the project who shared their views and experiences during this emotionally turbulent time for them. For starters, it was fascinating in many ways to experience such openness and solidarity with people who had been our enemies for decades, during a long and protracted cold war, and the buildup of one half of the most destructive stockpile of weaponry that mankind had ever created. But what floored me was their perspective on the satellite nations of the Russian empire, such as Estonia, Latvia and Lithuania. After decades of dominance and control by their giant neighbor to the east, they were in the process of breaking off from the Soviet Union, declaring independence, and striking out on their own. These young Russians spoke passionately about how, in a time of crisis such as this, these countries would return to the aid of Mother Russia, helping her to build a new society during her transition and transformation.

It was quite clear to me that this was ludicrous, given the deep-seated hatred and resentment felt by these people toward a brutal oppressor and an occupying force that had denied them basic freedoms and independence for the entirety of their existence. I was struck by the amazing ability of all homo sapiens in whatever system of beliefs we grew up with, wherever we happen to live on this large and diverse planet, to be convinced that our own ways are right and our own systems are the best, and ultimately the rest of the world will come to recognize that fact.

It dawned on me that we are all blind in a whole host of very important ways. More cracks in my stalwart adherence to the fortress of faith constructed around the WCG appeared. Like the Soviet Union, we had constructed a closed city, a fortress on a hill, unassailable by the outside world, based on internal logic and interpretation, much of which was self-referential. In our hermetically sealed environment we created our own reality. When an outsider looked into the Soviet system, the proverbial bread-lines were obvious proof that the emperor had no clothes. This problem was partially solved by not letting too many outsiders in, but more importantly not letting the insiders out, which is why my cousin's joke was so funny. But the parallels to the WCG were not yet quite so obvious.

Like those young, educated Russians who supported the Soviet Union, I was still an enthusiastic supporter of the WCG. Now I could claim to speak enough Russian to get myself into trouble, which added to the value that I felt I could contribute to the Work of God in the new Europe. This was on top of my ministerial duties, my increasing success with the German SEP, and my ability to travel and speak in a variety of foreign language countries that bordered on my area of responsibility. I was soon asked to travel to Estonia to support a small but growing congregation there. These were exciting trips, not only because it was a new, uncharted area, but because of the growing focus within the WCG on areas formerly under Soviet dominance.

Two Of Us

Victor Kubik was now assistant director of Ministerial Services in Pasadena, and he was of Ukrainian descent. I got to know him at some point, and hit it off quite well with both him and his wife, Beverly. He took a personal interest in the efforts in Estonia, and was also visiting with various Sabbatarian groups in the Ukraine. One of these groups numbered about 2,000, and our connection with them led to a startling comment at the Feast. The opening night message from the Pastor General was broadcast by satellite to most Feast sites around the world and played over the next day or two by video at all others. This was fairly advanced use of technology for the time and was intended to unify the WCG. In his message, Mr. Tkach made a throwaway comment that was to cause quite a stir.

In welcoming all of us he let us know that about "2,000 brethren are keeping the Feast with us in the Ukraine." This was the latest in a series of statements from Mr. Tkach that undermined key principles we all held dear; in this case our uniqueness, the exclusivity of those who had specifically been called into the WCG and God's backing of us, and only us, as the People of God. Could God really have brought others into a similar understanding outside our sphere of operations and influence? I immediately embraced the idea, but most others were skeptical.

In my view, the sign of the Sabbath predated and existed outside the WCG. We didn't define it, it defined us. God had likely revealed it to people behind the Iron Curtain not only to honor their faith, but to show us, as He had once shown Elijah, that God was not limited to work exclusively through one servant, no matter how special that servant might be to Him.[88] The message was clear. God didn't need us to do His Work so He was telling us to get off our high horse! And if we didn't get more serious about preparing for Christ's return, He would move ahead without us.

My approach from my first semester at AC forward was validated. HWA's challenge to do more in Scandinavia had led me to open up a major media door in Sweden, even if the WCG fumbled it due to petty politics and territorialism. I'd gone on to learn French and German and single-handedly doubled the circulation of *Klar & Wahr* through the newsstand program, only to see it shut down by those who lacked faith. I'd gone on to learn Russian and was positioned to be on the forefront of an expansion endorsed by the Pastor General. If that wasn't enough, I spearheaded improvements to our youth programs, growing the European resource base. My zeal and passion was irritating to some and had been resisted by the power structure within the WCG, but God was shaking things up outside and inside the church, indicating that He would push forward with or without us.

The dark side of my messianic zeal was a struggle with my personal health and increasingly, the health of my marriage. Like most WCG ministers, it was my wife's lot to manage the mundane matters of home and food as a second-class tagalong. I had been up front from the start of our relationship that the Work of God in Europe was my calling, and she had gone along with the arrangement. This old-fashioned patriarchal model had its roots in my dad's Swedish upbringing and it was reinforced within the WCG by referencing texts that were thousands of years old. She had willingly accepted a supportive, nurturing role with regard to my health, perhaps because she had seen her mother die of cancer, and she had a strong belief in methods of natural healing.

I dumped a large share of responsibility for my ill health on her and she assumed a martyr-like role, as though it were her spiritual burden to heal me through household structural and dietary efforts made more difficult by living in a foreign country. As a silent partner on ministerial road trips, she would read book after book on various aspects of health aloud. She would then implement the recommended programs at home, doing the work of purchasing and preparing the food. As unfair as this was to her, her understanding of the mechanics of health and cleansing were a real blessing and her desire to help

---

88. I Kings 19:18 and Romans 11:4

was genuine, enabling me to trust her despite a past that had trained me to distrust women. I made my share of changes, too, taking up swimming, getting on a weight-lifting program, and willingly participating in diet and internal cleansing programs under her guidance.

The progress of my condition slowed down, but did not stop. This focus on health was largely due to Mr. Tkach's priorities, but intellectually embracing them didn't mean fully understanding them. My core personality was not in alignment, and my focus on the work was spiritual workaholism. Recent research into motivation highlights how external motivators can become internalized by children, and then masquerade as intrinsic.[89] Deeply internalized spiritual behaviorism had turned me into a slave-driver, pushing myself to ruin. The more I learned about our ultimate goals in life, the more relentlessly I rode my own back about what needed to be accomplished. This psychologically unhealthy outlook exacerbated my genetic proclivity toward auto-immune disease.

Carry That Weight

I hadn't yet connected the dots between my belief system and my health. Instead, I become more aware that the Bible did not promise us an easy life and I began to compare myself to Paul, who suffered greatly. This kept me moving forward with my "very important" activities, despite sickness and near constant pain. It was fairly manageable during the day, when I was occupied and moving, but increasingly intolerable at night and lack of sleep was fueling a negative downward spiral. Even worse, I was frustrated and demoralized by the dismantling of the newsstand program and increasing political opposition to the success of my vision for the German SEP. But resistance to changing the tithing doctrine caused the worst of my distress, as I was being paid with money collected through a system I no longer believed in.

I drew an analogy to illustrate what was happening to the WCG. In physics and nature, principles of natural attraction and the balance of bodies in motion underlie the structure of the universe and everything in it. The WCG had its own closed system of rules and conditions holding it together. Within this system, people were held in orbit by the externally imposed gravity of rules

---

89. Alfie Kohn has written several books on this topic

and laws, which were now being removed. Commandments to obey, policed by the ministry, were being replaced with opportunities to do, governed by the individual. I was frankly happy to see a situation in which everyone involved was more likely to reveal the true nature of his or her alignment. With gravity removed, it would be faith and love that would counteract the centrifugal force that would otherwise fling the people and operations of the church into outer space.

And I thought about God's role as Revealer. We took pride in understanding the Sabbath, Holy Days, prophecies and many other things that others didn't understand. But I began asking people: "What is the most difficult thing for God to reveal?" The answer I supplied was, "The truth about you." This shift, the removal of externally imposed law, was important to help us all understand what we really wanted to do and be if the coercive fear, guilt, and control were removed. In this way, true love could grow as these negative elements receded. The question then became, would we stay faithful and replace these external motivators with internal governance mechanisms based in love instead of fear? The jury was out on this. Even my own reaction to all of this was not what I would have hoped to see.

David, a man after God's own heart[90], had proclaimed that his zeal for God had consumed him and that God was allowing him to suffer, particularly at the hands of others, for God's sake.[91] I had similar feelings, tied intimately to my declining health and a recurrence of my old victim mentality, which I was wearing like a martyr. Given the contradiction of what I felt was God's blessing on my efforts to serve Him, while my health made life intolerable and my future uncertain, something had to give. I made a conscious decision to follow the example of the prophet Jonah. He had been given an important task to fulfill, had refused, and in fleeing from God had been swallowed up by a great fish. His example played a critical role in Christ's claim to be Messiah, as highlighted earlier in this book, but his personal example is definitely not a positive one.

My wife took a more hands-on approach to the problem; she addressed the situation with Randall Dick, associate director of Church Administration—International. Her request for help was made without consulting me and was not entirely out of concern for me. She was getting increasingly tired of playing

90. I Samuel 13:14
91. Psalms 69:9

the role of minister's wife in Germany. Suddenly I was being encouraged to return to the U.S. in September 1993 on temporary disability. In any case, although adamantly opposed to leaving Europe where I had staked my claim to be a bold warrior for God, I was increasingly hemmed in by forces I couldn't fight. Despite having a name that means warrior, it was time to give up the battle I had been waging with myself, my wife, and now the administration, because God had failed to intervene and heal me. Now He could count me out. If God wasn't going to do more to back me up, then it was time to let the great fish swallow me up. God could come get me again when He was good and ready. I reluctantly agreed to return to the States on a leave of absence.

9

No Reply

After seven days He was quite tired so God said:
'Let there be a day just for picnics, with wine and bread'
He gathered up some people he had made,
created blankets and laid back in the shade.

—CRASH TEST DUMMIES: GOD SHUFFLED HIS FEET—

At the conclusion of SEP 1993, my wife and I traveled to the U.S. on a six month medical leave. The first stop was in Spokane, Washington. We would live with WCG pastor, Dave Treybig, and his warm, kind family, in order to visit several natural practitioners in the area. A naturopath diagnosed food allergies with blood tests, further restricting my already vegetarian diet. Then a holistic dentist replaced my mercury alloy fillings with ceramic while detoxification and cleansing programs worked to eliminate residual heavy metals and toxins, addressing underlying systemic weaknesses suspected of being contributing factors to my disease.

After a number of weeks in Spokane, we moved into temporary housing on the Pasadena AC campus where Dr. Ho and his team in Santa Monica delivered Chinese medicinal interventions, including daily acupuncture, cupping, herbal warming and potent herbal remedies for home use.

Dr. Robert

Dr. Ho claimed he inspired the fictional Dr. Ha in the Michael Keaton movie *My Life*, and was, in fact, treating various Hollywood celebrities. One leading lady who had recently peaked in popularity was being treated in the non-soundproofed chamber next to mine. She was obviously under the influence of something stronger than the herbal remedies and tended toward loud, colorful monologues. This added much needed comic relief as Dr. Ha and his team worked on me. Aside from Hollywood celebrity status, he claimed to be China's #2 rated acupuncturist for having perfected the "flying needle" technique, in which acupuncture needles were popped forcefully into the skin. I learned to count in Mandarin while more than one hundred needles were administered during my daily visits.

The herbal remedies were virtually undrinkable brews made from herbs, roots, and other hard to identify substances. These were packaged in quart sized Ziploc baggies in a natural state that often included small bugs that could not reasonably be separated from the contents, and were therefore dumped into the clay brewing pot along with the rest of the material. These herbs and bugs were then simmered for hours much to the detriment of the atmosphere in our apartment. The resulting liquids were then allowed to cool before being imbibed. One of these "teas" looked like motor oil and if you can imagine drinking slightly sweetened liquid tar, you can approximate the experience. The other concoction was more tea-like, but even harder to consume. It was so incredibly bitter that it was almost impossible to force down, but by holding my nose with one hand, I managed to swallow it without vomiting.

Cupping meant tossing flaming cotton balls drenched in alcohol into glass globes inverted on my back. The fire depleted the oxygen, creating a vacuum which pulled the skin into the globes. The purpose of this procedure was to improve the circulation of the spinal column area. The treatment also provided an unexpected side benefit to my daily swimming regime. Large purple bruises on my back left me looking like the victim of a giant squid attack or some horrible disease. Entering the college pool to swim laps chased others out, giving me all the space I needed.

Joking aside, each morning I worked to improve the time it took to swim a mile, seventy-two Olympic laps—a shorter time being a sign of progress. But swimming faster didn't solve the internal issues. My level of pain worsened as my time began dropping, which was followed by a relapse of sleeplessness and days in bed with a low grade fever, setting me back and forcing me to swim less aggressively again. As I struggled with this dynamic, Randall Dick asked me if permanent disability might be necessary, but I insisted progress was being made.

While these flare ups impacted my ability to continue with my regimen, I became aware that the psychology of striving to improve as judged by external criteria was a major component of my autoimmune disease. There was a tyranny inherent in performing to external measurements that were out of sync with what I really needed. I was not by nature an unmotivated underachiever. I wasn't failing to perform to some standard. I was internally sick, by any standard.

It began to dawn on me that my approach was part of the problem, which led me to focus on the pleasure of swimming, the art of the stroke, being in the moment. Swimming became dancing, and I began basking in the joy of motion through the water. I was determined to think differently, to view life as a pleasant opportunity rather than a challenge that must be overcome. Such a mental shift is incredibly difficult to achieve and progress was very slow. But it began to have as much, if not more, impact on my overall health as all the other treatments. The insight and determination to make a fundamental shift in my internal processing and experience of life itself was ultimately a major key to getting well.

The Feast that year was also a highlight, as Dad, Elinor Tobi, Julie, and even my sister Coby, along with their husbands and children, all got together in Victoria on Vancouver Island. The occasion for this family reunion was my return to the U.S., and they all came to hear me speak—even the ones who weren't WCG members. My efforts to get well seemed to be healing my broken family as well.

Baby, You're a Rich Man!

Another mind shift was taking place as well. My earlier aversion to consumerist, capitalistic materialism, fuelled by my experience in Sweden and later my spiritual focus, was now tempered by nine years in Europe. I was still a champion of the underdog and I still felt that those with wealth and power exploited and manipulated those who did not possess these advantages. But it was clear that in socialist systems opportunities for advancement were curtailed by systems and regulations that tended to keep everyone within a more limited range of material benefits. Eliminating extremes of poverty and riches somewhat perversely made it more difficult for those on the lower end to advance in comparison to those around them, despite ability, education, intelligence, or other advantages.

Ambitious Germans during the postwar boom years built a solid foundation for their financial future. But in the '80s and '90s one's opportunities were limited to working in someone else's empire. It struck me upon returning to America in the early '90s that life in the '80s and early '90s had been good to people financially. Many of my peers and associates from college, the church, and elsewhere owned their own homes and had nice cars and other material blessings. This made a big impact on me, because of my love/hate relationship with the material world as opposed to the spiritual realm.

Living in Alaska and my initial success at quickly achieving the vaunted level of journeyman food clerk at age twenty had been my own personal Egypt. Being flush with cash as a young, irresponsible, single man hid the degree to which I was becoming a slave within that system. At that time, I had followed in my Dad's footsteps in more ways than one, on track to repeat the errors of his youth, before I was liberated by my AC education. It contributed to the rejection of material goals and my move to Europe with nothing but a suitcase and a desire to serve God.

Then, as a married man, financial security became much more important and I found myself at war within myself over the issue of money and material success. Achieving success in Europe and what some considered a lavish ministerial lifestyle, with housing subsidy and a fleet car, was only an illusion of wealth. The house and car were not mine and very little cash was left over after food and other expenses. Extreme penny pinching on my part had enabled us to put some money away, but our assets amounted to less than $5,000. And now I was moving deeper into my Jonah phase, inviting the cares of the world and the deceitfulness of riches[92] to creep into my formerly ascetic and spirit guided life. This was partially due to my wife's dissatisfaction with her situation and my intense fear-based desire to keep her happy. This is an important backdrop to what was about to happen.

As my health slowly improved and my leave of absence was extended by two months to enable further recovery, I made a trip to visit Steve, my church friend from Alaska, whom I hadn't seen since the Feast in Czechoslovakia. He was living near Phoenix, a five hour drive from Pasadena, with his wife and two young children. They lived in a beautiful new 3-bedroom Southwestern style home in a very nice gated community. How had Steve, who had declared bankruptcy in his early twenties, had worked intermittently as a free-lance carpenter, and who had never been good with money, been able to buy this home?

Steve explained that he had bought his house with a non-qualifying loan in a government program for first-time home buyers and that many of the homes in the community had been bought with such loans. I was happy for Steve, but wanted in on the action. I wrote down the number on a for sale sign practically across the street from Steve. I planned to call from Pasadena, since I was leaving the next day.

The next day was January 14, 1994. Steve woke me up to tell me he didn't think I would be going home that day. California had been hit by a massive earthquake, freeways were down, and the city was in chaos. I thought it was a joke, but sure enough, there it was on TV, the Northridge Earthquake. For some WCG members this might have triggered a "prophetic rush"; my dad was probably sitting in front of his television announcing to whoever was next to him that this was the beginning of the Great Tribulation. I had learned not to view events through that lens and thought instead about how a large California earthquake would drive hundreds of thousands of people out of southern California, with many heading east, inflating property prices in Phoenix.

Instead of heading back to Pasadena, I called the number on the for sale sign. The seller wanted a check for $3,500 and a signature to take over the payments. Before I left Phoenix, that house was signed over to me and a couple

---

92. Matthew 13:22

of weeks later it was rented out, with Steve and Lisa as property managers. It felt very good to have made a wise investment for our future. Whether Dad and the WCG were right about the tribulation or not, I was spot-on about what Phoenix property prices would do. That $5,000 nest egg would hatch very nicely in a few years.

In my self-declared "Jonah Phase" I was no longer worried about God somehow punishing me. My early car chase episode and other experiences with God's direct intervention and protection along with faith in His love, kept me confident that when God wanted me, He would come and get me. What happened to Jonah was not that bad. Three days and three nights in the belly of a great fish was probably a piece of cake compared to ten months in a tent in Alaska or Dr. Ha's needles and brews! And Jonah was the Sign Christ gave of who He was. God still had plans for me, but I was just tired of chasing Him. He could chase me for a while.

We Can Work it Out

In the United States, I delivered several sermons generally supporting the changes and challenging the members. In one I compared us to a car with a defect and suggested that we were being recalled by our Creator. This play on words referenced the WCG experience of being "called to the truth" through a humbling repentance, in which we, per HWA, not only had been wrong but *were* wrong in God's eyes. Repentance was a personal recognition of disobedience to God, coupled with complete submission to God. Sadly, the new convert's submission to the Word of God was transferred to the WCG and its autocratic government of God structure. This created a hierarchy of people unable to see, much less admit to, a need for ongoing repentance and personal growth in understanding and spiritual discernment as opposed to blind obedience to an organization.

The metaphor of being recalled was to encourage admission of imperfection and inadequacy at all levels of the church, a difficult truth to swallow, but required if God was to reveal more to us than we already knew. I also used an example from a memorable sermon years earlier at AC. Christ, upon his resurrection, visited His disciples who had returned to their former professions after His death. He used the same physical circumstances to re-iterate His calling to them. Repenting once was not enough, especially if our new belief becomes "now I have the truth." Under Moses, God led Israel through the Red Sea, "baptizing" them, but when they emerged on the other side the real work began.

En route to the Promised Land, God protected and guided Israel with the cloud by day and pillar of fire by night symbolizing the guidance of the Holy Spirit. But under that system they wandered around for forty years in the desert and in the end only two adults, Caleb and Joshua, were allowed to enter the Promised Land. Even Moses was left behind. I drew parallels to the last forty years of WCG experience and the critical juncture we were now facing. My perspective drew the attention of several Pasadena leaders and I was offered two different WCG positions.

Henry Sturcke had replaced Tom Lapacka in Switzerland when Tom transferred back to the States to work for my former boss, David Hulme, managing international media. Tom had then, somewhat ironically based on his history in Europe, moved on to work on a more open and welcoming approach which included inviting people to church services. It was called the Open House program. Tom offered me a prestigious role, pastor of the Auditorium a.m. congregation, in what he called a Skunk Works project piloting a new type of WCG congregation. David Hulme, who I still greatly respected and with whom I shared a conservative streak, was skeptical about the direction Tom had taken after arriving in Pasadena. He advised me against getting involved in such a controversial project.

The other offer was to be the assistant director of the church's new Family Ministries, an outgrowth of Youth Opportunities United or YOU. In my interviews with Bill Jacobs, the new director, I quickly saw that our motivation and vision were in alignment. He wanted to re-integrate families within the WCG instead of continuing the current focus of serving different segments of the church population independently. The issue of family unity and reconciliation was an issue near and dear to my heart; it was a required step on my personal journey of healing.

Another reason to choose Bill's offer was my continued nervousness with where the main thrust of change was leading. Tom was consciously moving closer to mainstream Christianity which seemed to be throwing the baby out with the bathwater. I still believed the Sabbath, Holy Days, and the way of life outlined in the covenant with Israel to be a preferable pattern of worship. It was worth being different if the differences were meaningful and material. Fudging the Sign that Christ gave about three days and three nights, moving the day of worship to Sunday, then from Passover to Easter and giving up the Feast for Christmas were all out of the question. I was very positive about the cultural shift going on in the WCG, but overlaying fables about Santa Claus, bunnies, and eggs onto incorrect dates for Christ's birth and death muddied and distorted God's message to mankind. Distortion of Biblical fact, even if intended to popularize God, would ultimately lead away from God.

In Pasadena and surrounding areas, I continued to speak from a middle of the road perspective. My sermons focused on representing love to a confused world. This was controversial because we had our own definition of love, which was obedience to God's commandments (in particular, the Sign) and we believed the Bible revealed that the world would hate us for obeying them. So I asked the obvious question: "How on earth will we get to there from here?" I admitted that I had no clue, but I firmly believed God would lead us there. We were The People of the Sign. We knew God and He knew us. If we were willing to follow, it was only logical that God would lead us in the right direction.

Act Naturally

The Sabbath commandment was the "test" commandment, which the Judeo-Christian world rejected while also denying the specifics of the Sign Christ gave—three days and three nights. This made us utterly unique, confident that we were the spiritual Israel of God. We claimed the promises of the Old Covenant and the faith of the New Covenant. The Sabbath, inclusive of the annual Sabbaths—the Holy Days—was the cornerstone of this belief. The Tkachs were eroding this cornerstone. Since God honored church hierarchy, the messages emanating from headquarters had to be taken seriously. My understanding allowed for a Dr. Hoeh-like compromise, which I wove into sermons on being re-called as an example of spiritual growth. God had revealed through Moses that the Sabbath was a sign between Him and His people. It identified God as their God, and them as His special, chosen ones.

But I had come to view the Sabbath as a private matter, a private Sign between God and His people. The Sabbath and other laws help us establish our personal identities as individuals and families. It granted us security in our relationship with God, but was not intended for public consumption. God intended to elevate Israel as a model nation. People were to notice that Israel was blessed and acknowledge the blessings that flowed from cultural excellence. This initial attraction and recognition was not intended to occur due to public emphasis on any specific law such as the Sabbath, Holy Days, food laws, or tithing. Cultural excellence was to be an outcome. Israel was to be a light, not a loudspeaker. Our tradition, however, had encouraged us to unduly stress this private sign as a public proof in itself. It was the proverbial cart before the horse.

Jesus, on the other hand, did introduce a very public sign. His statement was "By this shall all men know you, that you have love one for another"[93]. The Sabbath was a private sign for us, something we clearly shouldn't obnoxiously broadcast. Christ's statement brought the focus to love, which is how others would be able to clearly identify us. Paul spoke of this as a more excellent way.[94] Love is the outward sign for public display.

This small concession to the changes made me an outsider to those most adamant about keeping our historical doctrines and identity intact. The strident nature of rigid doctrinal belief, typified by our incorrect and outdated focus on the Old Covenant Sign, separated us from each other. Understanding the New Covenant Sign could bridge gaps between us instead of blowing up our encampments.

Emphasis on our specialness and a bias toward exclusivity had led to an obnoxious attitude, despite our best efforts to remain humble. God was recalling us to prepare us for greater things ahead. He was working to help us become people of whom it could be objectively said, "They are full of love." Despite our opinion of ourselves as a loving group, there was little visible evidence, especially in the current environment of discord, but faith showed that this was where God was leading His church.

---

93. John 13:35
94. I Corinthians 12:31—introduction to the "Love Chapter"

The reactions to these messages were mixed. Two camps were building within the church and very few people saw any middle ground. A day of reckoning was coming, since WCG leadership was firmly in charge and was driving toward massive change. It was déjà vu on a grand scale. Some saw the Tkachs as kidnapping them away from their heavenly Father. Others saw the WCG as an alcoholic mother. There were variations of this theme, depending on which side you were on and how you viewed the opposing side. My focus on reconciliation was not surprising given the way divorce had ripped my parents and family apart. Middle children, in particular, tend to want everyone to somehow get along, but I was also a survivor.

I had to think twice about my next steps. Being stranded in Germany serving a church that was pulling the rug out from under my beliefs was a real possibility. In Pasadena a few leaders identified with what I was saying and encouraged me to keep respectfully pushing the envelope. Among these encouragers was Victor Kubik, responsible for U.S. church administration, and his wife Beverly. With friends like this, it made sense to stay closer to the epicenter of these momentous changes.

In Europe I had seen members suffering under the burden of the WCG and my autoimmune disease had forced me to deal with it. Mr. Tkach's priorities had pointed to a way out, starting with acceptance of the fact that I was sick and that it was my responsibility to get well. Dumping responsibility onto God for my illness with the excuse that I was doing His Work was insane. And dumping responsibility on my wife was the approach Dad had taken when he left Mom at home with the three kids while he was in Alaska.

These realizations came together as my insular black and white view of life through the lens of the WCG and its teachings was under attack. I wasn't ready to head back to Europe on a mission to save the world, but I was making tangible progress in the area of health and in my understanding of what God really wanted. I began to get excited about getting back in the saddle, albeit with a different focus.

We had begun to enjoy the relatively cushy lifestyle of the ministry in America, which involved fewer hours compared to the seven day weeks I'd been working for years in Europe. In Pasadena we had near perfect weather, friends, and my wife's younger sister, who had joked with her, as they talked about how wonderful it would be to move back to Pasadena, "You're living the dream;

forget about the fantasy." Now I was happy to help bring the fantasy to pass. I accepted the position with Family Ministries, and returned to Germany in March 1994 to conduct one last German/European SEP and coordinate our move back to the U.S.

Your Mother Should Know

Within Germany I was well respected by the members but viewed as controversial within the ministry. Coming back from Pasadena, some viewed me as tainted with the waves of liberalism spreading like cancer. Winfried Fritz had labeled me "Absalom," but with clarity that the church needed to express more love, I was now more confident in my approach, even proud to be identified as someone who expressed concern for the people. Obedience-based love disregarded the individual, whereas the love Christ demanded required understanding and awareness of individual needs and perceptions.

But in keeping with my conservative roots, my time in Pasadena also empowered me to resist the thrust of a European Ministerial conference in France, in which Dr. Stavrinidis was trying to indoctrinate the ministry in a new understanding of the nature of God. The ministry was sent a mind-numbing twenty six part lecture series Dr. Stav had recorded without an audience to prepare them for the live sessions and discussions. Most recognized the teaching as a not-so-subtle move toward the traditional Christian understanding of the Trinity, identified by HWA as a satanic deception.

At the beginning of the conference there was robust discussion with Dr. Stav, with me, Joel Meeker, and Henry Sturcke among those participating. Then Joe Tkach Jr. suggested to Henry during a break that it would be better if he arranged a private meeting versus asking questions in the group. Henry complied. During that same break, Victor and Bev Kubik encouraged me to keep up the fight. My relatively recent experiences in Latin Literature, which I had failed, and Biblical Scholarship, Dr. Stav's required senior level course in which I had earned an A, enabled me to use many of Dr. Stav's techniques against him. I had also just completed the book "*The Trial of Socrates*" by I.F. Stone, with its discussion of negative dialectics, an approach Dr. Stav used to cast doubt on virtually any proposition. The book showed this approach to be inherently difficult to use to prove something to be true, giving me a sword to use against Dr. Stav in this intellectual fencing exercise.

During the morning session, Dr. Stav had struck down some of WCG's cherished positions as based on metaphors and parables. In the closing segment he sought to settle his case with a series of Biblical proofs. I dismissed, one by one, Dr. Stav's list of final proofs as poetic references, metaphor, simile, and the like. Halfway through his list, Dr. Stav stopped to complain that if we dismissed the use of metaphor, poetry, and simile it would be impossible to prove anything from the Bible. It was an amazing admission, and it was surprising to see Dr. Stav. apparently oblivious to his obvious double-standard, and somewhat frustrated that he was suddenly no longer being allowed to have his cake and eat it too.

He asserted that what he was presenting was the most reasonable conclusion he could arrive at. I countered that while I respected his conclusion, I held a different conclusion to be more reasonable. So at least in Europe the WCG debate on the nature of God had ended in a stalemate, a considerable victory, given the effort and investment WCG leadership had expended to win the battle.

Around this time Vic Kubik asked me to pay a ministerial visit to one of the Ukrainian groups Mr. Tkach referenced in his Feast message. I obtained a visa but SEP and preparations to move back to the U.S. got in the way of my trip. But I learned that the group Mr. Tkach had discussed in the video, which kept the Holy Days, had been abandoned by us because they were in doctrinal disagreement with us on minor but visibly contentious issues like beards for men and head scarves for women. This was almost comical in its irony, since they mirrored our fundamentalist approach which imbued minor physical matters with enormous spiritual importance.

But why would Victor Kubik, whom I greatly respected, choose cultural conformity over something as important as the Holy Days? Instead of me visiting them, a minister named Vasily from the group he was working with was invited to speak in Stuttgart. This was how, on one of my last Sabbaths in Germany, the members in the WCG congregation I was closest to were somewhat shocked to be subjected to a sermon by a non-WCG Pastor that was full of tales of supernatural intervention with demons and alcoholics. The message was short on biblical relevance and long on dramatic but questionable claims to a direct connection with the spirit world.

This was the somewhat confusing situation my German brothers and sisters, whom I had grown to love, faced as I moved back to the U.S. They looked to me for guidance and leadership at this turbulent time, but I no longer wanted the responsibility of representing the WCG government of God hierarchy. In my parting message, I referenced my dad and his profession as an ironworker. He was comfortable walking along steel beams, twenty stories up, in an unfinished building, while most of us needed walls, windows, floors, heat, indoor plumbing, and carpets to feel comfortable up there. The law of God was like the steel structure, while love made the building livable. It was time for the WCG to become a more hospitable place. The other analogy I used was a simple foreground vs. background metaphor. Two pictures might feature the exact same things, love and law, but from two different perspectives. One showcased the law in the foreground hiding love in the background, while the other displayed love prominently, right up front. God had decided it was time for us to focus on true love.

But while talking about Dad, I felt more like Mom, abandoning people who depended on me.

The emotional pain of this situation was another reason I related to Jonah. I wasn't denying God, but was telling Him to come get me when He was ready to reveal Himself more clearly. In the meantime, the current WCG government of God hierarchy with its damned-if-I-do, damned-if-I-don't double-bind had blessed a transfer back to the States. My new role would be a meaningful and fulfilling one within the church and the Work of God that did not require me to operate within the chain-of-command, enforcing doctrinal change on the membership.

Fixing a Hole

That was how I justified my decision to leave Europe after God had called me and led me there to do His Work in exchange for a role as a young executive at WCG headquarters in Pasadena in the early fall of 1994. Other ministers and members had also found bigger loopholes that worked for them.

A minister in Oklahoma named Gerald Flurry had been disfellowshiped in 1989 for opposing the changes being introduced in the wake of HWA's death. His booklet *Malachi's Message to God's Church Today* claimed to be the "little book" mentioned in Revelation chapter ten. He and his sidekick pulled away about 3,000 members and founded the Philadelphia Church of God. This name referenced the church in Revelation chapter 3 that had the Key of David, which played heavily to some questionable prophetic speculations HWA had made about the history of the true church throughout the ages.

In 1989 I had felt the pull of such enticing claims, which appealed to sensitized feelings of ultra-exclusivity and inside knowledge shared by The People of the Sign. The booklet, however, was full of speculative manipulation of scripture that made sense only if you imagined that a lot of trivial WCG events were mentioned in archaic references by minor prophets in the Bible and the fantastic allegories in the book of Revelation. Aside from having embraced the first wave of changes, this approach didn't square with my understanding on many levels. It had more in common with interpretations of Nostradamus than a sound-minded approach to the Bible.

On December 10, 1992 a much more prominent man, Roderick C. Meredith, a charismatic, if somewhat eccentric forty year WCG veteran minister and evangelist since 1952 who had been a loyal lieutenant of HWA, was fired. He had often preached about staying in the WCG despite its checkered history, asking why anyone would leave the ship to swim with the sharks. Within a few weeks of getting himself fired, he had produced a thin and transparent booklet explaining his new view on church government and immediately founded the Global Church of God. This didn't have the exotic scriptural appeal of Flurry's approach, but provided a place to go for those looking for a top leader, with the charisma many had found lacking in the WCG ever since the ouster of GTA, who could also claim to hold true to the doctrines and principles of HWA. They could apparently overlook the fact that he had changed the one about the government of God, at least long enough to establish himself at the head of a new version of it.

Dr. Meredith's appeal had always seemed intellectually shallow and somewhat emotional, with a hint of chauvinism. He often emphasized his early experience as a golden gloves champion boxer, and wanted AC men to reflect a strong masculine image while women adopted a soft feminine approach. This ideal seemed more based on American romantic fantasy, in particular the classic Disney version of male/female relationships, than scriptural ideal.

I mention these things not to disparage Gerald Flurry, Dr. Meredith, or anyone who followed them, but to highlight the splintering that was taking place. Various flavors of the WCG experience were being presented to people who, while holding to the basic tenets of what I've labeled as "The Sign," were driven to choose between variations on a very similar theme. My efforts to reconcile with Dad and help bring our fractured family together within the principles of the WCG were being undone. Dad had abandoned the Tkachs some months before Dr. Meredith's firing, and had been increasingly vocal. He couldn't believe I could "go along with the garbage coming out of headquarters." The establishment of Global gave him a place to attend, if only briefly, and a position from which to voice his increasing dissatisfaction with me and my approach.

But aside from the personal pain of Dad and Elinor leaving the WCG and affiliating with Global, these little splits and small-scale defections were minor distractions. It was sad, but the approach and attitude displayed by those leaving was the reason I supported the changes in the first place. Gerald Flurry had an extreme and myopic view of scripture that read the most ridiculous things into the Bible, serving up a toxic, cultish poison. Dr. Meredith did not produce anything as patently false as *Malachi's Message* but carried with him many who tended to ridicule and judge others who were sincerely trying to get to the truth of the matter. The ego-driven hypocrisy of his rewrite of the doctrine of church government to suit his situation was clear to everyone except him and his followers.

So the departure by leaders of this nature, and those inclined to follow them, was therapeutic to the WCG at large, a minor bloodletting of the most contentious elements, those most resistant to the vision of becoming a church known for love. And in the newly formed Family Ministries department Bill Jacobs and I were working on programs to deal with an inadequate and increasingly fractured approach to the needs of families. We had Youth Educational Services for young kids, YOU and SEP for teenagers, Ambassador College (now an accredited university), and a variety of singles activities for those looking for mates. We were working to create an umbrella to pull all of this together to put a stop to the disintegration of families within the church.

We wanted to bridge the generation gap, help families communicate together, worship together, and create a common view and understanding of God and the church. Our goal was to create village events like the best WCG memories from my early teen years, where all ages were together and united in spirit and attitude. I could sink my teeth into this, introducing positive change as a way out of the belly of the fish. In line with this, I invited Joachim Kaiser from Stuttgart and Christian Steinman, a teen from Zurich, to join us at the Feast in Hawaii. We were weaving the church together across generational and geographical boundaries.

In Family Ministries we tried to avoid issues of doctrine, but as key doctrinal changes were being enforced, wiggle-room was disappearing. Many kids wanted fewer rules and restrictions, permission to attend or even play sports in school programs, go to school events on the Sabbath and basically be like their friends in the world. The answer to such questions had always been a firm and consistent "NO!" God required us to put aside our activities on the seventh day, including those that might be fine the other six days of the week. The seventh day was holy and we were to be wholly devoted to Him. Church administration was putting increasing pressure on Bill to loosen these restrictions and it became increasingly clear that WCG leadership wanted to make Sabbath observance optional.

Helter Skelter

On January 7, 1995 Mr. Tkach made an earth-shattering announcement in a sermon that was played in all churches. Out of nowhere, he decreed that tithing was voluntary. This was good news and although almost no one agreed with it, most people seemed to take it in stride and had relatively reasonable, if sarcastic, reactions. We had just closed escrow on a house in Pasadena the week before this announcement, and I recall joking, in gallows humor fashion, that although we were now under the New Covenant, my mortgage was based on laws defined in the Old. I was not the only one making jokes, as my wife related a conversation from the law office where she worked in which several attorneys were laughing at a report on this subject in the Pasadena Star News. They joked: "Church does away with tithing and wonders why income is down."

Then the other shoe dropped.

Mr. Tkach made a seemingly passing comment in a sermon given in a local area. In his opinion, there was nothing wrong with a member playing a round of golf on the Sabbath, provided it was done in the right spirit. The reaction to this minor and seemingly innocuous comment was visceral. HWA's beloved evangelist, Mr. Waterhouse, had given up a career in professional golf to come into the WCG. Every single member could have told a powerful story about what they had given up in order to enter into the covenant and join The People of the Sign through baptism by the WCG.

The die was now cast and everyone's worst fears were realized. A majority of the WCG was in violent disagreement. This should not have been surprising as our very identity was wrapped up in this point. The Sabbath was the Sign of the People of God. And we were The People of the Sign. The Sabbath sermon, as it became known, was the catalyst that allowed leaders within a disgruntled U.S. ministry to take action. They had been quietly networking behind the scenes, waiting for the right moment to leverage the regional pastor structure, in which fourteen men oversaw the activities of nearly three hundred full-time pastors and seven hundred local church elders (non-paid ministers). Mr. Tkach's comment allowed them to aggressively map out a loose plan, assessing the number of tithe-paying supporters they could expect if they were to orchestrate a large-scale defection. By Passover 1995, twelve of the fourteen regional pastors had formed a coalition that would result in the United Church of God (UCG). This was by far the largest defection the WCG had ever seen, essentially splitting it down the middle in an abrupt and unexpected divorce.

But these men had neither honored the government of God nor put their jobs at risk over the Sabbath in an act of faith, trusting in God directly. The timing of this and how it played out indicated that these regional pastors and other ministers cared most about maintaining their position and lifestyle, supported by the sheep they were supposed to be ministering to. It seemed evident that many had acted in bad faith, if they had acted in any kind of faith at all. It was reminiscent of what Dad had done in stealing us away from Mom, claiming he was protecting us from her. They certainly had good reason to do what they did, but their motives were mixed, at best.

This defection did not seem a genuine move to follow the direction of the cloud and pillar. The biggest indicator was that they offered no genuine answer to the conundrum of going against the government of God they had always preached and which they would still, in perhaps more subtle ways, expect the membership to follow. They offered no explanation as to why it was suddenly okay to disobey the top level of the hierarchy. I had certainly felt the pain of having a responsibility to those who looked to me for leadership, so I didn't want to judge them. I was admittedly playing Jonah myself. But instead of seeking answers from God, they pretended they didn't need to explain themselves. They felt justified in executing a political power play marketed as an effort to serve others, but orchestrated to preserve their own positions.

As I pondered all this, I traveled to the church's Minnesota SEP program I had last attended as an innocent fourteen year old camper. Dr. Nelson, who had been directing the camp in recent years, stayed on with the WCG to manage the camp, even though I recall his sentiments being more in line with those in the UCG. He and I had a good relationship, developed as I had looked to him for advice and support in building the German SEP program. His focus was on ensuring that all the campers and staff had a typical, positive, SEP experience, filled with activities, challenges, friends, and emotional support. His classic mantra "of all the places I could be, where I really want to be is right here" took on new significance that summer, as SEP was a chance to leave all the turmoil far behind.

I oversaw sailing and wind surfing and loved being back in nature with a great group of young people having a good time in a positive environment. While there, I also met a chiropractor, Dr. Jeff Maehr, who had responsibility for the health center. He had a new piece of equipment called a dark field phase contrast microscope which could analyze live blood samples. He analyzed and compared my blood to healthy blood, capturing the samples on a videotape. I was amazed at all of the problems in evidence, from uric acid crystals, to viruses, to red-cell clumping. Even though I was feeling much better, my blood was still very unhealthy. There was a scriptural correlation to this in which the Israelites were forbidden to drink blood, with the rationale that "the life is in the blood."[95]

Jeff gave me some enzymes and probiotics and in a ridiculously short period of time, something like sixty minutes, he took another blood sample

---

95. Leviticus 17:14

showing the uric acid crystals breaking up, the red cells declumping, and other encouraging changes in the sample. I took another full dose of these natural supplements before bed, and had the most wonderful night's sleep in years, with my back pain completely gone. The next morning I had an amazing burst of energy and vitality and signed up for a regimen with these products made by a company called Infinity². It felt like my health trials were definitively behind me, once and for all.

Returning to Pasadena, everything was changing. Bill Jacobs, director of Family Ministries, had resigned to join the UCG and I was named interim director. Joe Tkach, Jr. was the designated Pastor General, as his father was suddenly and unexpectedly dying of cancer. Detractors claimed that Mr. Tkach's death had prophetic significance or was related to a comment he had made that if God disagreed with what he was doing then God would remove him.

Joe, Jr. personally met with me to discuss the changes. He wanted me to know that they were really quite simple to understand and that he would be happy to walk me through them, if I was interested. I let him know that I appreciated this, but just didn't see it the way he did.

I was experiencing a near miraculous victory over my autoimmune condition but my spiritual identity crisis was becoming more acute. Many I respected in the WCG and with whom I had greater doctrinal affinity had left, while others I respected, such as the Tkachs and Randall Dick, were encouraging me to stay. I was re-evaluating my theological framework, which still held that the WCG was God's true church, along with the mandate to follow Mr. Tkach as the duly authorized leader. At the same time, I was increasingly uncomfortable staying, since my relationship with God and the benefit of the Sign of the Sabbath was at risk. My dilemma was underscored by the way Dad was harping on me to get out "before I became hopelessly deceived."

My wife and I were also increasingly at odds. She agreed with even the recent WCG changes and seemed more worried about the potential financial impact of my disagreement with my employer than anything else. When David Hulme was made President of the UCG, with Victor Kubik a prominent leader, it was tempting to join a new organization led by people I respected, who would welcome me with more than open arms. I was torn and didn't know which divorced parent to choose.

Regardless, my conscience no longer allowed me to draw a salary from the WCG, and beyond that I no longer wanted my faith tied to my paycheck. I felt no need to make a grand statement, but I did need to bring my life into alignment with what I believed on a spiritual level. God is much more concerned about what we do than what we profess, so I resigned in a way that I felt was respectful, staying to wrap up what I was working on for the WCG instead of rushing over to the rebels.

Let It Be

My last project in the WCG was a pilot series of intergenerational Bible Studies, designed to bridge the generation gap and improve family relations. These covered topics of interest to teens, using study guides and activities for them, their parents, and a facilitator to work though in small groups. Facilitated discussion of difficult topics under the guidance of a moderator could help get families that weren't talking to do so. I was reaching out to people who, like me, were struggling to make sense of the conflicting impulses.

And while Gerald Flurry was trying to convince others to follow him using *Malachi's Message,* the book of Malachi ends with an urgent appeal to turn the hearts of fathers to their children and vice versa[96], not to permanently sever these relationships. We needed to reconcile the beliefs we had in our heads with the feelings we held in our hearts. Not surprisingly, one of the intergenerational Bible studies focused on music, using the song *"God Shuffled His Feet"* by The Crash Test Dummies. The lyrics had clear implications for The People of the Sign.

After seven days He was quite tired so God said:
"Let there be a day just for picnics, with wine and bread"
He gathered up some people he had made, created blankets and laid back
in the shade.

The people sipped their wine and what with God there, they asked him
questions
Like: do you have to eat Or get your hair cut in heaven?

---

96. Malachi 4:6

And if your eye got poked out in this life Would it be waiting up in heaven
with your wife?

God shuffled his feet and glanced around at them;
The people cleared their throats and stared right back at him

The song summed up the challenge we faced when Mr. Tkach approached
the Sabbath day in a manner similar to the picnic analogy, not conscious,
perhaps, of the explosive reaction his seemingly casual remark was going to
launch. The facilitator's guide asked the parents and teens to give their opinions
on whether they liked the song or not, what it was about, and whether they
thought it was okay for a group to write a song portraying God in this way. The
intent was to raise the thorny and potentially explosive subject about Sabbath
observance (not to mention taking God's name in vain and so on) in answer
to the questions coming in to Family Ministries by using, of all things, a rock
song, by a group calling themselves the Crash Test Dummies.

Now I have no idea what the Crash Test Dummies were really thinking
about when they wrote the song. That is the nature of art. But they had somehow
magically stumbled upon a perfect expression of what the Sign was all about.
The had posed, in a perfectly detached and objective fashion, basic, honest
questions about the relationship between God and the people He had made and
how they should behave when they got together on the Sabbath.

My hope was that in exploring differences of opinion in a church setting
with a facilitator, a sharing of viewpoints would be possible. Since the song
somewhat innocuously touched on the meaning of the Sign, it might enable some
objectivity about our relationship with God and God's relationship with us. At
a minimum it might strengthen the bond between teens and parents, shrinking
the generation gap and weaving together the families of the Worldwide Church
of God. This approach was to be rolled out at all WCG Feast of Tabernacles
sites on my own twenty-fifth year observing it. This was ambitious, but it supported
Mr. Tkach, a name Gerald Waterhouse had famously proclaimed to mean
"weaver" in his effort to weave the church tightly together.

Instead, the weaver had torn the fabric of the church in two, causing me
to reflect on how the brothers of his namesake, Joseph, had treated the coat

of many colors.[97] And why had Mr. Tkach died of cancer just days before the Feast? Ron Weinland, another renegade WCG minister, claimed it was God's retribution, citing dates and circumstances to make this point. My experience with autoimmune disease implied it was more likely related to the agony of knowing that no matter what Mr. Tkach did, people would be terribly hurt.

I was again keeping the Feast in Hawaii, but the magic of the Island of Kauai, where parts of the *Jurassic Park* sequel *The Lost World* had been filmed, could not make up for the way the magic of the WCG had been gutted. Doctrinal changes had caused a mass defection of many people I had considered my closest and most trusted friends. The intergenerational Bible studies I conducted provided a chance for discussion, but they were wholly inadequate to even soften the blow felt by those who remained after the ripping apart of the fabric of the WCG.

My childhood was shattered by divorce, but with God as my Father and the WCG as my spiritual family, I had recovered. Now the church that had helped me find myself and regain my footing had cracked apart under my feet. Just as I had come to see that our path forward would be centered on love, a nasty divorce had split us down the middle and we were all forced to choose sides. Each side held the other responsible and we were all caught in an undertow of ugliness.

I had submitted my resignation prior to the Feast and was granted a severance package of one week of pay per employment year, or about two month's pay. That little buffer encouraged me to take an extra week of vacation on the Island of Maui, even though my wife had to return home for work. My resignation from the WCG, coupled with my decision to stay in Hawaii an extra week, generated an ominous tension in our relationship.

I had wanted to visit Maui ever since the Eagles referred to it on their *Hotel California* album as "The Last Resort." I had reached my last resort as well, in resigning from the WCG without a place to go. The dual meanings of my name are "wanderer" and "warrior." I was beginning to understand who I was, but I was still looking for a sign to guide me to where I belonged.

Flying from Kauai to Maui, I looked down at the ocean and felt broken inside, empty and lifeless—a spiritual zombie. Like Jonah in the belly of the whale, or Christ before the three days and three nights were up, I was stuck

---

97. Genesis 37

somewhere between life and death. *God Shuffled His Feet* was my only CD and it played over and over in my rental car as I drove in a daze to the golf course to play alone or to a restaurant to eat alone. Hearing it today still takes me back to the time and place where my quarter century of involvement with God's one true church came to a quiet end, as it had begun, at a Feast.

I had wanted to spend my first week free of the WCG alone in paradise so I could sort things out. I'd like to say I saw the light, but that's a lie. I was absorbed in a melancholy cloud. The music of the self-proclaimed Crash Test Dummies was a fitting soundtrack to my brooding over how a hundred thousand People of the Sign had been forced to risk the lake of fire by either leaving the one true church, or by staying in it while it abandoned the identifying Sign of the People of God. This divorce left a nagging question in its wake for us whichever side we chose.

Were those in the group I just left still The People of the Sign? How about those in the group I was considering joining? And what about me?

Why does the God Daniel called "The Revealer"[98] have such trouble showing us the truth about ourselves?

In that passage, God revealed Nebuchadnezzar's dreams to Daniel, but then turned around and told Daniel the meaning of the book was sealed, even from him, until the Time of the End, with a definitive "Go Thy Way, Daniel."[99]

The truth is that when it comes to ourselves, even when we aren't asking the wrong question we won't accept God's answer without a fight.

And when we feel cornered by God's answer, we often take issue with the messenger.

If you're anything like I was in 1995, God might deliver His answer in a hundred different ways, but another answer can still be found to suit you better than the one provided by the still, small voice.

And when all else fails and we're all out of answers, it's still very easy to simply ignore that still, small voice.

---

98. Daniel 12:47
99. Daniel 12:9

Acronyms Glossary

AC	Ambassador College	Private college founded by HWA
AICF	Ambassador International Cultural Foundation	Humanitarian arm of the WCG
GTA	Garner Ted Armstrong	HWA's Son
HWA	Herbert W. Armstrong	Founder of WCG
SEP	Summer Educational Program	WCG Summer Camp Program
UCG	United Church of God	Major split from the WCG
WCG	Worldwide Church of God	Church organization founded by HWA
WEP	Winter Educational Program	WCG Winter Camp Program
YOU	Youth Opportunities United	WCG Youth Program

CPSIA information can be obtained at www.ICGtesting.com
Printed in the USA
LVOW100137200412

278357LV00003B/1/P

9 780984 693801